WRITING GROUPS IN THE WRITING CENTER

Writing Groups in the Writing Center

Negotiating Authority and Expertise in Collaborative Learning

SARA WILDER

UTAH STATE UNIVERSITY PRESS
Logan

© 2025 by University Press of Colorado

Published by Utah State University Press
An imprint of University Press of Colorado
1580 North Logan Street, Suite 660
PMB 39883
Denver, Colorado 80203-1942

All rights reserved

 The University Press of Colorado is a proud member of Association of University Presses.

The University Press of Colorado is a cooperative publishing enterprise supported, in part, by Adams State University, Colorado School of Mines, Colorado State University, Fort Lewis College, Metropolitan State University of Denver, Regis University, University of Colorado, University of Northern Colorado, University of Wyoming, Utah State University, and Western Colorado University.

ISBN: 978-1-64642-765-9 (hardcover)
ISBN: 978-1-64642-766-6 (paperback)
ISBN: 978-1-64642-767-3 (ebook)
https://doi.org/10.7330/9781646427673

Library of Congress Cataloging-in-Publication Data

Names: Wilder, Sara Franssen, author.
Title: Writing groups in the writing center : negotiating authority and expertise in collaborative learning / Sara Wilder.
Description: Logan : Utah State University Press, [2025] | Includes bibliographical references and index.
Identifiers: LCCN 2025016634 (print) | LCCN 2025016635 (ebook) | ISBN 9781646427659 (hardcover) | ISBN 9781646427666 (paperback) | ISBN 9781646427673 (ebook)
Subjects: LCSH: Writing centers. | Writers' workshops. | Authorship—Study and teaching (Higher)—Evaluation. | College students' writings—Evaluation. | Academic writing—Study and teaching (Higher)
Classification: LCC PE1404 .W5336 2025 (print) | LCC PE1404 (ebook) | DDC 808.06/6378—dc23/eng/20250610
LC record available at https://lccn.loc.gov/2025016634
LC ebook record available at https://lccn.loc.gov/2025016635

This book will be made open access within three years of publication thanks to Path to Open, a program developed in partnership between JSTOR, the American Council of Learned Societies (ACLS), University of Michigan Press, and The University of North Carolina Press to bring about equitable access and impact for the entire scholarly community, including authors, researchers, libraries, and university presses around the world. Learn more at https://about.jstor.org/path-to-open/.

This work is licensed under CC BY-NC-ND 4.0.

The University Press of Colorado gratefully acknowledges the support of the University of Maryland toward the publication of this book.

Cover photograph by Qweek/iStock

Contents

List of Tables vii

Acknowledgments ix

1. Introduction: Studying Writing Groups as Communities of Practice 3
2. "People Thinking Differently About Writing": The Role of the Group Facilitator 35
3. "It's Not Necessarily Science": Disciplinary Clashes, Convergences, and Learning in Multidisciplinary Groups 65
4. Storying the Difficulties: Emotional Labor in Writing Groups at a PWI 113
5. Expanding the Boundaries of Writing Center Work 147

Appendix A: Interview Questions 165
Appendix B: Survey Questions 167
Appendix C: Survey Data 171
Appendix D: Codebooks 175
References 183
Index 193
About the Author 203

Tables

1.1. Dissertation writing group participants 25
1.2. Undergraduate thesis group participants 26
1.3. Second-year proposal group participants 27
1.4. Data collected 28
C.1. Survey respondents' demographics 172
C.2. Survey response data 173
D.1. Codebook for facilitator role and practices 175
D.2. Codebook for group feedback practices 178
D.3. Codebook for advisor talk 182

Acknowledgments

A project like this one, which is rooted in collaboration and which has carried me through my PhD and my first years on the tenure track, doesn't come together without the support of an entire network of people and places. To start, I'd like to thank the research participants who graciously allowed me to take part in their writing groups and who contributed their perspectives to this study. They are cotheorists, really, in this project of understanding what makes writing group collaborations work, what makes them difficult, and what sometimes makes them magical. I'm grateful to have been able to learn from and with them. I also want to acknowledge a number of organizations who have supported this project in its various iterations, including the IWCA, who supported the dissertation version of this project with a Ben Rafoth Graduate Research Grant, and the UMD College of Arts and Humanities.

This project began as a dissertation project, and it would not have been possible without the support of the people who guided me through my graduate program. A big thank you to Dickie Selfe and the rest of the writing center research team who worked with me to figure out how to study writing groups. My committee—Christa Teston, Jonathan Buehl, and Kay Halasek—gave generous, critical feedback on this study as it developed and turned into a dissertation. Most of all, a huge thank you and acknowledgment to my dissertation advisor, Beverly Moss, who guided me through designing and carrying out this project. Beverly's mentorship was—and is—priceless. She modeled generous, ethical research practices, gave the pushes that I needed to keep going, and offered the kind of feedback that not only made this project better but that made me feel cared for as a person and so made me a better scholar and teacher.

Unsurprisingly, this book has also had the support of a number of writing groups. Kaitlin Clinnin, Nora McCook, and Jennifer Burgess—thank you for helping me get the words on the page, and even more for the ongoing text thread full of updates on kids and pets and jobs that have kept me in good company throughout this process. To my writing buddies and Hufflepuff Book Club, Michelle Cohen and Liz Steinway, thank you for the long days in coffee shops, staving off the cold Midwestern winters. And thank you especially to Michelle, who offered such valuable, critical feedback on this work and whose friendship and support on the project have been constant and ever needed in the transition from graduate school to faculty life.

At University of Maryland, I've had the privilege of working with fantastic colleagues who have pushed my thinking and offered generous mentorship: Jessica Enoch, Vessela Valiavitcharska, Scott Wible, Linda Coleman, Michael Israel, Karen Nelson, and Angela Glotfelter. Thank you, also, to my junior faculty writing group buddies, especially Cecilia Shelton and Melanie Kill, who both offered feedback that helped shape what was a dissertation into a book. To Cecilia, thank you for being the colleague and friend who will talk through teaching, writing, parenting, and doing life on the tenure track. I want to say thank you, too, to Beth Godbee and Candace Epps-Robertson, along with all of the writing group members of Heart Head Hands, for holding space to write in community with others and to honor our needs as humans. Beth offered gentle yet critical feedback on portions of this work that deepened my thinking in a time when I was having trouble moving through my own anxiety.

I also want to acknowledge that this book and this job would not exist for me without a network of support, including the community I've found here: my neighbors, especially Grace Cheney, who watched over my tiny baby so I could get some writing done (or get some sleep), and the entire team at the UMD Child Development Center, who have provided loving care for both my children.

Last but most certainly not least, I want to acknowledge the support of my family in bringing this project to fruition. To my parents, who drove an RV from California to Maryland (twice!) to see us when it wasn't safe to fly, who have offered childcare and airfare and listening ears throughout the writing process, who cheered on every step, even when those steps took me into a career and a life on the opposite coast, thank you for your love and unconditional support. To my girls, Abigail and Josephine, thank you for the big hugs, for the pictures that have now papered over my filing cabinets, and for demanding the complete and utter presence that offers such incredible joy and keeps me grounded in what really matters. And finally, to my husband, Blake. Your love and support have made this possible. You celebrate the successes, and you calm the fears. I'm so grateful to do this life and this work with you.

Writing Groups in the Writing Center

1
Introduction

Studying Writing Groups as Communities of Practice

Scene: A small but comfortable group study room in a university library. Five undergraduate students and one researcher are grouped around a table. They have laptops out, using one to project a word document on a shared screen on the wall. The students are all working on undergraduate thesis projects, and they have come together on this Monday evening for their weekly writing group. One of the students, Marie, is the writing center consultant facilitating the group. At this meeting, early in the semester, they have been workshopping proposals for a campus-wide undergraduate research forum.

> ADANNA, AN UNDERGRADUATE ECONOMICS MAJOR: How do you guys come up for titles for your work?
>
> MARIE, THE GROUP FACILITATOR AND AN UNDERGRADUATE MAJORING IN PHILOSOPHY AND WOMEN'S STUDIES: The night before when I'm really tired. [*group laughter*]
>
> ADANNA: 'Cause this has actually been an ongoing project since the summer and it's probably had, like, seventy different names, so, like, I don't know, I know it can be changed as late as possible, but it'd be nice to like have something that I actually—like, that's catchy and I like.

MAGGIE, AN UNDERGRADUATE ENGLISH MAJOR: I kind of wait until I'm done with the paper. Sometimes it comes out of something I said in a paragraph that relates to my thesis or something like that. Like, I know I wrote about *Gatsby* or something about the ships being beat endlessly into the past, because it was related to, like, biography and stuff like that. But that didn't come down until the end, so it was a last line thing that kind of tied back to the title, so I don't know.

ELEANOR, AN UNDERGRADUATE MAJORING IN ENGLISH AND WOMEN'S STUDIES: I can't really help you. I'm horrible at titles, to be honest. Mine are always too long.

ADANNA: Yeah, and I can't say economists are very creative. I'll be like "Immigration and Economic Inequality." Bam. That's it. [*laughter*]

MARIE: I wouldn't do a creative title, because I don't know much about economics, but every paper I have read—

ADANNA: Not creative in the sense that "oh my gosh!" like, but not boring. A little something and you see it and you're like [*snaps fingers*] "okay, that sounds interesting" at the very least. Not "okay, that's nice."

MARIE: Yeah, I mean, titles in economics just seem a little more descriptive than they are anything else. So yeah, I wouldn't try too hard, I would just, in as few words as possible, describe what your project is and describe and use that as your title.

MAGGIE: I mean, I think your title sounds kind of cool right now.

ELEANOR: Yeah, I think it shows what your project's about, and that's what's important. It doesn't have to be something fancy. I mean it's economics, right?

ADANNA: I want to be a *cool* economist, guys. [*laughter*]

MARIE: Do that when you have a PhD though, not before.

ADANNA: I can do it now.

In this scene, we see and hear a student writing group do what student writing groups do: they come together and ask for insight into one another's writing processes and for feedback on their own writing. In response to Adanna's question, Marie, Maggie, and Eleanor offer their own experiences writing titles, express empathy for the difficulty of the task, praise Adanna's existing title and project, and try to account for disciplinary convention as they give advice. This exchange offers the group opportunities to collaborate on Adanna's title and also to reflect on disciplinary writing conventions and on their own writing processes. This exchange also shows these writers working out their own identities as emerging scholars and their relationships with each other in the writing group.

Perhaps most interesting in this exchange are the negotiations of authority that shape the collaboration and how those negotiations are part of the writers' emerging scholarly identities. Adanna sees her thesis as a piece of writing through which she can start to craft and perform her emerging identity as a "cool economist." The group, laughing together, recognizes and supports that goal. Interestingly, though, Marie's reaction, "do that when you have a PhD though, not before," combined with her earlier direction, sets up a negotiation of authority between Marie (the group facilitator) and Adanna that I would argue is tied to how Marie and Adanna differ in their relationships with their home disciplinary communities. Adanna, with what seems to be a bit more confidence in her ability to be a "cool economist" (and who, incidentally, had a very cool project), pushes back against Marie. "I can do it now," Adanna says, resisting Marie's directive. Marie, on the other hand, seems to value fitting into existing disciplinary norms in perhaps a less cool but also safer way before becoming more formally recognized as an expert. In this short exchange, then, we see a small community of writers who come together to share practices and feedback and who collaborate across disciplinary boundaries. As they do so, they engage in negotiations of authority and reflect on what it means to emerge as writers in their home disciplinary communities.

As I argue throughout this book, these negotiations of authority are central to writing group work, even in groups that might have tighter, more trusting bonds than the writers in the exchange above, who had only been working together for a short time. When I reflect on this exchange, I see it as a moment that offers insight into collaborative composition practices and into writers' emergence in professional and academic discourse communities. Further, I think that tracking these kinds of negotiations can help us understand the possibilities that writing groups offer for student writing support and for expanding our vision of what collaboration in the writing center looks and sounds like.

Collaboration and Authority in the Writing Center

Collaborative practice is the cornerstone of writing center work. In the writing center, people come together to improve their writing and to build expertise and confidence as writers. Scholarship in writing center studies has come to understand these acts of collaboration as ones that require complex negotiations of power, authority, and expertise among tutors and writers (Carino 2003; Corbett 2013; Dinitz and Harrington 2014; Grimm 1999; Kiedaisch and Dinitz 1993; Lunsford 1991; Nowacek and Hughes 2015). And yet, as a field, we have struggled at times to move beyond simplistic understandings of these negotiations. For example, the field still works to move beyond prescriptions that tutors engage only in nondirective practices (Corbett 2008, 2011; Denny, Nordlof, and Salem 2018; Nicklay 2012).

Jackie Grutsch McKinney's 2013 book *Peripheral Visions for Writing Centers* called on writing center researchers to tell a more complex story of writing center work, one that accounts for the many and varied practices of students, tutors, and administrators in writing centers. She argued that the field has been limited in its adherence to a grand narrative that "writing centers are comfortable, iconoclastic places where all students go to get one-to-one tutoring on their writing" (McKinney 2013, 5). Because we are preoccupied with this narrative, McKinney argued, we don't account for the many activities of writing center work that don't fit the narrative, and so we don't fully prepare future writing center administrators, nor do we communicate our work as effectively as we could to those outside of the center (whether faculty, administrators, or students). In their national survey of writing centers, Jackson and McKinney found that most centers offered some sort of group practice (workshops, group tutorials, etc.) and a significant number offered writing groups (Jackson and McKinney 2012).[1] By not accounting for practices, like these, that fall outside our grand narrative, we miss important opportunities to develop strong, research-driven practices that support those students or tutors who might not find the existing writing center comfortable, inviting, or aligned with their goals. Aligning with McKinney's call for an expanded view of the field are two bodies of writing center scholarship: one focused on empirical research to ground new theories and practices in the field (Driscoll and Perdue 2012; Kjesrud 2015) and one attentive to narrating and theorizing people's lived experiences in the writing center, focused especially on counterstories that center experiences of people of color in spaces where a majority of people are often white women (Denny et al. 2019; Faison and Condon 2022; Faison and Treviño 2020). Recognizing the limitations of current

---

1. Jackson and McKinney found that most writing centers engaged in some sort of group practice, including writing groups and workshops. Ten percent of survey respondents offered graduate writing groups, 8 percent offered faculty writing groups, and 13 percent offered some other type of writing group (Jackson and McKinney 2012).

theories and narratives of writing center work, both of these bodies of scholarship push for new and expanded guiding theories and practices in the writing center.

In the years since McKinney's book was published, we have weathered a pandemic. Writing centers, like most of higher education, pivoted to completing most of their work online. And now, we have trickled back, doing our best to support students, tutors, and staff during a time when many of us are preoccupied with safety, with little bandwidth to retheorize our core practices. And yet, many in the field also have taken the challenges that disrupted business as usual as an opportunity to talk about how to make our centers more accessible and equitable. A sampling of some of the writing center conferences in 2021 and 2022 shows how, as a collective, writing center administrators and tutors have been taking stock of who we are, what we do, and how we do it, questioning the assumptions that we come together to do in-person tutoring and what it means to make our work accessible in other ways:

- International Writing Centers Association 2021: "Together Again Apart: Reimagining Our Communities of Practice?";
- Mid-Atlantic Writing Centers Association 2021: "Access and Equity: Writing Centers in Times of Disruption"; and 2022: "Looking Back and Looking Ahead: The Writing Center's Past, Present, and Future";
- Northern California Writing Centers Association 2021: "Adapting to Intentional Student Support: Changes in the Writing Center";
- Southeastern Writing Centers Association 2021: "Trauma and Transformation: Writing Centers in an Era of Change"; and 2022: "Present Tense, Future Perfect: Shaping Purposeful Writing Center Practices"; and
- Pacific Northwest Writing Centers Association 2021: "Where Are We? Writing Centers as Sites of Existential Conundrums."

What I see in these conference titles is an interest not only in rethinking our modes of communication with students—online, hybrid, in-person—but an interest in what that means for our communities. Who is invited in, and in what roles? How do we make our practices accessible? How do we set up our practices with purpose and intention? Time and technology move quickly, and though our conference themes might now be full of questions about text-generating AI, I think it important to keep these questions about access, equity, and the human connections in our writing centers at the forefront of our work.

This book attempts to join these efforts to expand our view of writing center collaborations, to use research to carefully open up the richness of those collaborations, and to intentionally develop practices grounded in that research. Specifically, this is a study of writing groups sponsored—that is, advertised, formed, and facilitated—by a writing center. I examine what practices make up the work of writing center–sponsored writing groups and how those practices require tutors and administrators to adapt theories of writing center work. By closely examining the collaborative practices of groups, as well as one-to-one tutoring, writing center researchers may more fully theorize the complexities of collaboration among student-writers, tutors, administrators, and faculty in the writing center. In doing so, we are better able to implement programs that support students, tutors, and faculty from across campus as they engage in reading, writing, and mentoring.

Taking three groups as case studies—one group of second-year undergraduates enrolled in a program promoting student retention, one group of undergraduate researchers writing senior theses, and one group of dissertation writers—I use qualitative methods to study how students collaborate and negotiate their own emerging expertise as disciplinary writers and as readers of one another's texts. Drawing on observation, interview, and survey data, I track the ways that groups negotiate authority, navigate disciplinary difference, and experience emotions associated with the writing process and with writing center practice. I use the concept of "communities-of-practice" (Wenger 1998) as the theoretical framework to analyze these group practices as engagement in collaborative learning. In doing so, I contribute to theories of collaboration in the writing center and recommend practices for supporting student writers and tutors. I argue that writing groups offer a compelling site in which to study how writers collaborate across disciplinary boundaries, how writers emerge as disciplinary experts through collaborative practice, and finally, how writing centers might support such collaborations and learning.

Benefits and Challenges of Academic Writing Groups

Writing groups have received increasing attention in writing studies (Aitchison 2010; Geller and Eodice 2013; Moss et al. 2004) and, more specifically, in writing center studies (Cui et al. 2022; Hixson et al. 2016; Kinney et al. 2019; Kramer 2016; McMurray 2017, 2019; Phillips 2012; White and Miller 2015) as colleges and universities attempt to provide more and better support for student writers, particularly at the graduate level. Writing groups have been embraced because they can offer writers the benefits of both emotional and intellectual support. Several studies note the communal, caring, and trusting atmosphere that writing groups can provide (Beckstead et al. 2004; Day and Eodice 2004; Julien and Beres 2019; Kinney et al. 2019; Lassig et al. 2013). This scholarship highlights the important role that writing groups can play in countering feelings of isolation, particularly for graduate writers (Lawrence and Zawacki 2018). In addition to emotional support, writing groups can also become spaces that provide participants with unique opportunities to learn about their writing, particularly disciplinary writing conventions about which they may not receive explicit instruction (Gradin et al. 2006; Maher et al. 2008; Paré 2014; Phillips 2012; Thomas et al. 2004).

Writing groups have especially been embraced for helping graduate students gain authority as writers within their home disciplines. For example, Anthony Paré (2014) theorizes writing groups for doctoral students as important sites of "authentic social engagement" and thus learning in academic discourse communities. Following Claire Aitchison (2009), he sees writing groups as sites that can recreate the dynamics of peer review and prepare students to receive and make use of critical feedback. As Paré writes, writing groups offer students the opportunity to "see academic writing as what it really is, or really can be: a dialogue among colleagues" and, further, to "develop a sense of membership and authority" as participants in that dialogue (26). Similarly, Garcia, Eum, and Watt write that a multidisciplinary writing group allowed them, as graduate students, to role-play as experts in their fields (Garcia et al. 2013). They were able to engage as peer mentors while gaining confidence as emerging disciplinary experts. For the writers who took part in the above studies, one of the key benefits of writing groups was the opportunity to develop a sense of authority and expertise in the relatively low-stakes site of a writing group.

This kind of support has been offered as one way to increase diversity and equity in academia by providing sites in which writers both learn about and critique existing disciplinary writing conventions and expectations that overwhelmingly privilege white, standard, edited, American English (Kinney et al. 2019; Phillips 2012; Wilmot and McKenna 2018). Similarly, Beth Godbee found potential in collaborative writing conferences to counter what she calls "epistemic injustice," offering the graduate student women of color who participated in her study an opportunity to engage in feminist co-mentoring that reaffirmed their "epistemic rights, the rights to knowledge, experience, and earned expertise" (Godbee 2020, 36). In other words, a writing group can be a space that not only allows a student to practice being the expert but also invites participants to redefine, for themselves, what expertise might look like in their field.

The hoped-for outcomes of writing groups—providing students with authentic sites of social engagement around writing, developing writers' expertise and sense of authority, and supporting students in a safe, trusting atmosphere—are not always easy to attain. Implementing writing groups in the writing center also raises a number of challenges both for the center and for the writers who take part. For writing centers, one of the challenges is attrition in writing groups. Writing centers that are already under-resourced may not have the ability to put time and money into training and supporting tutors to facilitate writing groups that ultimately fail. As Claire McMurray (2019) notes, much of the (already limited) literature on writing groups narrates success stories, focusing on what works, yet sometimes facilitators and administrators find that writing groups fail as participants either never show up or drift away over time. It's difficult to find robust scholarship on why writing groups fail. In her small surveys of group participants and interviews with facilitators, McMurray (2017, 2019) found that group success hinged on the role of the group facilitator, the impact of the first meeting, and group negotiation of the structure for giving and receiving feedback. Further, participant satisfaction with writing groups depended on how well the group met participants' goals and expectations. Using a case study of a successful faculty writing group, Smith, Molloy, Kassens-Noor, Li, and Colunga-Garcia found that group members shared similar goals and values, appreciating, among other things, the multidisciplinarity, consistency, mutual support, and important opportunities for learning and professional growth offered by the writing group (Smith et al. 2013). These studies suggest that when participants in writing center–sponsored groups do not share (or do not come to share) similar goals, values, or expectations—when they don't form a community—groups are likely to dissolve.

Clearly, writing group members must find some common ground, some sense of shared purpose and expectations to collaborate successfully. For many successful groups, like those mentioned in the scholarship above that formed tight, trusting bonds, these shared values, purposes, and expectations might seem to come naturally, the result of a homogeneity in the group, for example when group members share the same gender identity (Kinney et al. 2019), or disciplinary background (Phillips 2012; Thomas et al. 2004). However, writing groups that experience challenges make plain the importance of *negotiating* for shared goals, practices, and values as group members navigate ideological differences and sometimes meet with real conflict between members.

Several studies of community writing groups have attended to these sorts of conflicts. For example, Jackson's (2004) study of groups in a prison classroom explicitly addresses conflict based on racial ideologies. Jackson contends that the ideology of writing groups, which rely on trust, mutual support, and engagement, runs counter to the ideology of a prison. Yet the racial ideologies that were enacted in conflicts among group members reach far beyond prison walls. Westbrook's (2004) ethnographic study of conflict in a self-sponsored community writing group also focuses explicitly on the diversity of group members' race and gender, theorizing the group as a contact zone. In focusing on difference and conflict, Westbrook and Jackson both aimed to fill a gap left in the research by its emphasis on the communal, caring nature of successful writing groups. These studies emphasize the importance of understanding how the particular social and institutional context of a writing group shapes group members' collaborative negotiations of conflict.

The negotiations of conflict and difference are also part and parcel of negotiations of authority that have the potential for the benefits of writing groups listed above. Foundational scholarship on writing groups has been somewhat suspicious of authority in writing group collaborations, viewing authority negotiation as a challenge and possible detriment to writing groups in institutional spaces. Anne Gere's 1987 text, *Writing Groups: History, Theory, and Implications*, drew a distinction between autonomous, semi-autonomous, and non-autonomous groups based largely upon their context inside or outside of the classroom. Gere theorized autonomous groups as those begun and sustained by participants themselves, such as the community writing groups that she took as the subject of "Kitchen Tables, Rented Rooms: The Extracurriculum of Composition" (1994). Non-autonomous or semi-autonomous classroom groups, she explained, were limited by how much they deferred to a teacher's authority. Gere's theorization of writing groups as socially situated and context-dependent was taken up in later literature on writing groups. Candace Spigelman's (2000) *Across Property Lines: Textual Ownership in Writing Groups* identified the challenges faced by classroom peer-response groups whose practice was overshadowed by the presence of the teacher and the classroom context. In the classroom, the usefulness of writing groups was limited by students' concerns about plagiarism, notions of textual ownership, and sense of the teacher as true expert and thus only source of authoritative feedback. Concerns about classroom-based groups, including those facilitated by course-embedded writing tutors, have centered around how well participants are able to manage and negotiate authority (Berkenkotter 1984; Corbett 2013; George 1984; Gere and Abbott 1985; Spigelman and Grobman 2005). These studies helpfully show how writing groups are context dependent. That is, they function differently in institutional spaces than they do outside of those institutions. It is useful, though, to unpack further how authority and power function in writing groups.

The scholarship above suggests that authority negotiation is a key practice for writing groups, a practice that can raise challenges for group members, but that also provides important benefits for student writers. The benefits and challenges of implementing writing groups point to several rich lines of inquiry for writing groups specifically located in the writing center. How does the location of the groups in the writing center, facilitated by a writing center tutor, impact the particular practices of the writing group? Like the classroom, the writing center is a site of negotiation, as writer and tutor bring different senses of authority and different experience and expertise to their collaborations. How do these negotiations of authority and expertise shape writers' and facilitators' collaboration in writing groups? Do existing theories of expertise and depictions of authority in the writing center account for group practice? What conflicts or differences arise as writers and tutors come together to read and respond to one another's work? For example, what sorts of conflicts or challenges arise due to disciplinary difference, and how are these negotiated? How might a writing group facilitated by a writing tutor support the emerging expertise of its members? What role does a writing group play in the larger writing life of group members and tutors?

In this study, I take up these kinds of questions by examining negotiations of authority and expertise among writers in writing center–sponsored writing groups. This study thus explores (1) how writing center–sponsored writing groups support the varied goals of group stakeholders (including group members, facilitators, and the writing center itself); (2) how participants negotiate authority, navigate disciplinary difference, and experience emotions in the writing groups; and (3) how identifying and describing writing group practices extends theories of collaboration in the writing center.

Theoretical Framework: Authority Negotiation in Writing Groups as Communities of Practice

To better understand how authority negotiation is at work in the writing groups and how the groups thus support writers' learning, I turn to *communities of practice* as a key theoretical concept. Theorizing writing groups as communities of practice is particularly useful for making sense of how learning happens through group interactions. Wenger, McDermott, and Snyder define communities of practice as "groups of people who share a concern, a set of problems, or a passion about a topic and who deepen their knowledge and expertise in this area by interacting on an ongoing basis" (Wenger et al. 2002, n.p.). Etienne and Beverly Wenger-Trayner further clarify that through interaction, communities of practice develop a "shared repertoire of resources: experiences, stories, tools, and ways of addressing recurring problems" (Wenger-Trayner and Wenger-Trayner 2015). In this model, learning happens not through transmission (for example, from teacher to tutor to student) but rather through participation in communities. As we act in collaboration with others in our communities and negotiate the meaning of our practices, we learn and we become expert in those practices (Wenger 1998). In *Writing Groups in the Writing Center*, I theorize writing groups as small communities of practice that sit in a liminal space at the periphery of the writing center and the home disciplinary contexts of writing group members. The groups bring together people who share a concern and set of problems about writing and who share experiences, resources, and ways to address those problems. The groups in my study were situated within the writing center, facilitated by tutors who were steeped in writing center theory and practice, and yet also connected to the discursive contexts of the writers' work.

Wenger (1998) initially theorized learning as situated in communities of practice through four key concepts: meaning, practice, community, and identity. In Wenger's model, learning occurs through a process of participating in shared *practices* with others and making *meaning* of our experiences with them through processes he calls "participation" and "reification." Participation is "taking part" in a process or practice with others. Participating in the writing center, for example, means taking part in the practices of a writing center—tutoring, posting on the writing center's social media account, observing a session, even answering the phone or socializing with other tutors—or in the more global writing center community by attending a regional or national conference, publishing writing center scholarship, or reading or posting to the WCenter listserv. Reification is the "process of giving form to our experience by producing objects that congeal this experience into 'thingness'" (58). For example, we might "reify" our practice through producing handbooks or, as R. Mark Hall theorizes in *Around the Texts of Writing Center Work*, lists of "valued practices" for observing writing center sessions (Hall 2017). As both Wenger and Hall make clear, however, reification isn't about ossifying meaning or practices but is an ongoing process of negotiation. For example, Hall's list of "valued practices" for observing tutoring sessions was produced, used, and revised through continued conversation with tutors. As a "temporary reification" (Hall 2017, 20), the list of valued practices became an object with which participants in the writing center negotiated the meaning of their tutoring practices and ultimately created a writing center that valued observation and inquiry. As individuals engage in the *community* of the writing center, participating in shared practices and negotiating their meaning, they also engage in negotiations of *identity* as members of that community. Tutors, for example, become active members in the community, learn through the practice of tutoring and through talking with one another to share resources and theorize their work. The writing center coalesces as a community of practice as participants engage together in theorizing and practicing their work as tutors, administrators, and writers.

By taking up communities of practice as a theoretical frame, I focus my analysis on the means by which writers and group facilitators develop and participate in shared practices, shared ways of reading, writing, and talking together. I examine how particular values, conceptions of writing, ways of reading and responding, and ways of theorizing work in writing groups become reified through group practice and negotiation. Finally, I ask what these acts of negotiation and participation mean for the learning of both group members and group facilitators, within the writing groups, the writing center, and their home disciplinary communities.

WRITING CENTER–SPONSORED WRITING GROUPS WITHIN A LANDSCAPE OF PRACTICE

In taking up Wenger's communities of practice (CoP) framework for understanding writing group work, I join a number of scholars who use this frame to theorize writing center work (Geller et al. 2007; Hall 2011, 2017; Phillips 2012) and to theorize writing and learning in academic disciplines and workplaces (Artemeva 2008, 2009; Dias et al. 1999). In *The Everyday Writing Center: A Community of Practice* (2007), Geller and coauthors introduced and popularized the idea of the writing center as a community of practice. They and others take up this model of situated learning because it can be a particularly useful tool for analyzing writing center work that has, at its heart, learning through collaboration and negotiation of meaning (Geller et al. 2007; Geller et al. 2011; Grimm 2011; Hall 2011, 2017). As Hall (2017) writes, "Rather than focus on individual knowing or tutor development, a communities-of-practice perspective turns our attention to the joint activities—the shared *practice*—of the writing center, the transactional process of becoming enculturated into that community, and the resources . . . which mediate that process" (20). To view the writing center as a community of practice helpfully frames engagement in shared practices as a means by which individuals entering the community continually negotiate their identities within the community and renegotiate these shared practices through participation in them.

The writing center scholarship that takes up the CoP frame tends to focus on administrators and tutors, with less explicit attention to student-writers. To some degree, this focus makes sense because communities of practice are built on consistent interaction among members, and administrators and tutors are consistent participants in the community (Wenger 1998). But what is the role of student-writers in this community of practice? Writers who come to tutoring sessions participate in writing center practice regularly, but they don't necessarily see themselves as members of the writing center community of practice. How do these students take part in the community? Shape the community? For Geller and colleagues (2007), they might challenge through "trickster" moments, moments that ask the tutor or administrator to reconsider their practices or frameworks, to see them through new eyes. In one-to-one models of tutoring, unless a student writer visits the center repeatedly, there isn't enough interaction for the writer to establish membership in the community.

Writing groups, however, do engage both tutors and student-writers in sustained interaction within the writing center. I argue that as engaged participants in writing groups, student writers negotiate meaning and participate in the community of the writing center through their interaction with other group members and facilitators. I consider the writing experiences they bring to these negotiations and examine how they engage in and potentially reshape writing center practices. Viewing writing group interactions as participatory practices in the writing center, we can observe how writing groups encourage students and tutors to establish membership, even fleeting or peripheral membership, in the writing center as a community of practice.

At the same time, group members are engaging in other communities of practice outside of the writing center through their writing. A doctoral student's dissertation chapter, for example, is meant to engage with practitioners in their home discipline. As a piece of scholarship, it engages in disciplinary discourses and also is an essential part of the writers' emerging participation in a disciplinary community. Writing dissertations and theses in particular requires that students begin to participate in disciplinary communities of practice and begin to develop a sense of identity as expert participant in their field (Paré 2011; Prior 1994). Within local contexts, students engage with professors as representatives of disciplinary fields and with each other through conversation around disciplinary genre conventions and expectations. When they bring these pieces of writing to the writing group, group members help them to negotiate participation in their home disciplines. Writing group participation is thus a form of peripheral participation in both the writing center and in the communities of practice that students engage with through their writing—their home academic disciplines or workplace communities. By considering writing groups as located at the periphery of the writing center and writers' other communities, this book attends to the way that participants' membership in multiple communities of practice, and their various levels of commitments to writing and to learning in those communities, affects their work in the group. In other words, I consider writing groups within a larger "landscape of practice" (Wenger-Trayner et al. 2015). Theorizing writing groups as communities of practice helps us to understand the significance of the writing groups' location in the writing center, to frame facilitators' roles, and to understand how participation in writing groups necessitates negotiation of expertise and authority and also leads to learning in and beyond the group.

In theorizing writing groups as CoP that sit at the intersection of the writing center and student-writers' other communities, I extend the work of several other scholars. Talinn Phillips (2012) found that multilingual graduate writing groups formed communities of practice that helped their members move more fully into their disciplinary communities. Phillips examines the "language of negotiation" through which these students engaged in legitimate peripheral participation (Lave and Wenger 1991) in their home disciplinary communities. Newcomers to a community engage in legitimate peripheral participation as they become expert; that is, rather than simply observing or receiving explicit instruction, newcomers begin by actually participating at the periphery of communities and gradually engage more fully, eventually becoming experts themselves. For Phillips, writing groups serve as small, low-stakes sites in which student-writers engage at the periphery of their home disciplines. Similarly, Kinney, Synder-Yuly, and Martinez found that their experiences forming and engaging in a writing group as a community of practice provided a valuable site of disciplinary socialization where they learned to interact as emerging experts in their discipline (Kinney et al. 2019). Both of these articles argue for the value of writing center–sponsored writing groups as sites of peripheral participation in academic disciplinary communities, but they are less focused on the impact of the writing center itself as part of the institutional context shaping writing group practices.

Brooks-Gillies, Garcia, and Manthey emphasize the importance of multidisciplinary writing groups as liminal spaces outside of traditional institutional authority and, particularly, the importance of the location of these groups in the writing center, facilitated by writing center consultants. Reflecting on what the writing center space affords writing groups, they write:

> Writing centers have a standing tradition of working with students at their point of need, whether that need is focused on what's written on a page or if that need is for emotional support and security. In addition, many writing centers employ students as consultants, so the very nature of the interactions that take place between consultant and client exist outside the traditional assessment and grading authority that exists within classes and departments. The graduate writing groups at the MSU Writing Center create rather unique institutional spaces, spaces that exist outside of traditional institutional authority yet inside the institution itself. Because of their nature, they provide graduate students with an important "bubble" in which those students can more objectively examine the practices expected by their departments, classmates, and especially advisors. Like Thesen (2014), though, we want to caution: "It must be said that the circle sometimes feels very fragile, and the flattened hierarchy of the group does not solve all problems" (p. 165). The groups allow students to come together to share and compare experiences, departmental and disciplinary practices, and of course writing knowledge with the hope that such exposure helps everyone become better scholars and professionals (Brooks-Gillies et al. 2020, 207–8).

Brooks-Gillies, Garcia, and Manthey's essay points us to the richness of the writing center space for writing groups, noting the possibilities for authority negotiation and also a caution against underestimating the difficulty of those negotiations by assuming a "flattened hierarchy." In this book, then, I build on their work, considering writing center–sponsored writing groups as at the periphery of both the writing center and of student-writers' disciplinary communities. I describe and theorize the practices and perspectives of writing group members in this liminal space, especially focusing on the challenges and conflicts that they encounter through this practice.

DIVERSITY, DISSENSUS, AND CONFLICT IN WRITING GROUPS AS COMMUNITIES OF PRACTICE

Theorizing writing groups as communities of practice, importantly, does not require that members of the community are homogenous groups of people, and doesn't necessitate the warm, fuzzy feelings among members that the term *community* often evokes. Rather, participants in communities of practice are connected through mutual engagement. The interrelations of members in a community of practice "arise out of engagement in practice and not out of an idealized view of what a community should be like" (Wenger 1998, 76). Writing center scholarship that has taken up this frame has also emphasized the way that diversity in the community of practice is actually essential to a dynamic and "learning-ful" (Geller et al. 2007) writing center. Geller and co-authors (2007) note that viewing the writing center as a community of practice doesn't eliminate "conflict, disagreement, competition, and disenfranchising hierarchical relations. Instead, we acknowledge that writing centers—like all communities of practice—are neither a haven for togetherness nor an island of intimacy insulated from political and social relations" (77). Following from *The Everyday Writing Center*, later scholarship emphasizes the importance of understanding how such conflicts, disagreements, and hierarchical relationships shape our everyday practice, especially when we take on the critical work of reimagining our centers to enact anti-racist pedagogies (Geller et al. 2011; Grimm 2011).

Despite the attention to diversity, dissensus, and conflict in Wenger's presentation of the theory and in the scholarship above, much of the literature on writing groups focuses on the communal, caring nature of these groups. Writing groups can be a powerful antidote to the isolation that often comes with writing, especially for graduate writers and others working on writing outside of a classroom. By attending to conflicts, challenges, and differences within writing groups, I don't mean to negate the importance of shared trust or the powerful feeling of camaraderie that can be so valuable for writing group members. Instead, I find that negotiating conflicts and challenges can be productive. By focusing on mutual engagement in shared practice and negotiation of meaning, the communities of practice framework allows for a conception of community that does not require homogeneity, whether of discipline, gender, race, or any other identity marker. It requires mutual engagement. The framework thus provides a means for understanding the practices by which group members manage dissensus, conflicting disciplinary expectations, and negotiations of authority as part of their community participation. This book engages in an analysis of how student writers and group facilitators manage conflict and negotiate authority as part and parcel of their group practice.

AUTHORITY AND EXPERTISE IN THE WRITING CENTER AND IN COMMUNITIES OF PRACTICE

A model of situated learning, the communities of practice framework provides a means for theorizing expertise as developed through practice and negotiation. In the CoP framework, old-timers in a community share their experience with newcomers, and newcomers also continually reshape the community. This framework is useful for considering expertise in the writing center and in writing groups because it offers us a different way of considering tutor and student expertise and authority, which have been fraught in writing center scholarship and in writing group scholarship.

As detailed above, writing group literature has been particularly ambivalent about the role of teacher authority in writing groups, positing a nonhierarchical group as an ideal. Writing center scholarship has been arguably even more uncomfortable with the idea of tutor authority, and its concerns are bound up in understandings of tutor expertise. Foundational writing center pedagogy posits tutors as peers who should use minimalist or nondirective techniques to maintain a nonhierarchical relationship between tutor and tutee (Brooks 1991; Bruffee 1984). Critiques of minimalist tutoring that advocate for allowing more directive tutoring strategies may move us closer to theorizing authority as negotiated through interaction. Peter Carino's "Power and Authority in Peer Tutoring" called for better understanding how power and authority are distributed in a session, arguing that rigid adherence to nondirective tutoring and total commitment to a nonhierarchical peer relationship between tutor and tutee masks the way that authority and power always already function in the tutorial, whether acknowledged or not. Carino concluded that tutor training should help tutors "recognize where power and authority lie in a tutorial, to what degree they have them, to what degree the student has them, and when and to what degree they are absent in a tutorial" (Carino 2003, 123). Carino's argument, persuasive in complicating a strict adherence to nondirective, anti-authoritative values, is also still predicated on a particular model of authority and expertise. In the above quotation, power and authority are held by tutor or student by virtue of their knowledge of how to complete the student's assignment. Rather than considering authority as held, by virtue of title or experience, I want to consider authority as constantly negotiated through interaction.

This understanding of authority as constantly negotiated is informed by feminist theories of authority in composition studies as well as in the writing center. In *Radical Writing Center Praxis: A Paradigm for Ethical Political Engagement* (2019), Laura Greenfield critiques both a conservative view of power and authority—which assumes that power and authority come from knowing and ascribing to a right way to speak, for example privileging a standardized English and the authority of a teacher—and a liberal view that is suspicious of power and authority, equating all authority and power with oppression, like the minimalist tutoring theories described above. Instead, Greenfield calls for a radical paradigm for writing center work that sees power as exercised (and not inherently good or bad) and authority as not inherent to people or institutions but residing in theoretically informed practices. Greenfield's argument recalls earlier attempts to reconceive of authority in composition studies. In 1993, Peter Mortensen and Gesa Kirsch called for a dialogic model of authority rooted in a feminist ethic of care (Mortensen and Kirsch 1993). For Mortensen and Kirsch, a better, feminist, dialogic model of authority would allow us, "in dialogue with others, to shape what authority does rather than simply attempting to alter what authority is" (566). To enact a feminist critique of authority in the composition classroom, Mortensen and Kirsch call on scholarship to "investigate the discursive practices writers use to invoke authority and the ways readers judge and respond to that authority.... By mapping the manifold ways in which authority defines people and relations of power—the discursive landscapes we and our students traverse—we can resurrect authority and make it more democratic, better suited to voices of both consensus and conflict" (568–69). More recently, in *Toward a New Rhetoric of Difference,* Stephanie Kerschbaum notes how difference is marked and negotiated in the context of student peer-review sessions (Kerschbaum 2014). Her exploration helps us see that even differences that might seem "prenegotiated" (like identity markers such as race, gender, and class) are given meaning through negotiations in ongoing interactions, inflected but not completely determined by existing cultural scripts. The move to retheorize authority, as Greenfield does in *Radical Writing Center*

Praxis, is thus part of an ongoing project in composition studies more generally. What I want to focus on in this scholarship is the idea that authority is not solely held by one person or entity, whether by virtue of their position in the group (the facilitator) or their expertise in writing (or particularly valued forms of writing), or their visible/invisible identifications (though these things matter), but rather that authority is negotiated through practice.

By considering writing groups as communities of practice, in which both tutor-facilitators and group members collaborate to develop their shared practice, I am interested in seeing how authority, power, and expertise are negotiated, shared, and performed. Throughout this book, I examine the conversational practices by which group members and facilitators negotiate authority over their texts and in the group. I see expertise not as an entity to be held but as knowledge in practice and as performed through negotiations of authority. However, these group negotiations and performances don't occur in a vacuum. Writing groups are situated within the larger institutional structures of the writing center and the university, and group members bring with them experiences and pressures from communities outside of the group. In this book, I examine students' and facilitators' sometimes clashing conceptions of authority and expertise, and ask what we, writing center professionals, can learn from how group members manage these differences, negotiate authority, and reflect on their own learning.

Research Site and Methods

WRITING GROUPS IN THE BIG STATE UNIVERSITY WRITING CENTER

This study examines writing groups located in the Writing Center at Big State University (BSU), a large Midwestern land-grant university. At the time of this study, the Writing Center was led by a full-time director and three to four graduate assistant coordinators and employed approximately thirty-five tutors (both undergraduate and graduate). Each year, the center conducted roughly 3,700 consultations through individual, face-to-face, and online meetings between tutors and clients.

Although well-established, the BSU Writing Center was experiencing a period of change at the time of this study, changes that in part prompted the expansion of its writing group program. The Writing Center was housed in the Writing and Research Center (WRC), a larger center for researching and teaching writing, that had also included the Writing Across the Curriculum

(WAC) program as well as a number of community outreach programs and digital media initiatives. In 2012, the WRC underwent major changes. It moved to a new location and cut its technology and community outreach programs, leaving two programs: the Writing Center and the WAC program. This shift, which scaled back the work of the WRC as a whole, also meant an increase in space and consultants within the Writing Center itself. This increase in resources, combined with additional funding earmarked for international student support (international students made up 48 percent of our sessions at the time), encouraged the center to concentrate new efforts on supporting international and graduate student writers.

At the time of my study, the BSU Writing Center was attempting to increase its offerings of writing groups, particularly to support advanced writers like graduate students and postdoctoral scholars. In the three years leading up to this study, the BSU writing center increased writing group offerings from just two dissertation writing groups to about fifteen, depending on the particular semester. During the spring of 2016, the primary semester in which I collected data, the Writing Center offered twenty groups, seventeen of which actually continued to meet throughout the duration of the term. During this period of growth, the Writing Center experimented with offering a number of different types of writing groups for writers of all ranks (undergraduate, graduate, and postdoctoral), from different programs (first- and second-year writing courses, ESL), and who were working on particular genres (dissertations, theses, grants, proposals, personal statements, journal articles). Through trial and error, the Writing Center dropped some of these offerings to focus on offering groups for writers working on long-term projects and who did not have other support in the form of a writing class.

Most of the groups offered by the BSU Writing Center at the time of this study had a similar basic structure. Each was facilitated by an experienced writing tutor and often included group members from a range of disciplinary backgrounds. Some groups expressly met to sit down and write together, spending only a small portion of the meeting setting writing goals and talking about writing process. Most, however, had feedback as a primary goal and practice. In these groups, one or two group members would distribute a piece of writing each week to be read ahead of a weekly meeting. Groups met for one or one and a half hours, and facilitators received one and a half hours of paid preparation time to read participants' work and keep up with group email. Beyond these generalizations, however, groups each developed their own routine and practices, led by the facilitator.

My Role in the BSU Writing Center

At the time of data collection, I served as a graduate assistant coordinator, after having worked in the BSU writing center as a graduate tutor and as a writing group facilitator, and my role in these positions shaped both the initial exigence for and the methods of this study. As assistant coordinator, I was responsible for scheduling and advertising writing groups, developing training and support for group facilitators, and administering an end-of-term survey to gather feedback from group participants. Additionally, I facilitated one group each term myself. It was my experiences as both group facilitator and as administrator responsible for the writing group program that prompted my interest in writing groups. Although I led a number of satisfying, successful writing groups, I also had experience with two groups that were less satisfactory to group members and that failed to continue over the course of the term. As a facilitator, I experienced a disconnect between writing center theory that had guided my tutoring work to that point and the practices I was engaged in as group facilitator. This disconnect and the need to develop better support for the massive increase in group offerings were the two exigencies that first led me to this project. I was responsible for training and supporting the group facilitators who took part in this study. As I analyze interviews with facilitators, in particular, I aim to account for my position in relationship to them, which may have influenced how they spoke about their work in the writing groups.

Recruiting Groups for This Study

In selecting my three groups for this IRB-approved study, I purposefully sought a mix of graduate and undergraduate groups to learn how writing groups might differ for participants with different goals, needs, and writing experiences. I began by recruiting facilitators who were willing to participate in interviews and have me observe their groups. I interviewed most facilitators before the semester began (described in more detail below), and then followed up to ask them if I could attend their group (choosing the groups I would attend based on scheduling constraints). If they agreed, I attended the first group meeting to introduce myself and the study to participants. In talking with the groups at those first meetings, I explained the purpose of the study, my role in the writing center, and the different possibilities for my involvement as a researcher in their group and their involvement in the research study. I then left the room while they deliberated about whether or not to allow me to observe the group. If all in the group were amenable to my observations, I continued to attend and observe all group sessions from that point on. I followed up with individual group members who were interested in contributing interviews.

Group Descriptions

The groups I studied varied in their makeup in terms of participants' race, gender, home languages, and disciplinary backgrounds. Below I describe the three groups that participated in this study: a dissertation writing group, an undergraduate thesis writing group, and a group of second-year writers writing grant proposals as part of a program promoting student retention. The information in the following descriptions reflects the ways that participants described themselves to me or to one another at the time of the study.

DISSERTATION WRITING GROUP (DWG). The Dissertation Writing Group met weekly for one and a half hours in a small group study room at the library. One participant each week would send the rest of the group a piece of writing before the group meeting. Group members committed to reading and commenting on drafts, bringing feedback with them to the group meeting, which was facilitated by an experienced Writing Center consultant. Table 1.1 describes the participants who took part in the DWG in more detail. Most of the writers in this group were well into the dissertation-writing process, though they had different amounts of experience with writing groups.

UNDERGRADUATE THESIS WRITING GROUP (UTG). The Undergraduate Thesis Writing Group formed under slightly different circumstances than the other groups. Partway through the previous term, two undergraduate Writing Center consultants, Maggie and Eleanor, approached me to ask if they could take part in a writing group to support their upcoming thesis projects. They also hoped to facilitate a group themselves eventually but were uncomfortable taking on the role of facilitator in their first group experience. Marie, another undergraduate consultant, who was finishing up her senior thesis, agreed to facilitate the group and herself took on the job of helping to recruit more group participants. Before the group was advertised outside of the Writing Center, Marie, Maggie, and Eleanor agreed on their roles as facilitator and group participants (rather than cofacilitating). Table 1.2 describes participants in the UTG.

The group met weekly in the same group study room used by the dissertators, for one and a half hours in the evening, the only time that could accommodate everyone's class and work schedules. The group's initial makeup

TABLE 1.1. Dissertation writing group participants

Facilitator
RADHA: A PhD candidate in literature, Radha had facilitated a range of writing groups, including dissertation and postdoctoral groups. Radha was an American woman of Indian descent.

Group Members
AHMED: Ahmed was PhD candidate in Veterinary Medicine. This was his first writing group at the Writing Center. Ahmed was an international student from Egypt. HOLLY: Holly was a PhD candidate in Art Education who also had participated in Radha's dissertation group the previous semester. She was a white American woman. PETER: Peter was a PhD candidate in Sociology. He had not yet worked with Radha, but had participated in several groups before, including one that I facilitated and one in which Emily participated. Peter was a white American man. EMILY: A PhD candidate in Women's, Gender, and Sexuality Studies (WGSS), Emily was in a writing group with Peter the previous term, though she had not been in any of Radha's groups before. Emily was a white American woman.

included students at very different points in the process of writing their theses. Maggie and Eleanor were just starting the process, planning to finish their theses the following academic year. They were using time in the writing group to begin research, do preliminary writing, and compose outlines. Andrew and Adanna had both completed abstracts at the time of the group. Adanna had completed her data analysis, and both of them were in the midst of drafting the thesis itself. Andrew, Adanna, and Marie were all readying themselves to defend their theses that semester.

About five weeks into the term, Andrew and Adanna left the group, explaining that they were juggling too many responsibilities (coursework, jobs) and could no longer commit to the weekly writing group. In consultation with the Writing Center director, the group elected to keep meeting throughout the rest of the term. Because Maggie and Eleanor weren't doing much drafting, many group meetings after Andrew and Adanna left were at least partially devoted to "sit down and write" time, in which group members worked independently and then came back together to share progress at the end of the meeting.

SECOND-YEAR PROPOSAL WRITING GROUP (SPG). This group formed in partnership with another campus program, which was designed to promote student retention. Students in this program lived in the same dormitory, attended co-curricular events, met in cohorts of about twenty throughout the fall semester, and wrote proposals for funding to complete a signature, "transformative experience" or project. Projects could include traditional research

TABLE 1.2. Undergraduate thesis group participants

Facilitator

MARIE: Marie was an experienced undergraduate consultant who had facilitated one group previously. She was double-majoring in Philosophy and WGSS and also writing her senior thesis. She was a white American woman, and she was the first in her family to attend college.

Group Members

ELEANOR: A junior English major and undergraduate consultant, Eleanor was just beginning her honors thesis in English. She was a white American woman.

MAGGIE: A junior English major and undergraduate consultant, Maggie was also just beginning an honors thesis in English. Maggie was a white American woman.

ANDREW: A senior completing his honors thesis in WGSS that semester, Andrew left the group five weeks into the term. He was a white American man.

ADANNA: A senior completing her honors thesis in Economics that semester, Adanna left the group five weeks into the term. Adanna was a Black American woman.

projects, internships, study abroad programs, creative work, outdoor leadership experiences, or community service. If their proposal was accepted, students were awarded up to $2,000 to fund their signature project. The Writing Center created a number of writing groups to help support students as they developed their proposals. The SPG I observed met weekly for one hour in the main Writing Center. Although the writing groups were voluntary, several of the students in the SPG signed up thinking that they were required; however, all of them elected to stay even when they realized the groups were not mandatory. Table 1.3 describes the SPG participants.

METHODS FOR DATA COLLECTION AND ANALYSIS

This study of three writing groups is grounded in a qualitative, inductive, and iterative approach to examining how participants engaged in the groups and made meaning through group practice. This study responds to renewed calls for empirical research in writing centers (Boquet and Lerner 2008; Driscoll and Perdue 2012; Gillespie 2002; Kjesrud 2015). In taking an empirical, qualitative approach to this study, I am interested in understanding the lived experiences (Denzin and Lincoln 2011) of writing group participants, and learning from the things they "do, say, and write, in day-to-day life" (Broad 2012). By systematically observing and analyzing the writing groups in these case studies, I have aimed to move beyond some of the initial assumptions that I had in my early group facilitation experiences (assuming that it must be best for the facilitator to speak as little as possible in the group, for example). Examining

TABLE 1.3. Second-year proposal group participants

Facilitator
ELIZABETH: A graduate consultant and PhD student in English, specializing in Rhetoric and Composition, Elizabeth had facilitated a pilot SPG the previous year. She also facilitated dissertation writing groups. She was a white American woman.

Group Members
VIHAAN: Vihaan was a second-year student majoring in Computer Science. His proposed signature project was a computer science research project. At the outset of the group, he was working with a professor to identify a suitable project. He was a male student from India.
JENNY: Jenny was a second-year student majoring in Mechanical Engineering. Her proposed project was a co-op (internship) with a well-known automobile manufacturer. At the beginning of the group, she had already secured her internship. She was a white American woman.
ANA: Ana was a second-year student majoring in Human Development. Her proposed project was an internship working in human resources. Throughout most of the term, she was interviewing for internships that would take place the following summer or fall. She was an American woman.
LINDSEY: Lindsey was a second-year student majoring in Chemical Engineering. Her signature project was a study-abroad experience in Greece with a special focus on engineering. Early in the term, she received confirmation of her place in the study abroad program. She was a white American woman.

writing groups as communities of practice put my focus on the practices each writing group engaged in together as well as my participants' perspectives on those practices. Finally, I was informed by theories of qualitative research design that insist on reciprocity with and for research participants (Powell and Takayoshi 2003).

Data Collection

Data for this book come from four sources: participant-observation of writing groups, interviews with facilitators and group members, documents from the groups and from the Writing Center, and surveys of participants in writing groups (see table 1.4).

PARTICIPANT-OBSERVATION. I attended, video-recorded, and transcribed group meetings from each of the three groups throughout the course of one semester.[2] Transcripts were written to privilege readability. I did not closely transcribe all ums, uhs, or back-channeling, except where it was especially

---
2. I attended all group meetings for each of my case study groups, with the exception of one DWG meeting.

TABLE 1.4. Data collected

Observations (field notes and video recordings and transcripts)	SPG	9 observations (9 hours)
	UTG	11 observations (16 hours)
	DWG	12 observations (17 hours)
Semi-Structured Interviews	Facilitators	Elizabeth (SPG), 2 interviews
		Marie (UTG), 2 interviews
		Radha (DWG), 2 interviews
		Yvonne (interview only)
		Shelly (interview only)
		Rachel (interview only)
	Group Members	Lindsey (SPG)
		Eleanor (UTG)
		Adanna (UTG) via email
		Holly (DWG)
		Peter (DWG)
		Emily (DWG)
Surveys	End-of-Term Surveys of all BSU Writing Group Participants	Autumn 2015–Spring 2016
Documents	Contextualizing Documents	SPG website and proposal guidelines
		SPG writers' in-process writing and finished drafts
		BSU Writing Center facilitator training materials

pronounced. I have noted extended silences and the number of seconds of silence. I also noted interruptions with an em dash at the end of the line. If participants were talking over one another (which was rare), I have indicated that in the transcript. Much more commonly, I have indicated laughter (of the group at large or of individuals), as well as reading aloud. In addition to recordings and transcripts, I also kept field notes as part of my observations. These field notes also included descriptions of the occasional informal conversations I had with facilitators or group members before or after the group meeting, as well as my reflections on my own experience as participant-observer.

My role in the groups was that of participant-observer, and the extent of my participation in the groups was determined in collaboration with each group at the outset of the term. I wanted to establish a reciprocal relationship with the members of these groups so that my presence would be a help rather than a distraction or a hindrance to them. Each of the three groups allowed me to record and observe weekly group meetings, but they also asked me to participate in their conversations, coming prepared to work with them during group sessions. The SPG agreed to allow me to analyze their proposal writing, while both the DWG and UTG preferred that I not include their unfinished writing in the analysis. They asked me to read and prepare for group sessions alongside them, offering my feedback as part of group conversation. Because I read work ahead of time, prepared my feedback, and shared comments in the group, I became a participant in group conversation. I generally did not share my own writing, but in all other ways, I became a participant much like the others in the group. As a contributor to group conversation, my comments make up part of the data alongside comments from group members and facilitators.

My level of participation both complicated and enriched my research. Among the dissertation writers, I was closest to being a peer, as I was also working on my dissertation and had worked with some of the writers before. I had previously taken a graduate course with Holly, one of the DWG participants, and I had facilitated a writing group in which Peter, another DWG member, had taken part. As I gave feedback in the DWG, I positioned myself as another group member and fellow graduate student, but my status as both researcher and writing center administrator complicated that role. In group meetings, I attempted to hold off on offering feedback, waiting first to see what other group members had to say and how the facilitator might invite me or other group members into conversation.

In both the SPG and UTG groups, I was even further removed from a position as just another participant in the group. As a graduate student and experienced writing center consultant and administrator, I had more experience with academic writing in the humanities and with responding to writing from across disciplines. When Marie, the UTG facilitator, introduced me to the group, she framed my role as both researcher and as experienced writer who could be a source of information about graduate school and graduate-level writing. Throughout the first several weeks, I was especially attuned to how and when I decided to speak up in the undergraduate groups. My field notes from these first weeks of all three groups reflect this attention and the uncertainty that I felt about it. I was aware, in the DWG and UTG, of waiting to offer a suggestion until there had been ample opportunity for everyone else to speak. In the SPG, I was anxious not to detract from Elizabeth's role as facilitator. In later weeks, these concerns are not as prominent in my field notes, though I did note moments in which writers seemed to feel free to disagree with or add to my suggestions. In both data collection and analysis, then, I have tried to account for my position and practices as participant-observer, attending to my own position as researcher and administrator, especially when analyzing negotiations of authority.

INTERVIEWS, SURVEYS, AND CONTEXTUALIZING DOCUMENTS. I conducted semi-structured interviews with facilitators and focal writing-group participants. Interviews were designed to elicit participants' perspectives on the writing groups, including motivations for joining or facilitating groups, their experiences in the group, and how they made use of feedback in revising their texts. Interview questions are included in appendix A. To contextualize my analysis of the case study group practices and perspectives, I also collected and consulted documents that contextualized the work of the writing groups. For example, I collected handouts used for training group facilitators, and I consulted the SPG program website, which included program and proposal descriptions and goals. Finally, I included data from end-of-term surveys sent out to all writing group participants (not just those groups I observed). These surveys elicited information about the overall satisfaction with the writing groups (see survey questions in appendix B). All responses were anonymous. Respondents were asked to take the survey if they had attended at least one writing group meeting.

Data Analysis

Informed by calls in writing center scholarship to rely less on lore and more on empirical research to theorize writing center practice (Driscoll and Perdue 2012; Kjesrud 2015), I approached my analysis inductively, grounding it in the data and using theoretical memos to reflect on data as I collected it. Through an iterative analytic process, I developed a coding scheme from the data rather than applying existing codes, following a similar process to the initial phases of grounded theory analysis (Charmaz 2008; Farkas and Haas 2012; Miles and Huberman 1994; Saldaña 2016). During my initial coding, I used both in vivo codes, which take their language directly from the data, and process codes, which use gerunds to describe action in the data (Charmaz 2008;

Saldaña 2016).³ For example, my list of initial codes included, among many others, process codes like "reading aloud," "explaining reading experience," and "resisting advisor" and in vivo codes from interviews such as "authoritative" and "stress-relieving."

Throughout data collection and analysis, I wrote short, theoretical memos to reflect on my developing codes and begin looking for patterns. I developed codes and grouped them into categories through constant comparison, testing the codes and comparing data from the initial open coding to the rest of the transcripts from group meetings, and finally triangulating observational data with interview and survey data (Farkas and Haas 2012). I looked for emerging categories and patterns—for example, feedback strategies used by group members, facilitator-specific strategies, and participant beliefs about their roles in the group—that I thought would help me account for how writing group members negotiated authority, how facilitators and group members engaged with one another, and how all participants navigated disciplinary difference within the writing groups. Finally, using the coding scheme I developed, represented in appendix D, I compared and contrasted group practices and perspectives in all three groups, using the communities of practice framework and writing center and writing studies theory to help interpret my findings.

I also took the opportunity, when possible, to member-check, or discuss my emerging findings with study participants (Merriam and Tisdale 2016). Toward the end of the semester in which I collected data, I spoke with the UTG about the emerging findings and about a conference presentation I gave on the topic, soliciting their perspectives. I also spoke with Radha and Elizabeth after the groups had ended, during writing center sessions in which they read and commented on portions of the work. Finally, during the final follow-up interviews, I took the opportunity to speak with Radha, Elizabeth, and Marie again about the findings as I had articulated them thus far.

---

3. Following Mackiewicz and Thompson (2015), who developed a coding scheme for analyzing talk in one-to-one writing center tutorials, my unit of analysis for the coding process was the topic episode, "strings of conversation that coherently address one subject" (16). Each topic episode could include either one or multiple speakers and could be explicitly closed (for example, when a facilitator explicitly told the group to move on to a new topic), allowed to peter out (when a group might fall into silence), or ended by a speaker who, within a single comment, might move from one topic to another or one strategy to another (for example, praising the writer, then asking a separate question).

Chapter Summaries

The following chapters of this book are organized around key findings of the study. Chapter 2, "'People Thinking Differently About Writing': The Role of the Group Facilitator," investigates the role and practices of writing group facilitators. I triangulate facilitator perspectives, gathered through interviews, with those of writing group members and my own observations of facilitator practice. Whereas facilitators were somewhat uncertain of their role and particularly ambivalent about their own authority or expertise in the writing groups, group members saw facilitators as a valuable source of knowledge about how to write and revise and how to read and provide feedback. This chapter argues that although facilitators, steeped in a tradition of nondirective peer tutoring, were ambivalent about their own authority, they actually engaged in important conversational practices that made use of that authority to scaffold writing group practice. In this chapter, I identify and describe the key practices that facilitators used to scaffold reading, writing, and feedback practices that would nurture a successful group. I group these practices into three distinct categories: logistical support, emotional and relationship-building support, and intellectual support for reading and writing across disciplinary boundaries. Thus, I theorize the role of facilitator as one that is less about attempting to mitigate authority so as not to overtake the group and more about actively finding ways to share expertise in writing, genre, and feedback, and to invite group members to take up, enact, and reshape those writing center practices.

Chapter 3, "'It's Not Necessarily Science': Disciplinary Clashes, Convergences, and Learning in Multidisciplinary Groups," investigates the challenges and opportunities that arose for group members as they collaborated across disciplinary boundaries. The chapter tracks moments of disciplinary conflict and examines the particular intellectual and emotional challenges and benefits for writers in multidisciplinary groups. This chapter argues that writing groups challenge each group member to act as expert in their home field and to perform their expertise through explaining their research and writing choices to the rest of the group. And yet, reading and responding as outsiders to other group members' writing was one of the key challenges articulated by the group members. Multidisciplinarity challenged group members to seek the rhetorical resonances across disciplines in order to write and revise together. As group members deliberate over revision choices, they also consider and make use of authoritative voices beyond the writing group, like their advisors. In observing students at different stages of their educations (second-year undergraduates, undergraduate thesis writers, dissertators), with different investments in disciplinary discourses and knowledge building, this chapter adds to the growing body of literature on literacy and writing development across disciplines. Following scholars like Roozen and Erickson (2017), I argue that the development of academic literacies is multifaceted, emotional work, and it takes place in community with others, even others outside the discipline. Thus, even though *Writing Groups in the Writing Center* uses communities of practice as a framework, it sees literacy learning within a larger landscape of practice, one in which writers' work and movement across and through multiple communities influences their emergence as participants in academic disciplines.

Chapter 4, "Storying the Difficulties: Emotional Labor in Writing Groups at a PWI," digs further into the emotional life of the writing groups, exploring the tensions that arose within and between group members' experiences of group practices. In particular, it stories difficulties around inclusion and exclusion in group dynamics, layering individual group members' perspectives and stories of group practice. This chapter attends to the key difficulties that participants expressed in performing the emotional labor that allowed them to navigate collaborative relationships in this institutional context: a writing center in a large, predominantly white research institution.

Finally, chapter 5, "Expanding the Boundaries of Writing Center Work," explores the practical and theoretical implications of this research for writing center scholarship and writing studies more generally. It synthesizes the arguments of the three previous chapters and takes up the practical implications for these arguments by offering some goals and possible activities for training group facilitators. While I don't offer prescriptive advice, which could never account for the many and diverse circumstances of different kinds of writing centers and institutions, I do explore some of the ways that this work helped writing group facilitator training evolve and the ways that it has impacted my own work with students in other spaces.

2
"People Thinking Differently About Writing"

The Role of the Group Facilitator

> I think writing groups are still a little bit new, and so we're still trying to figure out how to do them. For me, it's still a little bit of an exploration process. (Marie, UTG facilitator—interview)

> I try not to be too authoritarian in any way. So I guess I see my role as, y'know, holding them accountable, getting them to articulate their own goals [...] just really be a timekeeper in a lot of ways. [...] When I set up the group this semester, I kinda spent a day, just like the very first day, I asked, "what d'you want to get out of this session," like "how do you want it to be set up?" So hopefully, which isn't, like, too passive. But again, if they need me to take a more authoritative role, I definitely can. But I definitely want to start off with, y'know, "you don't have to be in this group, why do you wanna be here and how can we best structure this group to set up your goals?" (Elizabeth, SPG facilitator—interview)

As the quotes from their interviews show, Marie and Elizabeth—both group facilitators—expressed some uncertainty about their role, a sense of exploring tensions and feeling out practices as facilitators. In their explorations, they were working out what practices carried over from their tutoring practice into group facilitation, and how those practices fit within a theory of how group collaboration might work in the Writing Center. Elizabeth's explanation is rich with resonances from her peer-tutoring practice. Elizabeth was a graduate student in rhetoric and composition. She facilitated both the second-year proposal group that I observed and also a dissertation writing group. Her experiences facilitating groups for students who were true peers, perhaps even ahead of her in their doctoral studies, as well as groups for students who were far less experienced at academic writing, like the SPG writers, gave her a particular awareness of her own authority and sense of "peer-ness" in relationship to her group members. Like many of the facilitators I interviewed, Elizabeth emphasized the importance of centering group members' goals. She eschews "authoritarianism" and yet also finds herself in a balancing act between being authoritative and passive with group members: sometimes to the point of downplaying her role to that of "timekeeper," and sometimes recognizing herself as "holding [group members] accountable" or drawing them out.

Writing center folks will recognize in this balancing act some of the same tensions that we have worked through, as a field, in scholarship on power and authority enacted through directive and nondirective tutoring methods. This chapter explores the ways that facilitators understood their role, the blurriness of "peer" and "expert," the particular expertise that facilitators brought to the groups, and the groups' connection to the writing center as a community of practice. As I will explore throughout this chapter, facilitators often felt ambivalent about the negotiations of authority that shaped their work, and they struggled, at times, to articulate a cohesive understanding of their role. Interestingly, group members tended to speak of the facilitator role in quite different ways, pointing instead to facilitator expertise in writing and rhetoric or to the importance of facilitator authority in encouraging productive collaborations and supportive relationships among group members. In this chapter, I triangulate group facilitators' conceptualizations of their role with group members' perspectives on their facilitators; then, finally, I turn to the practices I observed in facilitators' interactions during group meetings.

The groups examined in this study represent just one approach to structuring the role of a writing group leader, but they offer a rich example of facilitation that also pushes writing center practitioners to rethink the roles and expertise of writing tutors. In her "pick-n-mix" typology of writing groups, Sarah Haas has suggested a range of models for group leadership, from a "start-up" leader who organizes the group, to an "expert" leader with expertise in writing and publication or in an academic discipline shared with other group members (Haas 2014, 35). The groups that I observed were facilitated by experienced writing center consultants who took on far more than an organizational or start-up role.

Although facilitators had insightful perspectives on writing groups in general, they often articulated their own roles in the groups as far less active and important than they actually were in practice. While facilitators themselves were uneasy with the idea of being an expert or authority figure, group members looked to facilitators not only for organizing the basic logistics of the group but also for expertise in writing, reading, and offering feedback. I argue that despite facilitators' ambivalence about their own authority, they nonetheless drew on their expertise as experienced writing consultants to scaffold the processes by which group members were able to form communities and give one another feedback.

The Tensions of Writing Group Facilitation: What We Already Know

Though writing center studies has made great strides in theorizing the role of the peer tutor, scholarly literature on writing groups is just starting to investigate and theorize the role of a writing group facilitator. In North American writing centers and graduate writing programs, there is very little scholarship that accounts for the role, often minimizing the work that facilitators do in such groups. We tend to assume, as Michael Pemberton writes, that writing consultants are "peripheral participants at most, typically acting only as facilitators in initial meetings and showing the participants how to comment on and critique each others' texts productively" (Pemberton 2018, 40). The peripheral role that Pemberton describes might well fit some groups, and certainly group members themselves do play a central role. However, I also think that "showing participants how to . . . critique each other's texts productively" can take a lot more active work on the part of facilitators than we realize or anticipate. In their 2015 essay, Stephanie White and Elizabeth Miller reflect on how their senior thesis writing group participants reported challenges with staying motivated and keeping their groups working productively without consistent facilitator involvement. White and Miller argued that as group facilitators, their first goal was to "put senior-thesis writers in the drivers' seat" of their groups, yet they also ultimately found that they needed to be more present than they had anticipated in order to give the groups more support (White and Miller 2015). I appreciate each of these pieces for their embrace of writing groups as a way to engage writers in social writing practices. What I find both interesting and telling about them is the initial assumption that it must be best to have the facilitators doing as little as possible. This attitude is very familiar. It was how I initially approached my own writing group practice, and it appeared frequently in facilitator interviews. However, it also minimizes the work and expertise it takes for a facilitator to know when and how to speak up, provide feedback on writing, or provide structure to the group.

The ambivalence around fully theorizing a facilitator role as more than a peripheral one is characterized by the tensions around authority explored in chapter 1. Facilitators and writing centers committed to peer collaboration are often suspicious of the authority that is enacted through leading as an expert. We saw this impulse in Elizabeth's opening reflection on her role, wanting to start with group member goals, wanting her group members to take ownership over the group, and avoiding being "authoritarian." The writing center (and writing center consultant-facilitators) wants the group members to critique one another's work, knowing that engaging in such critique offers many opportunities for learning. Yet sometimes students don't know how or aren't motivated to engage in this kind of critique, particularly across disciplines, and so, as this chapter explores, the facilitator often has a much more central role to play in the success of a writing group.

Other writing center scholarship offers small glimpses of facilitator practices but hasn't yet been able to fully theorize the role or describe practices in more detail. For example, in his chapter on supporting multilingual STEM graduate writers, Steve Simpson describes a "conversation starter" exercise led by the facilitator that helped group members understand one another's projects and experiment with different ways of explaining their research (Simpson 2018). Cui, Zhang, and Driscoll's recent empirical study of graduate writing groups used pre- and post-group surveys of writing groups led by writing center facilitators, finding that these groups were successful in helping the graduate students feel more confident, particularly in their goal setting, writing productivity, and mentality in approaching their writing projects (Cui, Zhang, and Driscoll 2022). Their study suggests that this model of writing group, with an involved facilitator who leads minilessons on writing and facilitates goal setting and peer review, was a successful one for graduate students.

There is a growing body of international scholarship on writing groups, particularly groups for graduate student writers, that does more prominently foreground the role of the facilitator. In her study of doctoral writing groups, Claire Aitchison (2010) found that facilitator pedagogy occurred in two distinct areas, first in keeping the group running smoothly—doing logistical, organizational work—and second in "direct facilitation of specific learning objectives" that emerged in real time in response to what happened in the group and which, she wrote, required a "high level of facilitator awareness" of learning needs, writing process, and a wide repertoire of teaching skills. Building on Aitchison's work, a number of scholars have begun to sketch out the importance of the facilitator role and the challenges facilitators face. Clement Mapfumo Chihota and Lucia Thesen identify tensions they felt in facilitating multidisciplinary graduate writers' circles, between the emotional work of nurturing laughter and community and the intellectual work of helping group members provide feedback across disciplinary boundaries (Chihota and Thesen 2014). In her chapter in *Writing Groups for Doctoral Education and Beyond*, Linda Li uses the concept of "scaffolding" as a metaphor for facilitating writing groups. She argues that by scaffolding the peer critique process, group facilitators can help address the major challenges facing writing group members, who bring to the group a great diversity of experiences with academic writing, experiences with English, expectations for the writing groups, and home cultures (Li 2014).

Like Li, I find the term *scaffolding* useful for theorizing the facilitator role, for several reasons. First, it dovetails with current scholarship on writing center tutoring, which uses the metaphor of scaffolding, borrowed from Vygotskian learning theory, to better account for learning in tutoring sessions (Mackiewicz and Thompson 2015; Nordlof 2020). Recent tutoring guides such as Fitzgerald and Ianetta's 2016 *Oxford Guide for Writing Tutors* have taken up the language of scaffolding to help provide tutors a way of thinking about their roles in a session. Second, "scaffolding" helps characterize the work of the facilitator as providing structure to the writing groups and recognizes their role in engaging group members in the practices of providing and making use of writing feedback. In this chapter, I flesh out the metaphor further by analyzing and describing the practices by which, I argue, the facilitators engaged in scaffolding group learning. I compare facilitator practices I identified as scaffolding group work to the scaffolding work that Mackiewicz and Thompson coded for in *Talk About Writing: The Tutoring Strategies of Experienced Writing Center Tutors*. In doing so, I interrogate the role of the group facilitator and consider the expertise that facilitators bring to their positions. This chapter thus explores how facilitators' work both affirms and challenges the norms of writing center tutoring, and so also explores the role of writing groups as part of a writing center community of practice.

Identifying, Describing, and Analyzing Scaffolding in Writing Groups

Through the analytic coding process, I developed a number of codes for group facilitators' roles and practices as well as for group member conversational strategies (see appendix D). One of the things that first struck me was that many of the conversational strategies facilitators used were similar to those we might expect in tutoring sessions, but it wasn't just facilitators using these strategies. Group members used them too. And yet there were also some conversational strategies that seemed specific to the facilitators themselves. To understand how facilitators were making use of tutoring strategies, I compared my initial codes to those developed by Mackiewicz and Thompson in *Talk About Writing*.

In their study, Mackiewicz and Thompson draw on a Vygotskian theory of learning to theorize writing tutors' work as scaffolding student learning. In this framework, Mackiewicz and Thompson write that learning develops "from a collaborative, context-dependent relationship between a student (a less expert member of a community) and a teacher or tutor (a more expert member of a community)" (3). The tutor scaffolds student learning by figuring out what the writer knows and pushing them to learn new skills or concepts within the "zone of proximal development." To do this scaffolding work, the tutor knows more than the student about writing or rhetoric and is able to help the student writer make connections between what they already know and what the tutor or assignment is asking the writer to learn. Mackiewicz and Thompson developed three categories of tutoring strategies through which tutors scaffold learning: instruction (telling or suggesting to a writer what to do, explaining a concept), motivational scaffolding (encouraging the writing and attending to the writer's emotions), and cognitive scaffolding (prodding the writer's thinking and encouraging writers to "find their own solutions to composing or content problems") (33).

Much of my coding scheme is heavily indebted to Mackiewicz and Thompson's work on tutorials. Strategies like "pumping" and "praise," which were developed as codes in their framework, also showed up frequently in writing group talk. And in fact, at times, I renamed my initial codes to align with theirs as a way of considering relationships between tutoring and group facilitation and also to help me refine my inductively derived codes. For example, "asking writer questions about project" became "pumping." As I will explore in more depth in chapter 3, both facilitators and group members tended to use many of those practices. And so, I divided the conversational practices into two categories: feedback practices that all group members used and practices that were specific to facilitators. As these categories emerged, I found that facilitators' practices were distinct from group members' because in addition to providing feedback directly to the writer, facilitators engaged in practices that scaffolded group members' feedback. Whereas Mackiewicz and Thompson's framework is focused on scaffolding learning for the individual writer in relation to their text, the scaffolding that facilitators provided was also to support group members' learning to provide feedback for one another. Facilitators prompted and supported the intellectual and relational work that group members had to do to collaborate successfully.

I further divided each of these sets of strategies into different types of feedback practices: logistical support, relational and emotional scaffolding (which includes what Mackiewicz and Thompson label "motivational"), and cognitive scaffolding.[1] I also, at times, saw the use of strategies such as "telling" and "suggesting," which Mackiewicz and Thompson categorized as "instruction." However, the label "instruction" didn't quite fit for the writing groups. Suggestions made by either the group facilitator or other group members were taken up, agreed with, disagreed with, and reframed by other members of the group. They seemed more contingent and carried less weight than the label "instruction" seemed, to me, to imply. Because group members were invited into the community of practice as full, active participants, the balance of power was different, and thus, the negotiations were different. In the next chapter, I attend more deeply to how the group members took up, debated, and used one another's feedback to write together. For now, I will focus on the facilitators' work as scaffolding for the group collaborative practice. As I argue over the course of the chapter, the codes and categories that emerged in my study show how group facilitators were drawing on and modeling their core practices as tutors to scaffold the group development and group members' ability to give one another feedback and to support one another as a community of writers.

---

1. In many ways, the distinction between "emotional and relational" and "cognitive" is a false one. In the next two chapters, I attend carefully throughout to the ways that the intellectual work of the group is also always emotional work. However, I also want to make sure that the work that facilitators do to encourage relationship building and motivation for the writing and the writing group is visible in the coding scheme.

Participant Perspectives on the Facilitator Role

FACILITATOR PERSPECTIVES ON THEIR ROLE: PEER FACILITATOR VERSUS AUTHORITATIVE TEACHER

As in the opening of this chapter, interviews with group facilitators showed them grappling particularly with uncertainty around their roles as authoritative or expert figures in the writing groups, with what it meant to be a facilitator, and with what practices would best put that role into action. All of the group facilitators[2] I interviewed were experienced writing center consultants, and most also had some teaching experience. And yet the writing groups challenged them to rethink their roles and practices in the writing center. As Geller and colleagues remind us, in communities of practice, it is not just newcomers that "have their understandings of their identities challenged [by] new ideas and experiences" but also that "old-timers can be newcomers too—when they encounter readings or situations that challenge them anew" (Geller et al. 2007, 56). The writing groups were such situations, challenging facilitators in ways that asked them to rethink their theories of writing center practice and their conceptions of themselves as peer tutors.

Facilitators' uncertainty in their approach to writing groups reflected the challenge they faced in doing new kinds of work in the writing center. The theories of peer tutoring that had guided their work in the writing center did not fully capture the breadth of their practices as I observed them in their group sessions. Both Marie and Elizabeth expressed worry over whether they were approaching the group in productive ways, asking how they compared to other facilitators in their practices. Several facilitators mentioned wanting more opportunity to talk to others more regularly and to be offered more formal training in running writing groups. In particular, they were concerned about enacting their roles as facilitators as opposed to teachers. Rachel was surprised "at the authority they [group members] were giving me," and reported taking several semesters to gain confidence as a facilitator.

The facilitators framed their work—their commitments, goals, and practices—largely in the language of their writing center training. This training was a bit suspicious of tutor authority and did not account for the complexity and nuance of facilitators' actual practices. In practice, Elizabeth, who was so careful to qualify her authority, took a strong leadership role in setting the agenda for the overall arc of the semester (deciding when to have each portion of the proposal—summary, personal statement, etc., drafted

---

2. I interviewed six facilitators, including the three whose groups I also observed.

and workshopped). That work, and the work of actually facilitating feedback, as I will show later in the chapter, went far beyond being a "timekeeper." Elizabeth's practices led to a really successful group, based on the group members' reflections, their consistent attendance and participation, and the state of their final drafts at the end of the group. And so, I would suggest that the binary language that Elizabeth uses to explain her role (authority vs. peer) wasn't particularly useful for her in conceptualizing her role in the writing groups. Her somewhat hesitant language shows her questioning how her own authority enters into group sessions.

The tension between authority and peer facilitator is the same difficult binary that has dogged writing center tutoring literature, between directive and authoritarian on the one hand (bad) and nondirective and student-centered on the other (good). In *The St. Martin's Sourcebook for Writing Tutors* (2011), Murphy and Sherwood emphasized how tutors must set up interpersonal relationships that foster shared dialogue and respect for a client's ideas. They wrote that "sometimes in a tutorial we need to overcome an assumed hierarchy of power. . . . A good question for tutors to ask ourselves is, 'who has the power in the collaboration and how is that power used?' . . . Are we acting as collaborators or as authority figures?" (12). Of course, it's important for tutors and group facilitators to consider how power is at work in collaborations, but that doesn't mean that making use of authority must be at odds with true collaboration. More recent tutoring guides and scholarship have moved away from the binary distinction between collaborator and authority figure. In *The Oxford Guide for Writing Tutors*, for example, Fitzgerald and Ianetta emphasize the asymmetrical nature of tutoring and, as mentioned above, use the concept of scaffolding as a way to conceive of tutoring sessions without reinforcing a binary between collaboration and authority. However, Elizabeth and the other facilitators I interviewed and observed—Radha and Marie—relied heavily on that binary to conceptualize their role.

Radha, the dissertation writing group facilitator, explained that she tried to avoid making the group feel like a classroom. Her goal, she explained, was "to help people think through their processes better. Depending on what their goal is, I basically make that the central focus and kind of reorient around that. [. . .] so I don't really have any goals other than 'are we getting through some writing' [. . .] and if possible, help you take a step back and reevaluate, like, your writing in general." Like Elizabeth, Radha sees herself as helping writers meet their own writing goals, putting what they want to work on as the central focus of a daily agenda. Radha actively resisted the idea that she had any authority or power in the writing group as a facilitator and set herself up in opposition to being a teacher in a classroom. As she explained to me, she tried not to make her voice the "primary voice because that can get really one-sided and very, like, classroom-y." Instead, she wanted to "let people talk," and not take over the group. She further distanced herself from a teacher role by saying, "They don't look to me for authoritative things that aren't grammar-related. [. . .] I don't think they look to me as like a 'so, you fix this, then.'" Her stance was "I'm not here to tell you this is right or wrong, I'm here to help you talk through your ideas and for you to be able to be a better writer, not for me to fix your problems, because I can barely fix problems of my own life-slash-writing." Radha's focus here is on mitigating her authority over writers' texts and nurturing students' agency, but in doing so she downplays the work she does to do help writers "talk through [their] ideas."

To be clear, I appreciate both Radha's and Elizabeth's perspectives, which echo important tenets of writing center work to foreground student goals and foster student agency. I don't think it would be effective for facilitators to come in and dictate to the rest of the group exactly what was going to happen and tell them every detail of what to do in their writing. However, Radha's insistence is curious to me because she doesn't, here, recognize the authority that she is able to exercise in negotiation with her group members, by virtue of both being official head of the group (what Geller and her coauthors would call the "structural leader") and having learned to read, write, and respond to others' writing both inside and outside of the writing center as an experienced tutor and as a doctoral student in English. Like Elizabeth, Radha is caught in a bind between authority-teacher-corrector and nonauthority-collaborator-peer. The binary, I argue, causes some dissonance for facilitators, not unlike the feelings of guilt that Jennifer Nicklay found among tutors, who worried about their occasional use of more directive tutoring methods, which, for them, seemed to fly in the face of nondirective collaboration (Nicklay 2012). Further, our preoccupation with the binary between authority and non-authority hides some of the important work facilitators do to scaffold writing group practices, work that I will explore in more detail later in this chapter.

Of the three facilitators, Marie drew the starkest line between herself as the tutor-facilitator and her group members. Marie had a particular investment in distinguishing herself from the members of her group, in part because some of them were peers that she knew in contexts beyond the writing group. Both Maggie and Eleanor, members of the UTG, were also tutors in the writing center. Marie was conscious of the fact that she was being paid to facilitate the group, while Maggie and Eleanor were not. Despite the fact that she was also an undergraduate student working on an honors thesis, Marie tended to position herself as separate from—and often more experienced than—the members of her group, rather than as a colearner. This impulse is understandable given the context and yet it also was somewhat difficult for Marie to manage the contradiction, because she was also committed to a sense of her work as non-authoritative.

> MARIE: I think, when you're sort of like the authority figure in a group, you can tend to think, like, "oh, it's all about me," a little bit, like you're on stage, but in a writing group it's really not like that, and even in a [one-to-one] consultation it's not like that. It's all about the other people. So I guess in some ways you're kind of like a parent, where you're thinking about your children and what could help them, and not really about you. And so, when I'm facilitating, I'm generally thinking, "OK, is there something that I can do to help my participants gain something?" and other than that, I just wanna make sure that the conditions are set, um, that they feel comfortable taking the lead.

In framing herself as a parent and her group members as children, Marie puts the relationship between group members and facilitators in more hierarchical terms than either Radha or Elizabeth did, even though the gap between Elizabeth and her group members in age and educational experience was much greater than that between Marie and her group members. At the same time, Marie didn't see her actions as taking center stage but instead as blending into the background.

Marie saw herself as quietly, almost invisibly, creating a space in which other group members could "take the lead" and give productive feedback. She explained that she thought facilitators "should sort of blend away, like we should be a little bit invisible in the process in writing groups." She named this work "passive actions," describing it as "doing a lot of work, but it's all behind-the-scenes work to make sure that everything's going smoothly and that you are creating conditions that people can share in" as opposed to "active actions," which "would be being authoritative in the facilitating." Marie's conception of facilitating was somewhat contradictory. On the one hand, she clearly delineated her role in a kind of hierarchy, and on the other, she eschewed "active actions" in favor of "passive ones" that would allow her to blend into the background.

When I collected data, the BSU Writing Center had just started steadily increasing its number of group offerings. Accordingly, we began to recognize a need for more robust training for facilitators. As we began to include a session in our pre-semester trainings on facilitating writing groups, we drew on some of the resources that facilitators had informally shared with one another over the years. We began developing documents that compared one-to-one tutoring and group facilitation. These documents first focused on logistics (managing attendance, for example) and then emphasized bringing the values of our approach to individual tutoring into the session (working with, not for). There was also general advice, reiterating that the goal was to get everyone to participate, to have an explicit discussion with the group about what good feedback looks or sounds like, to set an agenda for the group on day one, and to share resources on dissertation and thesis writing. There was, initially, very little actual guidance on what good facilitation looked like in practice, how to encourage strong feedback from group members, and how to redirect conversations when necessary. So it's not surprising that facilitators were thinking in terms of (nondirective) peer tutoring. Their training encouraged them to do that. The training materials emphasized logistical tasks and framed group facilitation in comparison to peer tutoring. These materials didn't answer the question of why we recommend particular practices and how they fit into an overall theory of writing center group work.

The uneasy conceptions of the facilitator role and theories about balancing authority and collaboration did not seem to help facilitators much. Uncertainty about their authority bled over into concerns about what to do when group members didn't show up or weren't necessarily contributing by reading and providing feedback for the rest of their group members. The suspicion of authority, I argue, was less productive for facilitators, keeping them stuck in the nondirective-versus-directive binary rather than offering them different ways to think about their own expertise as writing center consultants and ways that they might scaffold group practice.

To better account for the work of group facilitation and then consider facilitator training, I want to think a bit more carefully about Marie's "passive actions" and what her statements might point us toward in understanding the facilitator role. Leaving aside her worries about directivity, Marie's explanation of her "behind-the-scenes" work indicates that Marie is doing labor that she knows is invisible to others in the group. In fact, she values the fact that it is "invisible," that it "blend[s] away" into the background, even as she worried about whether her work was visible enough to merit her hourly wage. Recent years have seen a number of articles in the popular press about invisible work—the uneven mental load that many people, particularly women, take on in households: the labor of arranging appointments, nurturing children, keeping track of household supplies and pantry staples, maintaining social ties, and so forth. In the academic world, we might think of mentoring and administrative work that is so often either invisible or relegated to "service," thus undervaluing the complex emotional and intellectual work that people engage in as they perform these tasks. For group facilitators, I would argue that some of the work they did was similar to this kind of invisible work. As Marie said, they were creating conditions for effective collaboration. And that, as I explore in the next two sections, meant the emotional and intellectual work of scaffolding writing group practices.

In their interviews, most of the facilitators highlighted the importance of making the groups a positive emotional space, recognizing the potential of the writing groups to counter writing anxiety and isolation. Elizabeth, for example, mentioned wanting to make the writing groups a "stress relief" for both her dissertation writers and her second-year proposal writers, and she also emphasized the feeling of community that came out of the groups. Radha explained that "as long as they feel better about their writing, that's actually a great place for them to then keep writing. [. . .] So that, for me, is, I guess, the primary goal is to say, like, 'Do you even feel comfortable doing this writing?'" Similarly, Shelly, a PhD candidate, approached facilitating her MA thesis and grant writing groups from a place of empathy, remembering writing her own thesis and the first grant she wrote, and "how scary that can be, and the uncertainties and insecurities that come along with that. [. . .] So just being able to help someone else go through that and feel more confident makes me feel good." For these facilitators, much of the work of the group was in providing stress relief, empathy, and a way to nurture confidence for student writers.

Making the groups a stress relief and nurturing confidence wasn't always such a straightforward task, especially when group member needs or desires were in conflict. One of the key challenges that facilitators brought up was in managing people, particularly managing interpersonal conflicts. In their interviews, every single facilitator brought up the challenge of holding group members accountable for showing up and being prepared for writing group. All facilitators mentioned group members who would show up when it was their turn to have their work read and workshopped and who, on other days, would show up unprepared, if at all. For example, Radha told a story about one of her groups, in which a member seemed to have stopped fulfilling their responsibility for reading others' work ahead of time, and each of the other group members came to her individually to tell her they were upset about it and to ask her to handle this problem. Radha reflected,

> RADHA: I guess, like, I don't know how to balance that, still. It's such a weird fine line, 'cause you don't, like—as a facilitator, you're not a teacher.

Radha reveals two important aspects of the facilitator role. The first is that group members looked to her to help protect the integrity of their group meetings, to hold members accountable to agreed-upon group norms (such as reading group members' writing ahead of time). The second is that Radha felt a conflict between her role as non-authority in the group (not a teacher) and the imperative to do something to hold this group member accountable. And what would holding him accountable even look like? In Radha's situation, one option might have been a private conversation with the group member, asking him how group was going and what kinds of support he might need to be more prepared ahead of time. Or, perhaps Radha might have set time aside to ask all group members to assess their own participation in the group, to bring up any barriers to participation, and to explicitly address any issues that were arising. As I speculate about these possibilities, though, I don't want to downplay how difficult this work can feel for facilitators, who may not have experience mediating this kind of conflict and doing this kind of emotional, relational work. This sort of conflict is one where the writing center can put policies in place to help protect the groups and to take some of the burden off of facilitators. For example, a writing center can decide how many "no-shows" are allowed for a person to continue being part of a writing group. And they might offer a different kind of support to that person such as individual appointments or groups that operate on a drop-in basis where people aren't expected to read one another's work and that, perhaps, offer a bit more flexibility.

GROUP MEMBER PERSPECTIVES ON FACILITATOR ROLE: "WRITING PEOPLE"

As newcomers to the writing center, group members offered quite different perspectives on the facilitator role than the facilitators themselves. Rather than defining facilitators as either authoritative teacher or passive peer, group members tended to point to the practices through which facilitators brought their writing expertise to the group.

Emily, a PhD candidate in Women's, Gender, and Sexuality Studies (WGSS) and a member of the DWG, helped put into words the value that

Radha brought as a facilitator of the writing groups. Emily had taken part in several writing groups at the Writing Center by the time I interviewed her. She explained, "So, I thought, it's been really helpful having English students or people that are maybe thinking differently about writing than I do." She further specified:

> EMILY: So, what's been really helpful is, kind of, the attention to "what is this paragraph for" or "what does this sentence do," like, you know, this sort of more, like, technical writing terms that I'm not too familiar with. [...] So, it's made me more aware of that while I'm writing, where, I feel like, before, kind of, what I would do is just get stuff on the page, which is good, but I sort of would have a lot of fluff in there that wasn't cleaned up and wasn't focused enough.
>
> [...]
>
> But then hearing, kind of, from Radha and Elizabeth, for example, "well, but wait a minute, why is that there?" ... And I started reading stuff like that, reading, like, published people's articles, reading other people's writing like that and going back to my own writing like that and it's just helped me be more focused and try to be more intentional, I guess, with, like, what I'm putting on the page.

Emily explained that she valued facilitators particularly for the specific expertise in writing that they modeled in the writing groups. She explained how she began taking up particular vocabulary ("technical writing terms"—for example, she later discussed "signposting" as a useful concept), revision strategies (like reverse outlining), and ways of reading from the writing groups, and particularly from Radha and Elizabeth (who had facilitated one of Emily's previous groups). She began to think about writing differently and began reading with a greater awareness of writing structure and rhetorical choices.

Although Emily attributes Radha's and Elizabeth's expertise to being English students, I would argue that these are also practices that are especially valued in the Writing Center, practices that facilitators could bring to the group because of their expertise as writing consultants and teachers. Later in the chapter, I'll show how these types of strategies played out in practice in the observations, but for now, I want to focus especially on what Emily's comments suggest about the facilitator role.

Writing consultants learn to do the kind of questioning that Emily described in their day-to-day work in the Writing Center. They learn to have, at the ready, questions about purpose and audience and about the rhetorical effect of particular paragraphs, as well as strategies like reverse outlining.

So what Emily seemed to value the most in group facilitators was their ability to be what Nowacek and Hughes call "expert-outsiders." In their chapter in *Naming What We Know: Threshold Concepts of Writing Studies*, Nowacek and Hughes explain:

> Tutors draw on knowledge of writing processes and genres, as well as the affective, institutional, and ideological contexts for writing to inform their conversations with writers. . . . However because tutors cannot possibly hope to be content experts for every writer and draft they encounter, they can instead capitalize on lack of content knowledge to position the writers as bringing a different type of knowledge and the tutor as an interested, rhetorically savvy audience wanting to better understand that knowledge. (Nowacek and Hughes 2015, 181)

The rhetorical savvy—the knowledge of how genres work, of how to ask productive questions about texts, with an eye toward revision—is the knowledge of the expert-outsider tutor. It was this kind of expertise that facilitators modeled and shared with their groups, even though they downplayed it in their explanation of their roles.

Writing group members, like Emily, explained that they appreciated how facilitators took on leadership roles in the writing groups, sharing feedback in ways that pushed conversation forward. Emily explained that though she thought initially the facilitator would just be looking out for the time or a "figurehead," she was surprised that in both her groups, the facilitator was a person "who gives a lot of feedback." She said,

> EMILY: Both times, the facilitators have been pretty active and, kind of like, asking those extra questions if there's silence or confusion about a point, then jumping in and kind of pushing me or whoever's presenting that day to further articulate their ideas. [. . .] I think it's been helpful 'cause it's basically just an extra person to give feedback but then that person who's thinking almost larger-scale too sometimes. Like, "OK, is this what you're trying to say," or "it seems like what this person is asking is about this," so it's almost like a moderator for a conference panel or something like that.

Emily's explanation here contrasts greatly with Elizabeth's characterization of the role as being a "timekeeper in a lot of ways," and with Marie's focus on nearly invisible "passive actions." Rather, what Emily recognized was useful feedback and metacommentary provided by facilitators to help moderate group conversation.

Emily's comments give us a more in-depth look at broader trends in how group members at large seemed to respond to facilitators in post-group survey responses. The survey (see appendix B) was sent to all participants in writing groups that term (not only groups that I observed), and we received thirty-seven responses, for a response rate of 38 percent. Responses to the survey were overwhelmingly positive, particularly regarding the facilitators. Asked whether they agreed with the statement "I would work with the same facilitator again," for example, 83 percent of respondents strongly agreed and another 8 percent simply agreed. When asked for general comments about their experience in the group, eight of the eighteen people who responded mentioned the facilitator, specifically and positively, while only two brought up concerns about the facilitator.

When asked, "In what ways might your writing group have better served your needs as a writer? How might you improve your writing group?" of the thirty-one people who responded, eight said it was good as it was and that they wouldn't make any changes, five wanted to change the disciplinary makeup (mostly to group similar disciplines together), and four said a key challenge was attrition in the group or lack of commitment from other group members. Seven responses mentioned things that the facilitator could have done differently. These responses asked for more resources or specific lessons on writing from facilitators, or they critiqued facilitators for not being more engaged. In other words, they wanted facilitators to share knowledge about writing *more* than they were already doing. Far from seeing the facilitators as overstepping, these comments suggest, group members wanted facilitators to take on a bit more authority in setting up lessons, sharing specific resources, or managing discussion. Group members' expectations for facilitators, and their happiness with the facilitator's role in the group, centered on the facilitator as an expert in writing and as a leader in charge of group conversation.

Group members responded to writing groups as communities of practice with facilitators as experienced leaders in those small communities. Though the facilitators did not necessarily recognize themselves as leaders or as bringing a particular expertise to the groups, they did model strategies for reading and responding to writing and offered feedback that group members valued. Group members, by and large, were unconcerned about facilitator authority except perhaps to ask for facilitators to exercise more authority in the groups. They especially articulated the value they placed on facilitators as models for writing center practice.

Facilitator Practices: Scaffolding Writing Groups

Thus far, we have examined the facilitator role from the perspectives of facilitators themselves and of their group members. We'll turn now to the facilitators' practices as I observed them in the writing groups. Across all three writing groups, I found that facilitators engaged in conversational practices that scaffolded effective collaboration and feedback for the writing groups. As I examined these practices, I saw that each of them was contributing to different kinds of supporting and scaffolding work—logistical or structural support (establishing who will send writing and when, emailing reminders, timekeeping, establishing repetitive structures for group meetings); intellectual and cognitive (encouraging or modeling how to read rhetorically, how to give feedback, how to ask for feedback, reframing feedback); and relational or motivational (checking in with group members, inviting chitchat, sharing food, praising feedback, inviting metacommentary on group practice).

Of course, these dimensions aren't necessarily as clean-cut as they might seem. For example, modeling and moderating feedback is both cognitive and relational. When group facilitators praised group members' feedback, they both encouraged intellectual work and provided validation that could build group member confidence. Giving and receiving feedback is both intellectual and emotional work. Yet I make the distinction between cognitive scaffolding and relational scaffolding because I want to honor the kinds of expertise that group facilitators are engaging in to help scaffold group process. They put into action their expertise as writing tutors with knowledge of writing and writing process, and they carry out relational and motivational work (praise of writers and their writing, praise of strong feedback, and invitations to group members to express feelings about their writing).

STRUCTURING GROUP SESSIONS: LOGISTICS, DEVELOPING GROUP PATTERNS AND PRIORITIES, AND CHECKING IN

Like one-to-one tutoring sessions, the writing group sessions developed a rhythm and structure that began with an opening, a middle, and a conclusion, but each facilitator developed practices, particularly for that middle section, that were specific to their group. Most group sessions opened with informal chitchat about anything from the weather to TV shows to adventures in teaching. Facilitators often encouraged this, informally checking in with group members as they entered, or more formally beginning the meeting by asking how things were going, either with writers' projects or their personal lives or emotional states. As facilitators discussed in interviews, it was important to them to provide emotional support for their group members, and so, they took time to check in, to ask each group member how they were doing. At some point, each facilitator would do some kind of agenda setting, explicitly calling everyone's attention to the work under consideration for the day and perhaps putting it into the context of the rest of the semester's group sessions.

From there, the "middle" part varied by group and by day. The DWG tended to read each piece of writing aloud, one paragraph at a time, stopping to discuss each paragraph in turn. The SPG considered two writers' work each week, having planned well in advance which sections of their work were to be completed for each meeting. They read the entire section aloud and offered feedback on each writer's work in turn. The UTG was much more variable, but by the end of term, tended to include an extended period of time for independent writing and then for discussing whatever was coming up for each writer during that time. They also included more extended periods of time for "getting off-track," talking about anything from their favorite vegan snacks to what they were reading in their academic courses.

Facilitators, as they explained in interviews, did the logistical work of structuring group sessions. They emailed. They kept an eye on the clock, knowing when to switch over to discussing a different group member's work, and drawing the group back to the task at hand, if necessary. These somewhat mundane tasks did important structuring work for the groups, helping them to develop group processes, to keep feedback moving, and to motivate group members. These practices provided the logistical and emotional support that facilitators mentioned in interviews. By keeping time and providing the group with a basic agenda and a means of structuring conversation, facilitators helped groups establish patterns that worked for their particular aims and personalities. By continually checking in with group members, they invited group members to get to know one another and develop relationships that went beyond the transactional. They also sometimes opened up opportunities for group members to say when they weren't getting what they needed from the group.

FACILITATOR-SPECIFIC FEEDBACK STRATEGIES: SCAFFOLDING THE PROCESS OF GIVING AND RECEIVING FEEDBACK

Prompting Group Feedback and Reading Aloud

One of the most obvious ways that facilitators scaffolded group feedback was by prompting feedback from other group members. These prompts ranged from general to specific. For example, Radha would begin each feedback session by asking the group for their "overall" or macrolevel feedback on organization, key terms, or argument. As the group fell into a rhythm of reading aloud, after each paragraph was read, Radha would either provide her own feedback on the paragraph, followed by a question about what the rest of the group thought, or she would ask more generally for group feedback (e.g., "did anyone have any thoughts on that paragraph?"). Similarly, after asking the writer to read a draft section aloud, Elizabeth would first ask the writer what they thought now, having read it aloud, and then ask the group for their feedback on the draft.

Prompting group feedback was one way for facilitators to remind group members to give feedback related to the writer's goals, keeping the group focused on the agenda for the day. For example, after Holly expressed concern about how she was combining stories from her data with review of the theories informing her research, Radha prompted the group with a specific question about the paragraph under consideration:

> RADHA: Okay, so it seems like the kind of feedback that might be useful to you is for us to be like, "here's where this is a thing that you need to do here." Um, okay, great. So, then, the "on Fridays" paragraph, anything specific that you guys wanted added to that, or anything, like, signposting-wise that you need? This is a narrative paragraph, so I feel like, do you guys just want [to] just leave the narrative?

Radha thus directed group attention to the agenda she had developed in collaboration with Holly. They decided together to attend to how the narratives from Holly's study data were working in the context of her chapter, which was explicating theoretical terms. In her prompt for group feedback, Radha specifically asked the group members how they were responding, as readers, to Holly's narratives.

This kind of prompting also invited group members into the invention process with the writer. It provided cognitive scaffolding for the entire group, bringing the group members together in a moment of collaborative authorship. In another example from one of the SPG meetings, Elizabeth prompted the group to help Ana revise the wording of her personal statement:

> ANA: Yeah, there's a lot of, like, "guiding," "choosing," "changing."
>
> ELIZABETH: Right. So maybe even just taking a look at that first sentence there. [Reading aloud:] "So many people were vital to aiding in the development of my STEP experience." How, what might you do to make that a little more concise?
>
> ANA: Um, I haven't thought about it.
>
> ELIZABETH: Other thoughts, suggestions on [the sentence wording]?
>
> LINDSEY: Just saying, "many people were vital to development."
>
> ELIZABETH: That works.
>
> LINDSEY: Or "many people aided?" Is "aided" a word? [*laughter*]

In this example, Elizabeth first prompts Ana to make her own sentence more concise, a cognitive scaffolding move that we might expect in an individual tutoring session. When Ana isn't sure, rather than offering a specific suggestion, Elizabeth turns to the group, prompting their suggestions for Ana. Here, Elizabeth's conversational move to prompt feedback from the rest of the group invites the other group members into the "cognitive scaffolding" for Ana and her paper. The learning and revision process here is distributed across all of the group members, who are actively listening and engaging in the conversation.

Facilitators also used prompting to elicit agreement and disagreement about a particular point. For example, Marie prompted feedback from the rest of the group simply in asking if others had a similar experience reading Adanna's abstract:

> MARIE: But back to the writing, I am a little concerned or confused or something about the last two sentences because, when you say this way is counter to conventional wisdom, um, the two ideas there aren't immediately countered, to me. I'd also say, "counterintuitive," not "counter"— Would anyone else say that? Or am I just not . . . ?
>
> ELEANOR: No, to me, I think it was not enough of a transition there. Like, I see how utilizing that sentence works, but then when you switch that one, I kind of, like, I don't really see the connection, I guess.
>
> MARIE: I see the connection because she's saying, like, the method first, and then she's saying, "I find that higher levels . . ."

ELEANOR: I guess, a little more of a conventional ending, is what I mean.

ADANNA: Yeah, it's also another thing I feel like abstracts never really add, like, "well, in conclusion," like, I mean you can, but I haven't seen too many of those. Usually it'll end with what the finding is or the [implication], and that's another thing too, like the, the abstracts are hard to write because I'm still firming up my results, so yeah.

Opening up the group conversational space by asking them for feedback prompted Eleanor to offer a slightly different take on Marie's comment, leading to a conversation about genre conventions for abstracts. Finally, each facilitator would ask the group at large for any final thoughts before moving on to the next piece of writing, whether that was the next paragraph under consideration in the DWG or the next writer's work in the SPG.

Facilitators' prompts for group feedback were strongly influenced by their training as writing consultants and often linked to the practice of reading aloud. They prompted the group members for feedback, and when they prompted for specific kinds of feedback, they engaged group members in typical writing center practices (for example, responding as readers, offering multiple suggestions or choices for revision, and focusing on the writer's goals). In prompting group members for global feedback before reading the text aloud, Radha was adhering to pretty common advice in the writing center to tackle holistic concerns before attending to sentence- or paragraph-level revision.

Radha and Elizabeth both used reading aloud as a cognitive scaffolding tool both for the writer and for the group. Elizabeth made explicit the function of reading aloud to scaffold writer learning, asking each writer what they noticed and what they were concerned about after giving audible voice to their writing. Reading aloud also appears in Mackiewicz and Thompson's study of experienced writing tutors' sessions as a frequently used cognitive scaffolding strategy. Drawing on work by Paula Gillespie and by Leigh Ryan and Lisa Zimmerelli, among others, Mackiewicz and Thompson suggest that reading aloud generally allows the writer and tutor two modes of engaging with the text (hearing and seeing) and actively engages both tutor and writer in the session (as opposed to the tutor reading silently) (Gillespie 2002; Mackiewicz and Thompson 2015; Ryan and Zimmerelli 2010). Rebecca Block (2016) complicates this understanding of reading aloud in tutoring sessions, finding that reading aloud without a specific strategy for doing so could put the focus on sentence-level issues, at the expense of organization and argument. In sessions using the "point-predict" method of reading aloud, however, Block found that sessions were much more likely to address issues of content, argument, or organization.

Extending this discussion of reading aloud, I would also like to suggest that both Radha and Elizabeth used reading aloud to scaffold the group feedback. By reading aloud, they brought the text into the room, reminded members of what had been read, and used that as a jumping-off point to direct the conversation. At times, this move was the default and didn't seem particularly useful. For example, there were multiple times that Radha's group had nothing to say about a particular paragraph or had only general praise for a particular paragraph. However, used intentionally, reading pieces of the text aloud was a useful way for all of the writers to get started, it seems, giving everyone a way into a shared space around the text.

Praising and Reframing Group Feedback

Facilitators also commented on group member feedback in order to provide both cognitive and relational scaffolding for the groups. Sometimes they would praise group members to reinforce strong feedback; sometimes they would reframe a piece of feedback to make it clearer to the writer; and sometimes they would generalize a group member's comment, showing how it might be applicable to other situations. Radha was an effusive and enthusiastic facilitator, and she often praised her group members for their feedback and for their writing. For example, in one session, Radha described some of Peter's feedback for Holly as "really beautiful."

In a different group session, this one focused on Ahmed's work, Radha praised and then reframed Peter's feedback, reading back her notes on what he said. Peter had asked Ahmed a number of questions and then explained how he understood Ahmed's work.

> RADHA: So, I guess, where do you guys, in terms of this information, do you need this before here [in the paragraph they were discussing]? Do you want it before here in order to better conceptualize something else? Like, I think Peter had a really useful way of laying out of the story. Here's what Peter said: "We're studying MI, we have this methodology, which is, we used to do—what?" Sorry, I'm asking you [Ahmed].
>
> AHMED: DNA fingerprinting.
>
> RADHA: DNA fingerprinting. But technology got better and we realized it was insufficient because of the difference between detection and

differentiation. Now it's time for MI research to catch up to technology, here's the technology that we can use to provide reliable results. And that was the story, I feel like, you [Ahmed and Peter] laid out. Which, I feel like, doesn't quite match with your organization here.

Using her notes, Radha restates what Peter said and also articulates the problem that the group is addressing. She suggests that Peter's way of organizing Ahmed's literature review and statement of the problem was clearer than what was on the page. As an observer and participant in the session, Radha's conversational strategy was really clarifying for me, as it clearly summarized the group conversation up to that point. Radha reframed Peter's feedback in a way that all of the group could understand and could then use to suggest organizational changes for Ahmed.

Facilitators also reframed group member feedback to help writers see how it might be transferable to other situations. In the following example from the SPG, Elizabeth affirms Ana's feedback for Jenny and explains how other group members could apply the advice to their own projects:

> ANA: I agree, it just, like, obviously needs to be probably a little bit longer too.... I mean, it's close, but maybe just a little bit longer, and you could be like—like we said, adding more about the "super-mileage" thing.
>
> JENNY: OK.
>
> ELIZABETH: Yeah, and this is an advice for everyone in general. Like, if they give you page space, like, take all the page space you can.

By making the connection from the specific advice for Jenny to a general rule, Elizabeth offers the group knowledge that they can use in their own revisions and keep in mind if they go on to write future proposals. Reframing feedback to show how it is transferable to other group members' projects thus contributes to the goal of helping group members improve both the text at hand and their writing practices more generally.

Facilitators Modeling Feedback Strategies and Providing a Language for Talking About Writing

Facilitators (and group members who had participated in past writing groups) acted as models for group practice, showing group members how to respond to writing and engage in conversation about writing. As time went on, each group developed a shared language for talking about writing as well as the set of practices that guided their work together.

In the dissertation group, for example, the group learned to look for and talk about "signposting." In the following example, after Ahmed explained that he would prefer conceptual or organizational feedback first, followed by sentence-level, Radha reads his first paragraph aloud and responds in a way that models for her group members how to respond to Ahmed's request:

> RADHA: Okay, let's prioritize concepts, then. Okay, I will start, and then we can just go around the table. "Advancements of sequencing technologies over the last decade made whole genome sequencing a powerful tool. [. . .] We will discuss the technical integration challenges of this new technology and role of bioinformatics in tackling these challenges." So, I really like the last two sentences here. I think they're very useful in terms of signposting and, like, saying exactly what you're about to do. And I think they're also pretty accurate in terms of what you've gone on to do. So, that was really helpful. I think the first sentence was a little bit confusing because there's, like, two ideas in it, and it sort of threw me off because I was trying to figure out how to organize them. . . . I'm just wondering if there's, like, a way to kind of clarify that.

Radha's response does several things that would be familiar to an experienced tutor. She reads the paragraph aloud and follows up, first, with praise of something specific in the writing (in this case, Ahmed's use of signposting). Specific, focused praise is recommended by tutoring guides (Ryan and Zimmerelli 2010; Fitzgerald and Ianetta 2015). Radha follows the praise with an explanation of something that confused her, responding as a reader. Radha drew on her writing center expertise here, and her writing group participants followed her lead as they engaged in feedback.

Later in the session from which the previous example was excerpted, Emily provides feedback on a different paragraph, following the same structure as Radha used:

> RADHA: Thoughts? Concerns? Things that stand out?
> EMILY: I like the signposts a lot—kind of throughout. But I think it flows very well with your work and, kind of, like, the "however" and "this article," and "we discussed this" and, kind of, makes it very clear, the contribution—how this is going to make a contribution. I kind of thought the last sentence—two sentences—was kind of confusing. But you said sentence-level is probably something to fix, like, when you polish. I did have a question though. I was wondering—So, like, when you mention here, and I think earlier too, you say, like, in the middle of the paragraph on page 2, "changing the current paradigm blah blah

> blah, in addition to increasing efficiency, pathogen WGS is more cost-effective than traditional techniques." And when you kind of mention that [...] I was wondering, did you want to, kind of, throw in a little bit of what you're referring to? Is that something readers would already know? Because I kind of—I would have liked to read maybe, "more cost-effective than traditional techniques such as"

Like Radha in the previous example, Emily begins with praise for the signposting, identifying particular words and why she finds them helpful. Like Radha, she then follows up with a sentence she found confusing. Emily has several false starts as she explains her confusion and critique, hedging a bit by acknowledging Ahmed's goals for the feedback, and trying to direct her feedback toward the goal of deciding what readers might need to know in this sentence. Her feedback follows similar patterns to Radha's. It also provides an example of the kind of thinking that she mentioned in her interview that she appreciated: attention to "what is this paragraph for" or the "more technical writing terms" like *signposting*, that shaped how she responded to her own and others' writing in the group.

Perhaps the most obvious example of group members learning how to give feedback came in the SPG. On the first day, Elizabeth gave a great deal of direction because the group was not clear on what exactly the group was for or how it would run. They looked to Elizabeth to set up group practices and to explain what they would do as a group and why. In week two, the first week in which group members shared writing, they came prepared to talk, having read and prepared feedback for Ana and Lindsey on their personal statements.

> ELIZABETH: Since these are relatively short, are you willing to take some time and read it out loud to go through each draft? I mean, they're only about a page each. Um, I figure this time, we'll probably go until about 2:30, 2:35, something like that. Then we'll switch out, if that works for you.
>
> ANA: Okay.
>
> LINDSEY: So, well, wait, so like, did you edit mine at all?
>
> ANA: I read it, but the thing is, okay, it's kind of funny, sorry. I read it and then I was like, [inaudible] when I sent mine, then I was like, I forgot to edit yours, but like, I can.
>
> LINDSEY: Yeah, I didn't know, because I edited yours [Ana's draft] and put in, like, comments and stuff. So, like, [to Elizabeth] should I just send

that to her or should I discuss that? [...] I just didn't know, like, is she gonna tell me the stuff or should I just send that.

ELIZABETH: There are two different ways we could do this. So how it's worked in the past is that we'll get together, we'll talk through the comments, and then at the end, you send each other whatever comments or drafts that we have. I think that would probably be best.

This segment shows how important Elizabeth's role was in providing the logistical support that would lay the groundwork for her later scaffolding work (modeling and encouraging effective feedback). She had to give a great deal of direction to the group members, who didn't know what to expect or how to engage in the process. Elizabeth initially framed her first direction—to read the writers' drafts aloud and respond to them in turn—as a question, but not all of the speakers understood her. They talk not in terms of providing feedback or comments, as Elizabeth does, but of "editing" one another's papers and aren't sure if they are simply supposed to swap edited drafts or talk through their suggestions. They thus approach the group quite differently from Elizabeth and look to her to help them establish group practices. Elizabeth does so by providing knowledge of previous writing groups, suggesting when and how to discuss drafts, planning for time, and inviting writers to read their work aloud.

In contrast, a conversation from week six shows the writers engaged really fluidly in giving feedback, modeling much of that feedback on Elizabeth's. This conversation begins just after Ana has finished reading a revised section of her proposal aloud.

ELIZABETH: Yeah, good. Just, um, kind of connecting back to some of the things we talked about last time, you made a lot of really good, really effective changes, it seems like here. Especially, um, kind of, talking a little bit more about human resources things and especially when talking about your, um, STEP co-curriculars as well, it seems.

ANA: Yeah, I think it closed better. Makes more sense.

ELIZABETH: Yeah. Thoughts and feedback, or initial comments?

LINDSEY: Yeah, I think you did a really good job of, like, relating all the co-curriculars to what you're trying to do, your future career, and your internship. Like, I thought that improved a lot. And then, my only suggestion, honestly, was maybe, like, another sentence at the end to, kind of like, transition to the personal statement. But, I don't know, I still think it's good.

ELIZABETH: And that's something we can talk about too, when we do, like, the entire project at once and just, like, have a chance to read through the whole thing, yeah.

We can see Elizabeth's feedback here as a model for Lindsey. Elizabeth uses targeted praise, identifying a strength of the piece of writing, explaining that she thought the changes Ana made regarding her description of activities in the SPG program were successful. Elizabeth then prompts group feedback, opening the floor to others' feedback. What's especially interesting here is that Lindsey models her response after Elizabeth's. She also takes up the strategy of praising the writer, making Elizabeth's comment more specific when she says, "I think you did a really good job of, like, relating all your co-curriculars to what you're trying to do," and then follows up with a critique and a suggestion. So, Lindsey, Ana, and Elizabeth are engaging in practices that are common in the Writing Center, using them as core to the work of this small community of practice. Elizabeth's role in these excerpts also went beyond her role as a model for Lindsey. She also took a wide-angle view of the writing group, suggesting that they worry about transitions between sections later, thus keeping the group focused on the agenda for the day. Finally, Elizabeth also had to give much less direction for the group to get started in week six than in week two, asking in more general language for "thoughts, feedback, or initial comments?" So we can see that by week six, the group members were fairly comfortable giving feedback and taking it. Group members referred back to earlier conversations, building on previous interactions as they learned together. They had formed a community of practice that helped them develop strategies for giving feedback, reading others' work, and revising their own.

Implications for Facilitator Role: Writing Groups as Communities of Practice

The findings above show how the facilitators worked to scaffold the practices of the writing group for group members. In all groups, both facilitators and group members engaged in feedback practices that were modeled, prompted, and nurtured by facilitators. Facilitators provided logistical or structural support (leading agenda-setting and directing the group process), cognitive scaffolding (by prompting feedback from group members, by reframing feedback), and relational or motivational scaffolding (by praising feedback, by expressing excitement and interest, and by checking in with group members about their lives and about how the writing group seemed to be serving them).

Rather than eschewing all authority, as facilitators expressed some pressure to do in their interviews, I want to suggest that, in negotiation with group members, facilitators acted with authority as writing center consultants who are expert in writing center work and the process of writing. In doing so, they engaged their group members in feedback practices typical of writing center work. These findings invite us to think a bit differently about the role of the group facilitator. The goal, I think, is less about facilitators acting as minimally as possible or striving to keep their role peripheral to that of the group members, but more about leveraging their expertise to scaffold group practice, bringing group members into the practices of the writing center.

So what, exactly, is the expertise of a writing tutor and a writing group facilitator? I would like to suggest that the answer is an extension of Nowacek and Hughes's threshold concept of the "expert-outsider." The expertise in writing studies—in how to read rhetorically, how to talk about writing and writing process, and an understanding of genres—was necessary for facilitators to model, prompt, and reframe group members' feedback. I would add to this expertise in writing studies much of the motivational and relational work that is necessary for a group to cohere as a community of practice, such as checking in to encourage relationship building and praising feedback. In this chapter, I have tried to show facilitators' expertise as performed through their scaffolding practices—prompting, praising, and modeling group feedback as well as checking in with writers and inviting metacommentary on group process. I've highlighted the facilitators' expertise as writing center practitioners. And yet I also want to acknowledge that the writing groups pushed facilitators and made them, at times, uncomfortable and uncertain at the periphery of their usual writing center practices.

In training writing group facilitators, then, I think it's helpful to do a few things. First, group facilitators should be asked to reflect on their role as expert-outsider tutors. What strategies for reading did they learn as they gained experience as writing tutors? What knowledge of genre(s) do they have now that they may not have had before their work in the writing center? What kinds of emotional work do they already perform as tutors? This suggestion goes hand in hand with current calls in writing center scholarship for greater attention to reading as a central tutoring practice that needs support in tutor training (Block 2016; Greenwell et al. 2020; King 2018). Second, the role of the group facilitator should be framed as scaffolding group process. Tutors can then understand the group facilitator role as one that teaches and supports some of the key practices of the writing center. A writing group facilitator might ask whether or not members of the group have taken part in writing groups before or if they are comfortable giving feedback to people outside of their home discipline. And finally, a writing center might provide a new group facilitator, particularly a group facilitator with limited experience leading any kind of group or teaching, with some activities or exercises that can help them scaffold group processes. Such activities might help group members give one another background information about their projects, invite reflection on writing process, ask group members to develop a daily writing habit, help writers to get to know one another, and encourage group members to reflect on the learning that happens in group meetings.

Beyond these more practical considerations, however, there is still the challenge of exercising authority in "managing personalities"—holding group members accountable and handling interpersonal conflict. It's important, I think, to consider how we support facilitators in scaffolding group practices that ensure equity, accessibility, and inclusion in our writing groups. What happens when what one group member needs conflicts with what another group member needs? How are the interpersonal conflicts that facilitators are managing shaped by power dynamics inflected by race, gender, class, and disability? The following chapters explore these sorts of tensions and attend to the challenges that group members, especially, articulated in their experiences of writing groups.

3
"It's Not Necessarily Science"

Disciplinary Clashes, Convergences, and
Learning in Multidisciplinary Groups

Scene: The Dissertation Writing Group (DWG) is grouped around a table at their third group meeting. After some opening chitchat, Radha, the facilitator, calls the group's attention to the agenda for the day: offering feedback on a chapter draft from Holly's dissertation, an ethnographic exploration of play in early childhood art education.

> AHMED (VETERINARY MEDICINE): I have a question before—about the nature of your research. So, what are the methods you are using in your research? I noticed that you are telling us maybe a story about your experience and observing children doing different activities. [. . .] It's maybe a general question, but I—it's a new field for me too, but I'm questioning how you do this.
>
> HOLLY (ART EDUCATION): So, there's not a test, right? There's no true test. It's more descriptive. So, I take, so, some of the tools that I use, I take ethnographic notes. So, typically, after I visit the site, I will take notes. [. . .] I also use video and sometimes audio. [. . .] So, those are my two biggest tools for observing. And then, I would say, I use theory and historical understanding of art education as, sort of, tests—to sort of test it against or work against. So, these are—this is not a science . . . and there is—there is this gray area, like, it's my interpretation.

https://doi.org/10.7330/9781646427673.c003

[...]

AHMED: I think this is—I like this too much, because in your field, you are able to have your own perspective about things.... But in the medical field, you have to be on the same track as people who invented it two hundred years ago. You have to follow the same methodology and the same methods to reach—to prove or disprove a hypothesis. But in your field, you are more free to say what you think about it, and just—may use different theories to interpret what you think. It's a very good—I like this. I like it.

In this small slice of conversation, we see Ahmed and Holly engaged in one strategy we would expect to see from collaborators from very different fields: explicit conversations about disciplinary difference. Faced with the task of offering feedback on writing in an unfamiliar field, Ahmed opens group conversation by inviting Holly to explain the theoretical and methodological commitments that inform her work.

Most interesting to me is how this moment illustrates the kinds of knowledge that are put into practice through multidisciplinary writing groups. Holly, the writer, is asked to perform as the disciplinary expert in the room: she has to explain her methods and, in doing so, is invited to make explicit the values and assumptions that guide research in her field. Holly explained her research by defining it against a scientific, positivist paradigm. In addition to simply giving background information to Ahmed about her project and the expectations for research in her field, this exchange gave Holly an opportunity to practice her own expertise—showing her understanding of the landscape of academic research while also articulating her own research paradigm, as the expert in the room. For Holly, this was a particularly useful opportunity. All semester she was navigating sometimes conflicting feedback on her work from different committee members, and more than once, she mentioned feeling uncertainty about genre conventions for her dissertation and a great deal of pressure to simply be done before her funding ran out. It was especially important for her to have opportunities to develop her confidence as researcher and author of her work.

In asking the methods question and in his response to Holly, Ahmed displays his characteristic curiosity and intellectual engagement with work that differs very much from his own. He also, I would argue, shows skill in working across difference. He recognizes the limits of his own experience with English-language research writing in the humanities or social sciences (something he spoke about with the group), and so he opens group conversation by inviting Holly to clarify the disciplinary expectations guiding her work. He actively listens and responds, showing that he values Holly's expertise and showing his own ability to engage across disciplines. Further, he offers a description of methodological commitments in his own field. This exchange, then, shows Ahmed and Holly together developing knowledge about the expectations for research writing across fields. We see, in this exchange, how explicit talk about academic work in different disciplines allowed for a social, collaborative development of genre knowledge that was essential for the group members in giving feedback across disciplinary boundaries. It also gives a glimpse of how these exchanges offered valuable opportunities for student writers to develop their own sense of themselves as disciplinary experts.

Many of the writing groups at Big State brought together writers like Ahmed and Holly from a range of programs and disciplinary backgrounds, and this multidisciplinarity offered opportunities for collaborative knowledge-making and negotiation of scholarly identity, even as it challenged many participants. The prospect of reading and offering feedback across disciplines could inspire a great deal of anxiety and uncertainty among writing group members. With the support of their facilitators, group participants had to find ways to effectively read and offer feedback on work in unfamiliar fields on unfamiliar subjects. These practices offer rich insights into how expertise in writing, genre knowledge, and academic disciplines develops in writing center spaces, both for tutor-facilitators and for student-writers.

Throughout this chapter, then, I trace the practices by which writing groups negotiated differences in disciplinary expertise and what those practices meant for group participant learning. As in chapter 2, I triangulate facilitator perspectives, group members' perspectives, and my own observations of the writing groups to explore the intellectual and emotional work of multidisciplinary collaboration. This chapter thus examines how participants felt and thought about multidisciplinarity and then explores the sequences of feedback that made up group collaborations across disciplinary boundaries.

I found that participants in the groups generally were more anxious about giving good feedback than about the quality of the feedback they received. They pointed to reading across disciplinary boundaries as both a key challenge and an opportunity for learning. In practice, group members and facilitators developed strategies for negotiating disciplinary difference—including explicit talk about disciplinary genre conventions and implicit conversational moves that allowed group members to negotiate authority and expertise as they collaborated. These negotiations of expertise were in relationship to one another and also to absent-yet-present others, such as dissertation supervisors. Group collaboration thus offered insights into emerging scholarly identity for student writers, as they took on expert roles and mediated the voices of experts from outside the group.

On Multidisciplinarity in Writing Groups

The literature on multidisciplinarity in writing groups thus far is mixed. Although some studies report a preference for discipline-specific groups, many indicate potential benefits of multidisciplinary groups, especially for graduate writers, in providing a space to learn about academic discourses and genres and to begin developing their professional identities in those discourses (Guerin et al. 2013; Kaufhold and Yencken 2021). As seems to be common among writing center–sponsored writing groups, the writing groups in my study were multidisciplinary more to accommodate scheduling than for any intentional pedagogical purpose. Yet, like others, we came to find that the multidisciplinarity of the groups, though presenting some challenges, also offered rich opportunities for collaborative learning. Brooks-Gillies, Garcia, and Manthey argue that multidisciplinary writing groups function as liminal, "in-between" spaces, outside of students' departments and the more usual spaces of disciplinary writing (Brooks-Gillies et al. 2020). By providing such liminal space, groups offer students a chance to write away from department politics or the immediate assessment of someone with direct power over them and their place in a program. Brooks-Gillies and co-authors suggest that multidisciplinary groups in their program gave participants practice at being the "expert" in the room, rather than the mentee to more experienced disciplinary experts. Similarly, Cuthbert, Spark, and Burke argue that multidisciplinary writing groups provide a "level playing field" in which graduate students might develop a professional identity and develop their writing (Cuthbert et al. 2009).

Other scholars have had more mixed feelings about multidisciplinarity in writing groups. Colombo and Rodas suggest that there needs to be a "close distance" between group members' disciplines (for example, bringing together students from different subdisciplines within the humanities, such as History and Religious Studies, perhaps, whereas Chemical Engineering and Philosophy, for instance, might be too great a divide) (Colombo and Rodas 2021). Participants in a recent case study by Kirsten Wilmot said that although they valued opportunities to learn about other fields, they didn't find cross-disciplinary peer review activities very useful (Wilmot 2018). Kinney, Snyder-Yuly, and Martinez (2019) suggest that sharing a disciplinary background was important to the way that their group supported disciplinary becoming.

Part of what might make multidisciplinary groups successful is simply group members' dispositions toward the task of working across disciplines, not unlike the role of student dispositions in new writing situations, documented in the literature on writing transfer (Driscoll and Wells 2012). Trixie Smith and co-authors identify shared values around multidisciplinarity, learning (about writing and about other campus work), respect, and consistency, among others, as what made their faculty writing group successful (Smith et al. 2013). Such mixed accounts of multidisciplinarity in writing groups indicate, to me, a need for a systematic investigation of how student writers navigate disciplinary difference in writing groups. Much of this literature has also been focused on graduate students, with some on faculty. In this chapter, then, I explore how disciplinary difference was navigated in writing groups, how participants felt about it, and the opportunities it offered for learning among writers at very different stages of their academic and professional lives (second-year undergraduates, undergraduate thesis writers, and dissertators).

The major themes in the literature—writer-as-expert, developing professional identity, gaining rhetorical knowledge, and the challenging potential of crossing disciplinary boundaries—also arose in the data that I collected through interview and observation. In this chapter, I start with participant perspectives, describing the key benefits and challenges of multidisciplinarity as participants articulated them. The main contribution of this chapter, however, is bringing together participant perspectives with observation to understand how the key themes listed above were enacted in practice. I analyze group collaborations, particularly those in which disciplinary knowledge and expertise became salient to the group. In doing so, I attend to the ways that cross-disciplinary collaborations required intellectual and emotional work, experienced amid feelings of vulnerability, anxiety, (growing) confidence, and gratitude.

Expertise and Genre Knowledge: Writing in Communities of Practice

Because this chapter considers the negotiations of authority and expertise that characterize multidisciplinary groups, I want to explain, briefly, my conception of expertise as it was practiced in the groups and as it is theorized in this chapter. Guided by the communities of practice framework, as well as writing studies scholarship on transfer and disciplinary emergence, I understand expertise as enacted through practice, emergent for individuals in communities with others, and performed rhetorically as part of authority negotiations.

In the community of practice framework, we become more experienced, more expert, within a particular community by gradually participating, first peripherally and then more centrally within that community. In an academic context, writing is a central practice of most disciplinary communities. The literature on writing and disciplinary becoming emphasizes active participation through various writing genres, gradual emergence of expertise, and, increasingly, interplay of literacy learning from multiple communities (Prior 1998; Roozen and Erickson 2017). Expertise, then, isn't just knowledge of concepts but knowledge in practice and in community with others.

In their synthesis of literature on expertise, Yancey, Robertson, and Taczak note that experts have developed and make use of extensive writing knowledge. They also note the importance of an ongoing stance of noviceship, being open to new learning when writing in new genres and new situations. Drawing on the National Research Council's 2000 *How People Learn: Brain, Mind, Experience, and School,* they note a number of characteristics of experts that are especially relevant to writing group work:

- Experts notice features and meaningful patterns of information that are not noticed by novices.
- Experts have acquired a great deal of content knowledge, organized in ways that reflect a deep understanding of their subject matter.
- Experts' knowledge cannot be reduced to sets of isolated facts or propositions but instead reflects contexts of applicability—that is, the knowledge is "conditionalized" on a set of circumstances.
- Experts are able to flexibly retrieve important aspects of their knowledge with little attentional effort.
- Though experts know their disciplines thoroughly, this does not guarantee they are able to teach others.
- Experts have varying levels of flexibility in their approach to new situations (Bransford, Pellegrino, and Donovan 2000, qtd. in Yancey et al. 2014, 39).

I'd like to draw attention to several features of this list, as they intersect with what we know about how students write and learn about writing. First, knowledge is important, but expertise is about "retrieving" and using that knowledge in various situations. As Negretti writes, "Academic writing is complex. . . . Expert writers not only possess a variety of knowledge types, but they also know how to use and adapt them" (Negretti 2021, 172). As we grow in expertise within a particular community (say, an academic discipline), we are able to exercise our knowledge, perform our expertise, with relatively little attentional, conscious effort. That is, as is often noted in the literature on graduate writing support, experts in a particular discipline have developed a great deal of knowledge of particular genres that they put into practice when they write and read, but they may not be able to consciously articulate that knowledge to newcomers. This is significant to the writing groups for two main reasons. First, both the undergraduate students and the graduate students may have received relatively little explicit instruction about the genres in which they were writing. Second, the writing groups, by presenting group members with writing from somewhat unfamiliar rhetorical contexts (a different discipline) and asking them to provide formative feedback on that writing, are asking group members to participate in a new situation by drawing on or developing knowledge from multiple domains. Group participants are being asked to *provide* feedback *in the writing center*, not just to receive it as student-writers. And, further, they are being asked to write with others *in a different field*. In group practice, then, we'll see group members practicing expertise as they draw on prior knowledge and collectively developing expertise in the practices of the *writing center* as well as the conventional writing practices of their academic disciplines. A participant in a writing group thus makes use of knowledge from at least two different domains: their home discipline (the community for which they are writing or the genre of their writing) and the writing center (the community in which they are currently acting in the group itself, learning to engage other writers by reading and offering feedback on unfamiliar writing).

The writing center has long been a fruitful place to study how student writers develop and make use of different kinds of writing knowledge. In their 2022 *CCC* article, Angela Rounsaville, Rebecca Lorimer Leonard, and Rebecca Nowacek suggest that the writing center is a "uniquely synchronic" space, in which "tutors and writers bring their own disciplinary expertise to bear on single writing events (the text or task at hand)" and "multiple academic discourses converge for collaborative exchange" (151). Their article reflects on the ways that writing transfer—which I'll roughly define here as recontextualizing prior knowledge from one writing situation to another—is relational, even collaborative, embedded in communities. As has been suggested in much of the scholarly literature, writing transfer is a complex act that draws particularly on genre knowledge and is also dependent on the writers' dispositions (Driscoll and Wells 2012; Reiff and Bawarshi 2011; Yancey et al. 2014). Like the Writing Center more broadly, the writing groups I investigate in this book offer another view of that synchronous space in which writers (with a range of experiences and dispositions toward the writing group tasks) are bringing together their disciplinary knowledge and experiences and, I would argue, together developing that knowledge and the participants' expertise in and beyond their disciplines.

In the writing groups, as I'll argue below, genre knowledge was a particularly important part of the puzzle of how group members navigated disciplinary difference. In their article "Teaching and Researching Genre Knowledge: Toward an Enhanced Theoretical Framework," Christine Tardy, Bruna Sommer-Farias, and Jeroen Gevers (2020) put forth a theory of genre knowledge that is really useful for considering how the writers in these groups make use of prior knowledge and how they develop new knowledge and practices through group participation. Tardy and colleagues' framework consists of five key components:

1. Genre-Specific Knowledge: multidimensional knowledge of a specific genre, including a number of domains such as formal (conventions of content, organization, style, etc.), process (for composing, distributing, etc.), rhetorical (discourse community), and subject-matter knowledge; can be tied to one language; writers might be most familiar with a genre as it is enacted in a particular language.
2. Genre Awareness: understanding how genres work, theoretically; a "broad understanding of rhetorical contexts and how writers may effectively respond to exigencies within such contexts" and a framework for analyzing genre contexts (Tardy et al. 2020, 296).
3. Metacognition: "a writer's ability to consider and regulate cognitive processes while planning or writing."
4. Recontextualization: the process by which writers draw on prior genre knowledge each time they compose in or otherwise enact a genre (transfer).

5. Multilingualism: "dynamic and socially oriented ability to participate in social practices involving two or more languages or language varieties" (303)

Throughout the following analysis, we'll see examples of group participants discussing formal conventions of their writing, expectations of their disciplinary community for research methodologies and ways of knowing, their linguistic and academic backgrounds in relation to the writing at hand, and the strategies that they develop for approaching reading and writing tasks in the group. Thus, we'll see, in real-time composing interactions, the ways that the group members implicitly and explicitly draw on genre knowledge as they participate in writing groups. As we saw in the opening of this chapter, this was a distinctly social and collaborative act.

So, writing expertise is enacted through activating genre knowledge, and it is emergent, as writers continually encounter new situations that challenge them, again, to adapt that prior knowledge. It is also, in these groups, performed for and with an audience of other group participants.[1] In the writing groups, then, expertise is not only about recontextualizing prior genre knowledge for a new piece of writing or activating and developing an awareness of academic genres. It is also about performing as an expert in the authority negotiations that guide group practice.

Participant Perspectives on the Benefits and Challenges of Multidisciplinary Writing Groups

BENEFITS—DEVELOPING EXPERTISE AND CONFIDENCE IN A LANDSCAPE OF PRACTICE

In both surveys and interviews, group participants identified the benefits of multidisciplinarity as improving the clarity of their writing, becoming more knowledgeable about research and writing in other disciplines, and gaining confidence in their own writing and expertise. In response to the open-ended question "Many of the Writing Center's group include writers from multiple disciplines. Please describe your experience working with writers from different disciplines in your writing groups," survey respondents were generally

---

1. In her 2010 book *The Rhetoric of Expertise*, Johanna Hartelius argues that expertise has a rhetorical dimension; it is exercised and persuasive both through an individual's experiences and knowledge and through their performance of an expert ethos.

positive.[2] About two-thirds (twenty-three of the thirty-four in multidisciplinary groups) emphasized the usefulness of multidisciplinarity. The final third were either negative or mixed in their responses, emphasizing the challenges of providing feedback to others across disciplines.

The first benefit of multidisciplinarity named by survey respondents was learning to write more clearly and articulate the significance of their project in simple, straightforward language. One respondent explained:

> When we began there were two of us from social science (though the other student was far more qualitative than I), and two from the humanities. It was super, super helpful to have the humanities students' opinions and eyes on my work. It helped me reduce my jargon, work on my grammar and passive voice, and overall help me see the forest for my little, bitty tree.

What is most illuminating here is that the respondent mentions not only pushing for sentence clarity or clearing up unnecessary jargon (though both are good things for this writer) but helping to "see the forest," to more clearly articulate the stakes of a project. This is an important task for communicating with discipline-specific audiences as well, and one of the major tasks of writing a dissertation or thesis.

Survey respondents' other key benefits of multidisciplinarity were (1) denaturalizing disciplinary conventions and (2) gaining confidence as a writer and researcher. The following excerpt from a survey response, for example, indicates both intellectual and emotional benefits to working with writers from across disciplines:

> Working with writers from other disciplines was helpful for my writing and academic development in two ways. First, seeing writing conventions from other disciplines helped make the conventions of my own discipline (conventions that had become routine and hard to recognize) more vivid. Recognizing that I knew what the conventions of my discipline were gave me the confidence that I do know what I am doing. Second, working with writers from other disciplines benefitted my ability to talk about the writing on the page. Being able to explain what counts as knowledge in my

---

2. After writing groups had ended for the term, the survey was distributed to all ninety-seven writers who were signed up for a writing group during that semester. Thirty-seven people completed the survey, for a response rate of 38 percent. About half of the respondents were graduate students, another quarter were postdocs, and the remaining quarter were undergraduates, plus one staff member. Respondents came from at least twenty-two different academic programs and ranged in disciplinary background. Of the thirty-seven respondents, only three indicated that their groups ended up including only people who were in similar fields.

discipline and why the arguments I'm making are significant improved my sense of mastery over the writing in a broad sense.

For this writer, the effort of reading across disciplines was rewarded by an increase in self-confidence in their ability to contribute meaningfully to their field and to communicate about their work. As I will show in more detail later in this chapter, the writing groups asked both the undergraduate and the graduate writers to step into the position of expert in their disciplines and their projects. In addition to gaining confidence, I would argue that they are also drawing on and developing genre knowledge and gaining a broader understanding of the landscape of academic work. In the descriptions, above, we see traces of genre-specific knowledge: the formal and rhetorical features of the dissertation in a particular field, and a sense of how those are similar to and different from the same genre (dissertation and research writing) in a different field. Thus, this student is also articulating genre awareness and a growing ability to state, declaratively, what they know. The survey response suggests that the interactions with students and writing from other disciplines were particularly useful in both developing and recognizing this knowledge.

In the edited collection *Learning in Landscapes of Practice: Boundaries, Identity, and Knowledgeability in Practice-Based Learning*, Wenger-Trayner and coresearchers (2015) take up the task of exploring what it means for people to take part in multiple communities of practice and how they navigate multimembership. The collection of essays highlights the challenges and the potential of boundary encounters among practitioners from multiple communities. They suggest that brokering boundary encounters helps people to develop knowledgeability about a landscape of practice, rather than competence in one particular community. The writing groups offer that kind of space, allowing group members to develop shared knowledge of how to respond to writing (as we saw in the previous chapter) and of the genres of writing and kinds of work that people do in other spaces in the academy.

PARTICIPANT PERSPECTIVES: THE CHALLENGES OF MULTIDISCIPLINARITY

Many of the negative or mixed survey responses to group multidisciplinarity had more to do with the confidence that the writer brought to *giving* feedback and less to do with the quality of feedback they *received*. Participation in these groups prompted the kinds of emotional responses we might expect to see from people encountering a boundary like anxiety, curiosity, or interest. Four survey respondents indicated that they would have preferred working with people from the same or a similar field. One wrote, "I enjoyed the people I met. However, sometimes it was challenging to provide feedback on my colleagues' work because the discipline differed dramatically from my own (i.e., very technical science writing of my peers was different from my qualitative social sciences writing)." Others wrote, "it was hard for me to provide much useful feedback for them," and "I think that it was important for me to get better acquainted with writing from other disciplines. However, I don't feel that I was able to provide as valuable feedback to those groups as I would have been able to provide to a science-based discipline." Although these negative or mixed responses to multidisciplinarity made up about one third of survey responses, overall 89 percent of respondents positively valued the feedback they received from their group members.[3] So, although most people valued the feedback they received, many participants were far less confident in the value of their own feedback for others.

These responses dovetail with what I heard in DWG and facilitator interviews, where reading surfaced as a key task and primary challenge in graduate and postdoc groups. Writers in all three case study groups had to develop methods for reading that would help them respond to their peers with valuable feedback, a mode of reading practiced and valued in the Writing Center. Emily describes her experience:

> EMILY: I would say, sometimes it is a challenge to read stuff from people in other fields. Especially, like, science-y stuff. [. . .] Or, like, Holly's, for example, sometimes it was difficult, some of the philosophical stuff, theoretical stuff. It was difficult, so sometimes it's just kind of, um—it takes more energy and effort to read stuff in a different field.

Emily articulates here the investment of intellectual labor, the energy and effort that it took to read work in other fields. What Emily (and, I think, the other survey respondents as well) articulates is the challenge of crossing disciplinary boundaries through reading. I would argue that this struggle—in reading material, understanding it, and also offering suggestions to improve it—has at its root reading as a disciplinary practice. Further, the intellectual work of reading across disciplinary boundaries has an

---

3. On a five-point Likert scale, 65 percent of respondents strongly agreed and 24 percent agreed with the statement "I felt that my group members' comments were useful." Eight percent neither agreed nor disagreed, and the remaining 3 percent (one respondent) disagreed.

emotional component as well, impacted by the dispositions that students brought to the task.

In contrast to the dissertation group and the survey responses, the undergraduate groups did not emphasize reading as a key challenge. The SPG members, reading and providing feedback on relatively short sections of proposals, written for a non-discipline-specific audience, did not complain about the effort and energy it took to read one another's work. There was less of a time investment. The UTG did discuss reading practices, but once Andrew and Adanna left, the group primarily worked as a sit-down-and-write group—with less sharing of written drafts, and thus less reading of one another's writing. In the DWG and other graduate groups, however, reading presented a key challenge, particularly as writers encountered texts that were unfamiliar.

Reading, like writing, is a social practice, and thus reading, like writing, is shaped by the contexts of the writing group and by the contexts of participants' home disciplines. Ellen Carillo has argued persuasively for better accounting for varied reading practices and for developing a metacognitive framework to help students read for different purposes and contexts (Carillo 2015, 2016). Cynthia Shanahan, Timothy Shanahan, and Cynthia Misischia's cross-disciplinary study of expert reading practices found that experts in history, chemistry, and mathematics took very different approaches to reading articles in their respective fields (Shanahan et al. 2011). By the time that group members join a dissertation writing group, they will have begun to develop strategies for reading within their home discipline. They will have completed coursework and, likely, preliminary exams that require them to learn to read within a disciplinary community of practice. So, too, do participants in a writing group need to learn to read within the *writing group* community—with an eye toward helping the writer develop their text. In entering the writing center, group participants had to learn to read and respond similarly to writing tutors—as outsiders who nonetheless could comment on and contribute to the writing. This wasn't easy. It was the work of crossing boundaries and becoming part of a new community of practice. It was also a practice of recontextualizing genre knowledge. In meeting these challenges and learning from them, group members had different stances or dispositions toward the task that, I argue, helped and hindered them in developing strategies for participating in the writing group.

Emily, in particular, developed strategies for reading that helped her to engage productively in the group. Although Emily identified the task of reading outside of her own field as a challenge, she found strategies for reading that made the task manageable. As she talked about these strategies, Emily revealed her disposition toward this task; she valued it as helping with her own writing and she persisted, despite difficulty, by trying out different reading strategies. She was motivated to read her group members' work not only because she wanted to hold up her end of the deal (an exchange of feedback) but also because it was, for her, an opportunity for learning in itself:

> EMILY: It [multidisciplinarity] kind of forced me to articulate my ideas to people that weren't maybe reading all the same stuff I was reading. And then I got to see their writing, which was a bit hard at first to read, but it was actually really productive to see how other people of different disciplines could be really concise. It would make me realize, "OK, I'm being way too wordy for this," and then, um, try to be more concise maybe.
>
> SARA: So, when you were reading other peoples' [. . .] how did you figure out how to read those? You said it was a little difficult at first?
>
> EMILY: Yeah. So, Ahmed's was especially difficult, and then Peter had been in the writing group from before, so I was kind of used to some of his writing, and then Holly I hadn't met before. But, for Ahmed it was really difficult because it was—it seemed like there was a very strict organization to his writing. [. . .] I would try to read the beginning and the end of what he said, you know? And then try to see, kinda, repetition, what argument carried through in his abstract and then conclusion, and then skip over some of the little details, right? I would kinda look for where his arguments were and then what his contributions were, how he was articulating that. So, I thought that was really helpful 'cause that's something that I struggle with in my writing. [. . .] Sometimes I would Google stuff too, if I didn't know terms and things.

Emily had concrete strategies for reading Ahmed's work, for example, reading the beginning and the end, looking specifically for argument and contribution, and skipping over some details while looking up what she needed to. In other words, she scanned for the rhetorical moves in Ahmed's writing, and she went on to say in her interview that she did the same when reading Peter's and Holly's work. Emily's explanation shows that she had some persistence as well as a basic understanding that, regardless of the discipline, each group member's academic writing was likely to share some formal features (an introduction and conclusion) and some key rhetorical moves (articulating argument and contribution). Further she valued the labor she performed to read others' work, not simply as an exchange of feedback but because it was a learning opportunity for her in itself. She saw the task of reading others' work as an opportunity to learn something that would improve her own writing.

It was important for Emily and others to see reading and offering feedback as a useful learning opportunity in itself, rather than as a transactional means to an end. Composition scholarship as well as scholarship on learning in communities of practice emphasizes the stance or disposition a newcomer to a community might take in relation to the new identity or practices that they are asked to perform. A person might take a novice stance, relying on others' judgments and expertise within the new community, or a resistant stance, rejecting others' judgments about appropriate behavior (Wenger-Trayner et al. 2015). In a writing group, for example, a new participant might rely on or resist a facilitator's explanation about what constitutes useful feedback. Similarly, scholarship on transfer of learning in writing studies emphasizes the affective and motivational aspects of how students approach a new writing context or task and make use of previous knowledge (Driscoll and Wells 2012; Yancey, Robertson, and Taczak 2014). Students must identify the task they are approaching as relevant to past and future work and be confident in their ability to complete it, even as they seek out help from others. Writing group participants could see the work of reading and offering feedback as either aligning with their overall goals (improving their writing, getting writing completed) or as peripheral to them (simply something they had to get through in exchange for help on their own work). Emily found that the task of reading unfamiliar writing did align with her goals and help her with her own discipline-specific writing. She valued the act of reading across disciplinary boundaries in the writing center as relevant to her reading and writing practices in other communities of practice, and further, she had a sense of self-efficacy that prompted her to find reading strategies that helped her with a difficult task.

Other writers had different dispositions toward the tasks of the writing group and engaged in different strategies. Ahmed, in particular, expressed concerns about the group. Like the survey respondents, Ahmed was especially concerned about being able to offer others valuable feedback. In the third week of the group, the first that the group provided feedback on an extensive piece of writing, Ahmed raised his concern with the rest of the group:

> AHMED: I have a comment. [. . .] I was concerned about the formulation of the group, and the—the specialties of everyone. And I read this first sample, so I found it very—it's the first time to me to read English literature

other than medical literature. It may be a problem for me because I am an international student. I don't know. I enjoyed reading it, but I don't feel that I am able to give any critiques that may be useful to Holly or something that she could use. I enjoyed reading, I tried, but—and I got what she wrote, but I understand some words are new for me, because they are like "epistemology" or something like this. So maybe that's a big difference. [. . .] I think the greatest thing in our group is making a peer review, but the peer review has to be useful. For Holly, I don't think I would be useful at all for peer review. I don't know if you would be useful for me. I don't know if my writing will be hard for you to judge.

Ahmed's concerns echo the concerns expressed in the survey results about being able to offer useful feedback. His comments also point to the layered experiences and expertise that Ahmed had, as international student, a multilingual speaker and writer, and as a newcomer to the writing groups. Ahmed was concerned, and I don't want to downplay his concerns. He was highly motivated to do the peer review—it's what he wanted from a group to begin with—but he knew how much work it would be, and he knew that it had to be useful. And this, I think, points to the knowledge that Ahmed was bringing with him. In addition to his knowledge of specific genres in his field (and in other genres in different languages), Ahmed signals a metacognitive knowledge. He knows that his experience with academic genres in English has been entirely medical literature, and so he has a sense that the genre-specific knowledge he might need is either tied partly to other languages (that is, he has more experience of nonmedical literature in other languages) or that his English-language genres might be too far afield. And he recognizes that the cognitive load (the effort and energy that it will take him to do this work) might be more than what he is willing to put in. Tardy and co-authors (2020) consider multilingualism as one key component of genre knowledge. Summarizing relevant literature, they write, "cross-lingual acts of recontextualization may be more demanding than recontextualization processes within the same language (variety), given the expanded linguistic repertoires and the possibly diverging (cultural) conventions writers must negotiate" (303). Thus Ahmed's concern about the difficulty of the work dovetails with what others studying multilingualism, genre knowledge, and writing transfer have suggested—it's especially difficult work to read and write across genres and languages.

Although Ahmed framed the task and the language difference mostly as a problem (and potentially a problem unique to him in this group), the literature on multilingualism also suggests that there are some real benefits to multilingualism, such as "refined awareness of different rhetorical patterns, audience expectations, and composing process knowledge, potentially resulting in increased writer agency and enhanced creativity" (Tardy et al. 2020, 304). In other words, Ahmed had a lot of prior knowledge built from his experience of learning to read and write in multiple languages that he could bring to his work in the writing group, even if he didn't frame this experience as a resource in his comment. We saw his skill at navigating boundaries by asking questions in the opening of this chapter, and by voicing concerns, Ahmed also showed a maturity and skill in addressing potential difficulties explicitly and in good faith.

In response to Ahmed's concerns, Radha and the group members did not explicitly address language difference but tried to reassure him and point him to possible ways of engaging. Radha explained, "I noticed that you said that there were parts that you really enjoyed also, so I think that's—in terms of critique, that's actually the easiest way to start, right? Is to be like, 'look, this paragraph was really great because it was so clear, and I enjoyed reading it because this was the point that got across,'" and later, "I definitely see what you're saying. I think there are ways to kind of develop a way of reading that's not necessarily content-based," and she explicitly planned and set aside time to discuss the concerns again at the end of the meeting, after he had a chance to experience what the group might be like. Holly also chimed in, telling a story about her first experience in a previous writing group, of the difficulty she had of getting through "dense" writing on an entirely unfamiliar subject. There was, though, perhaps a missed opportunity here to cue both Ahmed and the rest of the group to develop "genre awareness" by pointing to the kinds of rhetorical features that might be shared (or not shared) across writing from different disciplinary contexts. In other words, while Radha explained that there were other ways of reading, she (and I and the rest of the group) didn't fully describe those other ways of reading or the genre knowledge that informs them, at least not in that moment.

However, Ahmed did, both in this session and in later group sessions, find ways to contribute. He offered feedback about his reading experience (articulating a structural concern about Holly's paper). He also made connections to others' work based on his own personal knowledge and experience. Ahmed's experience of this challenge, though, seems, at least at first, to have been characterized by apprehension. He does, also, raise the possibility that this labor presents a more challenging barrier for him because it was his first encounter with academic literature in English in fields beyond his own.

For Peter, the challenges of a multidisciplinary group lay in what he saw as group members' lack of confidence in their understanding of the standards of another field, leading them to be too generous or lenient in their reading:

> PETER: I guess I feel like I've been kind of lucky 'cause for the most part I've been interacting with people who even if they're, like, a music major, their dissertation or thesis or whatever the project's called still sounds to me like the sociology of culture or something like that. [. . .] Um, I think this last time, with the, like, what was he doing?
>
> SARA: Veterinary medicine?
>
> PETER: Yeah, that was actually, I think everybody else was, like, following along way better than me. I was like, yeah, I was really out of my wheelhouse with that, so that was one instance, but I think maybe one [challenge] was, you don't know what the standards are [. . .] and, um, kind of being really generous, and I'm like, "oh no, I actually need you to be really rough on this, because it is supposed to be really tight and make sense by itself."

Peter articulates several emotional elements that make multidisciplinary work challenging. One is about confidence with reading research that is disciplinarily closer to his own, as social science and humanities research was to his home field of sociology than Ahmed's work in biological sciences. Peter's stated way of engaging with writing—reading as a sociologist—didn't work as well for him when reading Ahmed's work. Yet, in practice, his methods of engaging with Ahmed in the writing group were consistent with the ways he did so with others in the group—asking questions around points of confusion, listening carefully, and restating what he heard. We'll see in the next section how Peter and other group members did this work. For Peter, the real challenge of multidisciplinary groups was getting an honest assessment that gave him the benefit of the doubt based on difference in fields. All of these accounts emphasize emotions, the feelings that bubble up around multidisciplinary work. For these group participants, the work of drawing on and developing genre knowledge was also emotional work: it was about relationship building, about confidence in their own reading ability, and about interest in learning from the challenge.

Group Practices: Developing Genre Knowledge Through Feedback and Deliberation Across Disciplinary Boundaries

I observed a number of practices by which group members offered feedback and wrote together across disciplinary boundaries. Most obviously, they explicitly discussed disciplinary differences, talking about methodologies; genre conventions for their dissertations, theses, and proposals; and their own goals and identities within their fields. However, I also examined how group members navigated disciplinary differences implicit in their conversations. Group members engaged in two recurring sequences of feedback strategies that also allowed them to work across disciplinary boundaries, coded as follows: Pumping + Project Explaining + Suggesting and Responding as a Reader + Suggesting, each of which could then be followed up with Agreement and Disagreement from the rest of the group.[4] In the following sections, I'll work through examples of each of these patterns in different groups. Although these patterns could show up between members of the same discipline too, in this chapter, I focus on moments in which participants navigated disciplinary difference. What's most interesting to me are the implications of each of these feedback sequences for what they asked of group participants. These writing group practices required writers to act as expert disciplinary representatives, and they required group members to read and listen for "rhetorical resonances" across disciplines and to gather enough confidence to articulate their reading response and make suggestions, even if they felt unsure and unqualified.

EXPLICIT CONVERSATIONS ABOUT DISCIPLINARY DISCOURSES

We saw in the opening exchange of this chapter how members of the DWG had explicit conversations about disciplinary difference and the sorts of research and expectations guiding their dissertation writing. The explicit conversations about disciplinary difference and expectations also gave some insight into how each group of students was understanding the role that disciplinarity played in their writing and their own growing sense of expertise as they emerged as participants in disciplinary discourses. In the undergraduate thesis group, writers were just starting to gain a sense of how scholarship

---

4. To code for this, I did two levels of coding. First, I coded the feedback strategies that emerged through group conversation, as detailed in chapter 1 and represented in appendix D. Second, I flagged passages that stood out to me as ones in which group members' differing expert knowledges of a particular academic genre, discourse community, research methodology, or subject seemed especially salient to the conversation as Multidisciplinarity.

contributes to a conversation, and how the conversations in each discipline were shaped by different commitments, expectations, and values. In the early days of the undergraduate thesis group (before Andrew and Adanna left), the students benefited from multidisciplinarity because it made those different methodological expectations clearer.

In the following excerpt, Andrew articulates his understanding of the differences between writing a thesis in English and writing one in Women's, Gender, and Sexuality Studies (WGSS), in an effort to help Eleanor focus her topic and develop a more specific research question.

> ANDREW: Are you writing this in the Women's Studies department or the English department?
>
> ELEANOR: Well, I'm trying to do—I'm getting more women's studies readers, but I'm going for both. So one of my advisors is in both. She does feminist literary criticism. So, it is mainly within English, but I'm making it as intersectional as possible. Literally and . . . [laughs]
>
> ANDREW: So, I ask that question because eventually I'm pretty sure you have to designate. And so that would kinda change, like, the requirements, like, what your defense would look like. 'Cause if you're doing it in Women's Studies, then you're definitely looking more at theory and that aspect of the literature, and you're also going to have to bring in a lot of other scholarly works that are looking at these books. Whereas within English, I would guess, from my understanding, you are interpreting the text and the narrative and the construction, so I guess that's also helpful, to think about which approach you're going to bring? [. . .] And I guess the other thing I would say is that these [topics in Eleanor's outline] are all, like, super interesting and, like, connected, but what are you trying to—Like, what's the question in all these sections? Because that's what's gonna drive your research and your, like, reading of the novels. [. . .] I understand what you're looking at, but what do you want to find out from what you're looking at?

Andrew's comments demonstrate his perception of subtle differences between WGSS (his own field) and English studies and how those differences might shape Eleanor's project. He identified a different set of primary texts (theoretical texts vs. literary texts) and a different methodological approach (reading and juxtaposing theories vs. using a theoretical lens to analyze literary texts). Andrew's understanding of the subtle possible differences between WGSS (already an interdisciplinary field) and English was remarkably sophisticated for an undergraduate student. Whereas Andrew seemed to have a strong sense of how questions, subject, and methods would together drive a research project, Eleanor was still just getting a sense of specific texts and topics that interested her, without a unifying question that prompted a particular type of analysis. Eleanor's sense of the difference between pursuing honors in Women's Studies and English was through who her advisors were, rather than a sense of how that choice might shape her research process.

FEEDBACK SEQUENCES: INVITING WRITERS TO PERFORM EXPERTISE, LISTEN FOR RHETORICAL RESONANCES, AND CO-AUTHOR REVISION SUGGESTIONS

Often the practices of collaborating across disciplines might not include explicitly talking about difference but, rather, actually listening for what Gradin, Pauley-Gose, and Stewart call the "rhetorical resonances" across disciplines. In their essay, Gradin and colleagues write that writing groups "surface, de-codify, and denaturalize" the generic features of disciplinary writing "in order to reveal rhetorical resonances in the seemingly different discourses" (2006, n.p.). In other words, the groups offered members a chance to compare how different disciplinary communities respond to the exigencies of communicating research methodologies and findings, and thus to understand the rhetorical effect of features of their writing.

In this section, I show how the exchanges of feedback in writing groups enabled students to listen for rhetorical resonances. These exchanges could take a variety of forms, but I focus on the two sequences of talk that group members used to engage one another's projects and to direct their feedback: (1) Pumping + Project Explaining + Suggesting, and (2) Reading Response + Suggesting. In both sequences, group members could follow up one anothers' comments with expressions of agreement, disagreement, further questions, and so on. Often the writer (and sometimes the facilitator) would also take notes on the conversation, trying to record the various suggestions the group came up with. And so these sequences engaged the group in a collaborative invention process. Each of these sequences of feedback required different kinds of knowledge, different performances of expertise of writer, group members, and facilitator. Writers were called upon to explain their projects as the disciplinary expert in the room. Group members had to be curious, listen attentively, and have the courage to make suggestions that recontextualized their genre knowledge for a writing situation in an unfamiliar field and that openly showed the limits of their knowledge.

Pumping + Project Explaining + Suggesting

In this sequence, a group member would ask the writer a question intended to draw out the writer's ideas around a particular topic or sentence. Most of the time, the pumping question would be followed by the writer's explanation of the project. The most useful suggestions that followed would be those that showed how the group member was listening to the writer's explanation and that used the explanation to shape a suggestion. I'd like to suggest that these kinds of pumping questions enabled group members to listen for the "rhetorical resonances" between genres of academic writing across disciplines. For example, they might listen for how a "gap" is created in the existing literature and how the writer filled that gap.

In the following section, Peter asks pumping questions to get Emily to articulate the significance of her approach and her contribution to the literature on a particular film.

PETER: Hang on, I have a question.

RADHA: Yeah?

PETER Um. So, from this paragraph, like, I guess . . . what . . . like, so you're saying that you're, you're, you're saying that *Imitation of Life* is a marriage movie?

EMILY: Mm-hmm [*affirmative*].

PETER: Um. I guess, what is that? Can you just talk to me about that a little bit?

EMILY: Yeah. Like, why does it matter that it's a marriage movie sort of?

PETER: Yeah.

EMILY: Um, so . . . this probably will be also a little revised as I figure out the link to the other chapters so that, that's part of the problem, maybe it's not that clear, but I . . . The reason I'm saying it's a marriage movie is 'cause most of the feminist scholarship talks about other things, like, they kind of, they might mention, "oh, she has this proposal," but um, but I'm saying [. . .] so, I think, now, the whole focus of the larger dissertation is: marriage, um, at this, in this, like, the civil rights era, marriage, right? And so, it's like, centering around the Loving [v. Virginia] case, and how, like, essentially, I don't know, this pop culture, Hollywood, and law are kind of engaging the same kinds of conversations, and so, by saying, like, you know, other people say it's a movie about mothers or about work and stuff, so I'm saying, like, actually it's a movie about marriage also, right?

PETER: Right, right.

EMILY: Um, yeah, so actually that's why I do need a stronger word than "skirt." Does that make sense, kind of? Um . . .

PETER: Definitely, I . . . yeah. Um, so just, kind of, maybe some suggestions as you're revising it is, kind of, um, maybe in the middle of the page—"In this chapter, I argue that *Imitation of Life* is a marriage movie of sorts"—like, maybe if you, um, just, kind of, within that sentence, saying, like, "whereas other people haven't addressed marriage, um, like, I do see this as a marriage movie."

EMILY: Okay.

In this sequence, Peter asks Emily a pumping question, to "talk to me" about *Imitation of Life* as a "marriage movie." After hearing her explanation, he suggests making Emily's point of departure from previous scholarship more explicit in her writing. The dissertation writing group worked together to help the writers articulate the unique contribution that their work was making to the field. This was often the focus of the DWG, as it was the focus of what dissertators were trying to do with their dissertations: figure out where their work fit and how they fit as emerging scholars in that field. This sequence (Pumping + Explaining + Suggesting) required Emily to perform her expertise in her subject area. She explained her subject knowledge—what others had said about *Imitation of Life*—and also worked to develop her growing sense of the significance of her interests and argument within her field. Peter offered suggestions for language and organization to help Emily mold her explanation into a recognizable gap in the research (whereas other people haven't addressed marriage, she did see it as a marriage movie). In doing so, Peter showed that he was listening for a particular kind of story—a story about the intervention Emily was making.

Peter's suggestion also includes what Melody Denny has termed the "oral writing-revision space" (OR). In her 2018 study, Denny used conversation analysis to identify and theorize the OR, a discourse feature of writing center sessions in which writer or consultant tried out, rewrote, or repeated possible revisions for the text at hand. This space, she argues, provides writing center researchers a way to investigate scaffolding in writing center sessions, showing, as it does so, how consultants and writers were working through revision together in real time. In Peter's suggestion, above, we can see the OR when he suggests "within that sentence, saying, like, 'whereas other people haven't addressed marriage, um, like, I do see this as a marriage movie.'" Peter's suggestion repeats Emily's earlier articulation of the significance of her claim in relation to the literature on the film. I call attention to this feature to emphasize the ways that group members were composing together. This discourse feature was part of the talk of both group members and facilitators, distributing the revision work among multiple people present in the group and allowing group members a moment to play as and with the author. In this case, developing that suggestion required Peter to make use of his genre knowledge and required Emily to articulate her subject matter (and genre-specific) knowledge, as well.

The SPG group also featured pumping sequences to tease out necessary knowledge from the writer, even though they weren't necessarily engaged in research writing for a discipline-specific audience. And, although they weren't engaged in disciplinary writing, this sequence still featured in moments where discipline-specific knowledge was pertinent to the conversation, and it showed how the second-year students were navigating disciplinary identity.

For example, Vihaan, who was requesting funding to pursue a research project for his "transformational experience," needed to describe his project, and so he had to describe research in his field as well as its significance to him as a student. In the following excerpt, Elizabeth, the group facilitator, and I both ask Vihaan a series of pumping questions, trying to prompt him to brainstorm aloud at a time when he was having trouble identifying a particular research project and professor to work with:

> ELIZABETH: Without knowing exactly what you're going to be doing, um, what sort of "transformative experience" are you looking for, or hoping to get out of it?
>
> VIHAAN: Um, well, mainly, like, learning the professional skills needed for software development. Or, um—the social side, probably just working with the professor, so I'll start building a network. And, well . . .
>
> SARA: Can I ask the question in a different way?
>
> VIHAAN: Sure.
>
> SARA: Um, so, why do a research project instead of the internship that you've already got?
>
> VIHAAN: Well, I wanted to do the internship, but it's paid, and it's paying enough. Yeah.
>
> SARA: OK, so, but like—beyond the practical reason, what could you imagine as an answer if you had to give a reason? Why not look for another

internship that's not paid, right? Um, or study abroad, or any of these other options. You wanted to do a research project. Why?

[*eight seconds silence*]

SARA: You might not have an actual answer yet either, but that might be one of the questions that you want to answer, right? Because you have a lot of options, right? A lot of options. So, what is it about research that interests you?

[*nine seconds silence*]

SARA: I also don't know what research looks like in your field at all, so that might be another way—um, what does research look like in software development?

VIHAAN: Um, it's mainly just finding more efficient ways of doing things rather than making something completely new. Like if there's an algorithm to solve a certain kind of problem, then research should be trying to make that more efficient. [. . .] So, most of the research is like that, trying to decrease the time.

SARA: Who defines the research problems in the field? Is it professors? Is it people who are, like, using the stuff and saying, like, I can't get it to do what I want in the time I want to do it in? These are questions that might not make any sense at all because I know nothing about this, but, um, I don't know.

VIHAAN: Um, well, for the projects I was considering, most of them are stuff the professors decided to do. But, um, the internship deals with business solutions, and in that case, it's the clients who decide how they want the program to work.

ELIZABETH: So, for your interest, do you see yourself kind of more in the business side or on the research side, you know, ten years down the road or whatever?

VIHAAN: Probably the research side.

ELIZABETH: Oh, the research side? OK. Have you had a chance to do that before, other than in coursework, or?

VIHAAN: Not the exact same type, but I've done some, um, testing projects, um, for a company that makes, like, practice test sets for the SAT.

ELIZABETH: Okay, so you're coming into this already with—with research experience. Like, is that the sense of—this is not going to be transformative in the sense that it's your first research project?

VIHAAN: Not my first research project, but the first one of this type.

Elizabeth and I ask Vihaan pumping questions about research in his field. We initiate the explicit conversation about discipline-specific research practices, listening to his responses for any hint of a story of transformation (one of the key values of the proposal audience) or at least for material that he could use to begin describing a potential project and its value to him as a budding researcher or professional. Elizabeth and I, who at the time were both graduate students in rhetoric and composition and experienced writing consultants, would have most likely had a stronger grasp of how disciplinary values might generally shape research projects, but we were newcomers to computer science. This excerpt highlights how all of us relied on Vihaan to provide information not only about his project but also about his field and its norms. Even as a second-year undergraduate, Vihaan was able to give some general ideas about what research looks like in computer science, even though he had a harder time articulating his own interests within that field. This could be because of the nature of undergraduate research in his field, in which a professor would give him a small portion of their own research project to work on. From Vihaan's perspective, he just needed to get someone to agree to let him work with them. It didn't seem to matter much to him what the specific project was. From our perspective, it was important, for the purposes of his proposal writing, that he explain why he was committed to that particular project and why it could be transformative to him. We were asking Vihaan to step into a role as more of an expert in his field or at least to take more agency and ownership over his research project experience. We were listening for a narrative about what he was hoping to get out of this research project that his coursework and other internship couldn't offer him.

Responding as a Reader + Suggesting

The other sequence of feedback strategies that emerged from the data was offering a reading response, followed by a suggestion. In the following example from the UTG, Andrew offers his response to Adanna's abstract.

> ANDREW: My only question is, your first sentence. Like, [*reading aloud*] "understanding is critical," so, just what is it critical to?
>
> ADANNA: Yeah, that's a good point. Initially, because I met with my advisor just to kind of talk about how I should structure the abstract and like I was going to put like economically, geopolitically, but I was like I'm not going to have enough space. So I might include that just to be more clear.

ANDREW: Cause I think I understand why it's important as you keep reading but just because of that sentence, how it's structured, I feel like it's just like cut off cause it says "will be critical" and left saying to what? So that's why.

Conversation then continued as the group debated suggestions for a change in verb tense. In this case, the differences in discipline may not seem to matter so much to the group members. The audience for the abstract that Adanna is workshopping, like the SPG's proposals, is for a more general audience. However, in both cases, group members are reading about an unfamiliar subject, from an unfamiliar field, asking questions, and offering suggestions. In addition to asking the writer to provide expert information on their subject and on disciplinary norms in their field, the group process asks the group members to exercise the courage to say, "I found X confusing," or to trust themselves as reasonably competent readers, to trust that the feedback they give might be productive or useful for the writer. As we saw in the interviews and survey data above, this wasn't easy for all group members. It could be intimidating. We often talk about the vulnerability that writers feel in sharing their work, but group members in this study shared that they often feel as vulnerable in offering feedback.

Difficulties of Navigating and Negotiating Multidisciplinary Expertise

I turn now to an example from the dissertation group that illustrates some of those anxieties and some of the difficulties that arose, even with the strategies for feedback that the groups developed. In this conversation about one of Peter's chapters, we'll see some of the same kinds of feedback (reading responses, explicit conversations about genre and disciplinary difference), and we'll also see group members agreeing and disagreeing about the best way to move forward. Throughout, I'd like to draw attention to the emotional and dispositional elements of the exchange. I'd like also to draw attention to how inefficient this process is. Bringing multiple people, from different fields, together to discuss writing was not efficient, if all we wanted to do was get Peter's dissertation in the best shape possible as quickly as possible. But the extended deliberation, I would argue, created rich opportunities for collaborative learning. The following excerpt, longer than the previous ones, is both extended and a bit convoluted. In this example, the DWG is discussing one of Peter's dissertation chapters, and Radha and Emily have been encouraging Peter to be more explicit about the argument and contribution of his chapter in his opening paragraph. As conversation continues, I (Sara) try to map out how I understood Peter's existing introduction's structure, currently stretched over the first four paragraphs of the chapter:

> SARA: So, it sounds like, to me, this, it seems like, so you have your, like, you've got that kind of funnel structure, where you start out, like, particularly broad in the first paragraph. You get a little bit more specific, and then you have the more specific statement of the problem, and then you get into what your thing addresses, right, in that fourth paragraph.
>
> PETER: Yeah, yeah, yeah.
>
> SARA: So, it sounds like everyone just wants a little bit more here [in the first paragraph] of, like, what you're doing.
>
> PETER: Right.
>
> [...]
>
> SARA: So, are you basically trying to, like, replicate this [the structure of paragraphs 1–3] but in sentence one, two, and three instead of, and then, like, give it, like, like, as if it's an abstract of, like, what's about to come next, kind of thing?
>
> PETER: Um. Y—yeah. What do you think?
>
> SARA: Yeah, I mean that's a—
>
> PETER: Is that okay?
>
> SARA: That's what I was hearing, so that's what I was, I was trying to, like, ask. Does that make sense?

In this moment, I was trying to clarify two things: the existing structure of Peter's work as I had read and understood it (a funnel structure stretched over four paragraphs) and the change others were suggesting (to state the problem more specifically in the first paragraph, rather than waiting to give that statement until the end of the fourth paragraph). In this exchange, I began by stating my own understanding of Peter's work and then restating the feedback I had heard thus far. I also gestured toward genre-specific knowledge, comparing Peter's proposed revision to an abstract at the beginning of an academic article. What I didn't say, and likely should have, was that I didn't completely agree with that feedback. In fact, I had been fine with the organization of the introduction as it was. As a reader, I hadn't had a problem with the organization, but as a contributor to the conversation, I was hesitant to contradict the feedback that Radha and Emily had already given. That hesitancy was both because of my own uncertainty about the validity of my reading and also because I didn't want to undermine the group facilitator. Peter, sensing my hesitation, then followed up, asking questions to draw out a more forthright explanation:

> PETER: So, are you, are you thinking like, I, I guess—Who, who, who are you th—like, you, you kind of agree that I made the first paragraph, I mean, to say what I'm, what I'm doing.
>
> SARA: I don't know.
>
> PETER: You don't know?
>
> SARA: I don't know.
>
> PETER: Okay.
>
> SARA: I, I have—
>
> PETER: Wait, have you read it and you, you didn't think this was a problem?
>
> AHMED: What I think here is there is a confusion between, um, uh, the traditional form of an abstract at the beginning of the paper and introduction.
>
> PETER AND SARA: Mm-hmm.
>
> AHMED: What I see here is this one-and-a-half pages is, kind of, introduction, maybe for introduction—
>
> PETER: Right, no, this isn't a, I guess I didn't, I don't have an abstract for this.
>
> AHMED: So, you didn't, uh, it will be here, or not?
>
> PETER: Yeah, it will.
>
> AHMED: It will.
>
> RADHA: Oh, you will have an abstract?
>
> PETER: Yeah.
>
> AHMED: So. And the abstract will, it will be three hundred or, or so words.
>
> SARA: Mm-hmm.
>
> AHMED: And he will have all these parts, uh, together, so he will have the currently two sentences for the introduction, then the research problem, what is it?
>
> RADHA: Mm-hmm.
>
> AHMED: And then your approach, or methodology. Then your main results and applications. So, these are the five components for each abstract.
>
> RADHA: Mm-hmm.

AHMED: And what you are trying to do here, and then this, the title for this is introduction, and in the introduction, once I read this paper, and abstract, I kind of know what he's, what the problem he's discussing, and what, uh, all, what it's about.

SARA: Right.

AHMED: And then, in the introduction, I'm ready to have some, uh, the [*unintelligible*] you are talking about, that you need to introduce some words, some sentences here or here.

SARA: Mm-hmm.

When Peter actively solicited some other opinions, Ahmed articulated more clearly what I had been tacitly implying—Peter did not need to start with his argument in the first sentence when he had it clearly stated just a couple of paragraphs later, especially if his work was to include an abstract. In doing so, Ahmed draws on and shares his genre-specific knowledge, providing a counterpoint to the rest of the group. Later on, Ahmed jumped in to disagree with some feedback Radha and others were offering Peter along similar lines, again offering genre knowledge specific to academic research papers in his field as a comparison and resource from which to draw in this situation.

AHMED: So, uh, they are, they are trying to put your contribution in every paragraph, but at the end though, if you did this in each paragraph [*laughs*], you will finish your paper in the first, uh, in the first introduction.

[GROUP MEMBERS]: Mm-hmm [*affirmative*].

AHMED: I think, so, um, my suggestion is to have something like this in here and in closing. I don't know if this works for these papers or not, this last paragraph, but you put a summary for your work and th—that's what we do in our field. And rather than introducing it in each . . . I—I think the paragraph is complete. It's good.

RADHA: Yeah.

AHMED: Um, then, this contribution will be here, which is introduction to . . . at the end of this. When we briefly uh—[*inaudible*] study, not in—not introduced everything in, in the titles.

RADHA: This is, I think, a field thing [*group members agree*], um—because I, I think in English it's—You do, like, a quick and dirty lit review, but for at least, like, the things that I've been reading more recently, they tend to be, like, "I'm gonna say this in, like, two or three sentences and get it out of the way." And then it jumps straight into "And these are my thoughts, this is, like, my analysis, this is my contribution."

GROUP: Mm-hmm [*affirmative*].

Throughout these exchanges, it was important to dig into the different reading responses and how they were shaped by each group member's expectations for the piece. These moments offered opportunities for group members to articulate their readerly expectations and to address disciplinary conventions shaping those expectations. This was a space for them to articulate genre-specific knowledge, and perhaps, through comparison of how each field accomplished rhetorical tasks, to develop a greater genre awareness. It was also especially important for group members to voice disagreement in their readings of the projects. Even though I struggled to articulate a dissenting opinion, Ahmed did take up my question and provide a stronger counterpoint to the group's initial ideas for revision. Radha then was able to respond by framing the disconnect for us as a "field thing" and leaving the question to Peter, now that he had all the information from each of his readers.

AUTHORITY NEGOTIATION AND EXPERTISE IN RELATION TO OTHER COMMUNITIES OF PRACTICE: PRESENTIFYING ADVISOR AUTHORITY

So far, we've seen how the group processes invited writers to take on the position of disciplinary expert and invited group members to read critically, offer feedback, and negotiate possible courses of action. Group members asked the writer to think aloud, and then they echoed back or wrote down what they heard. They found the rhetorical resonances that would allow them to help the writer shape a piece of writing to meet its rhetorical purpose. These sequences of feedback brought forth a number of possibilities for revision, and they asked the writer to hear multiple readers' responses and, perhaps, to filter or translate them in order to make a decision about what to do next. But, of course, the writers weren't working in a vacuum. They weren't actually the sole representatives of their discipline with direct involvement on these texts. They also were writing for an audience of advisors and committee members, who had important roles as readers and supervisors. Those supervisors assessed whether the texts met the expectations necessary to secure funding, prove the writer worthy of undergraduate honors, or grant the writer's doctoral degree.

In this section, I turn to how the writers spoke about and managed the influence their advisors had on the group. In their 2021 article "It's Crowded in Here: 'Present Others' in Advanced Graduate Writers' Sessions," Kranek and Carvajal Regidor argue for greater attention to the "present others"—advisors, committee members, colleagues, etcetera—who, though not physically present, still actively shape writing center sessions with graduate writers. Drawing on a study of graduate writing consultations, they argue that individuals like advisors, who were part of writers' direct feedback networks, were present for these writers in the session. They write that "engaging with graduate writers' texts and present others that surround them provides a valuable opportunity to support these writers more holistically" (63). These present others are part of the emotional space of the consultation as well as the interaction and negotiation between tutor and tutee. Similarly, Hansun Zhang Waring (2005) draws on a case study of a graduate writer and writing consultant, finding that the writer invoked her advisor's authority to resist the tutor's advice. The absent-yet-present advisors and committee members were also significant to writing group talk in my study, especially for the DWG and UTG.[5]

In a previous article published in *Written Communication* in 2021, I argued that group members leveraged the authority of their advisors to negotiate authority within the writing groups, particularly in moments where disciplinary expertise was salient. I drew on a concept from organizational communication, "presentification," to understand how talk about advisors functioned as part of conversational authority negotiation. In their 2009 article, Benoit-Barné and Cooren define presentification as "those ways of speaking and acting that are involved in making present things and beings that, although not physically present, can influence the unfolding of a situation" (10). In the writing group conversations, advisors were made present to legitimate, shape, and challenge the feedback given and received in writing group conversations. These negotiations also opened up opportunities for the groups to mediate advisor authority, to offer writers a means of reflecting on and rethinking relationships with advisors. In this section, I explore and build on that argument, putting it in context of the multidisciplinary work that we've explored thus far and attending to the emotional work that happens with and through authority negotiation.

---

5. Talk about advisors also featured heavily in the SPG but was more about navigating the administrative requirements of their program. Faculty advisors in this program weren't linked to students' majors or disciplines.

Advisor Authority in Use: Legitimating, Shaping, and Challenging Group Feedback

Citing advice from an outside authority was one way for writers across groups to legitimate their own and others' feedback. In the following example from the UTG, Andrew presentifies his advisor as he makes a suggestion for Adanna. By citing his advisor, he lends weight to his own reading of her abstract for an undergraduate research forum:

> ANDREW: I think also, uh, just considering what your abstract will look like at the end of a project is going to be very different from what you're submitting to the poster forum. 'Cause that's something that I'm keeping in mind and my advisor has told me, is like, "you're writing this for the forum. You're not writing this as a part of your thesis yet." You can use it later, but that's the advice she's been giving me, which is why I asked that question, 'cause I had to use a lot of language that is not what's gonna be in my abstract of my actual paper, because it's much more words than it needs to be, because I can't—when the forum views it, it's not gonna be history professors or women's studies professors or econ professors, necessarily. You're gonna have people who are, like, chemistry professors reading this, so for me to use, like, "heteronormativity" doesn't really fly 'cause it doesn't compute.

Over the course of this piece of feedback, Andrew links himself both to his advisor and to the eventual readers of this abstract. He is able to anticipate the questions that readers, like chemistry professors, who have general academic expertise but not expertise in the subject area or discipline, might have. Andrew uses his advisor and own writing experience to justify and lend credence to his advice about word choice. Andrew's sound advice—for Adanna to consider her audience of readers from outside of economics—could stand on its own, but he chooses to cite a recognizable source of authority for the genre knowledge that he relays, rather than relying solely on his own reading experience.

Similarly, group members wanted to use advisor feedback to shape their own feedback, to make their own feedback as useful as possible for the writer. In a different exchange from the DWG, Peter attempts to use Holly's concerns about her committee's advice for her literature review to shape his suggestions:

> PETER: I think—it seems like one solution would be to integrate your observations [into discussion of theoretical concepts]. My—the way—what I'm inclined to do is, kind of, orient it, you know, let's say your advisor

says, "no, don't bring in the observations, I'd rather that come in a separate chapter." But just kind of—if you could just orient the reader and be like, "So, the reason why it's important to, you know, the reason why this approach is important is because it has all these strengths, but it also has these shortcomings, which I will address in the next chapter when I try to, like, make—kind of correct those shortcomings."

Here, Peter voices Holly's advisor in a hypothetical piece of feedback and then uses that to make his suggestion for how to orient readers in what was fast becoming an unwieldy review of past literature. Peter was sensitive to Holly's need to meet her committee members' expectations, as well as the stress she was feeling as she neared a deadline for this piece of writing, and he shaped his feedback accordingly. In this example, as in the previous one, advisors were invoked in ways that departed from Waring's observation of using advisor authority to resist tutor advice. Here, they are used to lend weight to advice and to help shape or frame the feedback.

Examining more contentious exchanges of feedback for instances of presentification also shows how advisor authority was made present in ways that deflected or challenged feedback offered by the group. In the following example, Eleanor, a third-year undergraduate student beginning her English thesis, closes a topic episode by summarizing her advisor's guidance to deflect advice from Marie, the group facilitator. In this early group meeting, Marie challenged Eleanor to more clearly define her use of the term *intersectionality*. In response, Eleanor voiced her advisor's guidance to defend her current focus and process:

> MARIE: I'm not entirely convinced that you're using "intersectional" in the way that people normally think of it. [. . .] I would go through and pick out the words that you think need definitions, do some reading on what the literature around it is. Definitely looking at the work of Kimberlé Crenshaw, whether or not you've read—
>
> ELEANOR: Actually, I have.
>
> MARIE: —her work a million times, do it again. Do it again. Read things that people have written about her work and just figure out what you really take—what your interpretation really is of intersectionality and how that's working in your project. Also, I've never heard of "cyborg feminism" before, so I'd kind of like to hear more about that.
>
> ELEANOR: I can send you a reading.

MARIE: But whether or not I know anything about cyborg feminism, I think it's still good within your thesis, and even in the outlining stages, to have those definitions at hand.

ELEANOR: I do kinda have a list [of terms]. It's just it's been changing a lot because I'm trying to cut down and so, like, when I was talking to [an advisor] last she was like "you need to focus on voice, I think that will really help you."

In this exchange, Marie and Eleanor negotiate authority as they recognize or doubt who holds expertise in the conversation and decide how Eleanor might best move forward with her research. By summarizing her advisor's direction to focus on "voice," Eleanor chose not to take up Marie's suggestion to focus on defining key terms, particularly "intersectionality." Eleanor's responses and voicing of her advisor's perspective deflected Marie's feedback. Furthermore, in offering to send Marie a reading on cyborg feminism, Eleanor did offer help in the form of sharing a resource—and yet she also one-upped Marie by displaying her own expertise in feminist theory. Eleanor ended this episode of conversation by voicing her advisor's guidance without ceding authority to Marie.

Later interviews revealed that this exchange was deeply shaped by Marie's and Eleanor's relationships with advisors; they both took on authority by enacting a teacher-like role. During her interview, Marie explained that she had been trying to address what she saw as a problem Eleanor had: using buzzwords. She empathized, explaining, "I used to do the same thing, but I learned to not do it after a couple embarrassing papers being turned in to a professor who was like, 'Don't do this.'" She identified the use of buzzwords as "a confidence issue," explaining that she thought Eleanor was using such words in a "fake it 'til you make it kind of way." Although Marie was able to identify with Eleanor, she directed Eleanor to interrogate her terms, performing the role of the teacher who told her, "Don't do this," rather than of a fellow student writer. Reflecting on her experience as a facilitator in a later interview, Marie also explained that she actually regretted the way that she sometimes felt herself in competition with Eleanor, especially when it came to "sounding smart" by using challenging terminology. Eleanor's interview confirmed Marie's hunch that Eleanor was using terms like *intersectionality* in a "fake it 'til you make it kind of way." Eleanor explained that in talking to advisors, she wanted to "sound smart" and "make a good impression." She also was frustrated that her advisor "assume[d] that I know" how to use "big concepts" such as intersectionality or postmodernism. When asking her advisor for help, Eleanor reported that he would tell her to "just read these three sources" when she wished he would unpack them with her. Eleanor, like her own advisor, offered to send Marie a reading on an unfamiliar concept. Whether helpful for them or not, Eleanor and Marie relayed professors' feedback in the group. Eleanor also explained that she later found the group a helpful space to talk through and "make more sense of those concepts" that were driving her thesis, and Marie did eventually find the group rewarding because they "talked about a lot of interesting things and learned interesting things to read with each other." In the early group conversation, however, both Marie and Eleanor direct one another to resources rather than talking through a particular concept or sharing similar writing experiences.

The tendency in the undergraduate group to point one another to resources was indicative of a larger pattern of looking to outside resources to solve writing problems. These resources included readings as well as people, such as librarians and graduate student colleagues. Marie, Eleanor, and Maggie referenced advisors in ways that indicated that they saw advisors as resources who could solve writing problems for them. This example of using advisor voices as challenge points us to the emotional experiences of these advisor invocations. There were a lot of feelings around self-confidence and competition or comparison with others bound up in this process of identity formation for these particular undergraduate writers. In the next section, I attend to how the writers understood themselves in relation to their readers and sources of authority related to their projects outside of the writing group.

Looking for the "Silver Bullet": Resource Sharing and Advisors as Problem-Solvers in the UTG

As emerging scholars in their fields, the undergraduate writers especially relied on advisors to lend disciplinary or subject-matter expertise that they themselves had not yet developed. For example, Eleanor spoke of her advisors as actual stand-ins for disciplinary knowledge in the construction of her thesis.

> ELEANOR: I have two advisors. So I have one, [Advisor 1], who is the postmodernist, and he's been giving me a lot of information about what postmodernism is in literature and how I can connect feminism with it through [Advisor 2]. 'Cause [Advisor 2] is the one that knows feminist literary criticism. So, with them I really get this combination of both sides.

Eleanor's language, to "connect feminism with [postmodernism] through [Advisor 2]," refers to her advisors as actual points of connection to bodies of work and conversations that come together in her thesis. She doesn't frame herself as the agent who forges a connection between the two subfields.

Maggie sometimes drew on an advisor's guidance in ways that could constrain group feedback and even seemed to impede her own research progress at times. Maggie had initially hoped to write her thesis about Scout's character in Harper Lee's *To Kill a Mockingbird*. Following her advisor's assessment that there was probably not anything left to contribute to scholarship on Scout, Maggie embarked on a project investigating the book's publication history, incorporating its reception and the reception of the recently released *Go Set a Watchman*. This type of research was much less familiar to Maggie. She relied on her advisor for his knowledge of the field and for sources with which to drive her research:

> MAGGIE: Surprisingly there's not a lot of books out there about *To Kill a Mockingbird*. BSU only has, like, six books. And we [Maggie and her advisor] were trying to look into the collection in the Rare Books Library and, like, there's not a *To Kill a Mockingbird* [in the Special Collection] and so, there's also, like, no Twain author series. 'Cause my professor was kinda like looking through it, he's like, "oh there's no Twain author series, there's no [Special] collection," and so it's just kinda like—there's not a lot out there.

Maggie relied on her advisor to point her to databases and other sources. Here, she summarized his assessment of the library holdings to support her statement that "there's not a lot out there." Maggie did not seem to keep looking for sources beyond this, however. Although both Eleanor and I, at different times throughout the semester, urged Maggie to consult a subject librarian, who might help her widen her search to find useful primary and secondary sources, Maggie stuck to her advisor's brief search and assessment of the field until much later in the semester. This invocation of advisor as source of disciplinary knowledge was not productive in this instance, because it appeared to predispose Maggie to avoiding the additional work the rest of the group thought would be useful to her.

The emphasis on finding resources approved by Maggie's advisor was intensified by her expectations for the writing process. During one session, Maggie explained that she was having difficulty making an argument out of the few articles she found in 1960s newspapers:

> ELEANOR: I think the subject librarian would definitely be the most helpful.
>
> MAGGIE: OK.
>
> SARA: Yeah, and I mean, you're finding sources. It's not like you're not finding anything. It's not going to be a magic bullet that suddenly gives you an answer.
>
> MAGGIE: Mhm. Yeah, and that's what I'm, like, looking for. Because I'm so used to writing papers based off of "oh I found this quote. I can make an argument out of this." This is—there's no quote I can make an argument about, so.

Maggie's usual method of writing papers did not work for her thesis, which required her to piece together insights from primary and secondary sources to build a much longer paper and argument than her course assignments had required of her thus far. Although, in the above excerpt, I suggested that Maggie would have to treat her sources differently, she continued to look for what she later called a "silver bullet" article. Both Maggie and Eleanor struggled at times to articulate their own key interests or purposes in their projects and relied on advisors and other outside sources of authority for direction and disciplinary knowledge. In particular, they asked for resources (like Maggie's "silver bullet article" or Eleanor's numerous secondary sources) that would be the key to their theses. Naming advisors as stand-ins for disciplinary knowledge and sources of solutions for writing problems could constrain the ability of the writing group to talk through possible solutions and ideas, allowing the writer to ignore suggestions and ideas that might have been more productive.

Mediating Advisor Feedback and Authority in the UTG

As facilitator, Marie sometimes responded to these less productive invocations by trying to mediate advisor authority. In the following excerpt, after Eleanor had talked at length about her thesis, Marie prompted her to separate herself from her advisors:

> MARIE: One thing I've heard a lot in your explanations is, you're talking about what your advisors are sort of saying and what they want. Um, it's OK to want what your advisors want, but I think that maybe sitting down and really thinking about what you want from this project might be helpful, because you don't have to agree with your advisors. I mean, they're your advisors so you kind of want to give them something that they're gonna like, but they might be really, really open to seeing something different.

In this instance, Marie pushed Eleanor to think through her own ideas and goals for the project. Marie made an important move here, inviting Eleanor to use the group as a space in which to practice developing ideas and building authority based on her own interests and expertise. Marie thus encouraged Eleanor to take more ownership over her project. Resisting or reframing the voice of the advisor, as Marie did in this example, provided writers opportunity to develop their own sense of authority in collaboration with the group. Facilitators in both groups were more likely to prompt resistance, rather than the writer initiating that resistance herself. Writers might ask questions and express uncertainty about advisors' comments and expectations, but it was most often facilitators or other group members who encouraged writers to negotiate with advisor voices.

Advisors as Problem-Posers in the DWG

Overall, dissertation writers explicitly drew on advisors in their speech less often than the undergraduate group, yet advisor authority was still an important part of group negotiations. Like the undergraduates, the graduate writers most frequently referenced advisors as guides to the writing process. However, with more experience as researchers and writers, dissertators tended to rely less heavily on advisors to solve problems for them. They more often seemed to understand their advisor-guides as problem-posers, pointing to the writing problems that needed to be solved next. In the following examples, I begin by considering how group members referenced advisors, in order to productively define writing problems and shape feedback. I then turn to an example of how, even for graduate students, reliance on paraphrased advisor guidance could limit the usefulness of group feedback.

Although graduate researchers looked to advisors for guidance, they tended to frame advisors not so much as problem-solvers but as problem-posers, who helped push projects along. Often, these references were productive for the group and for the writer, providing guidance that shaped group feedback. For example, during a group session focused on her work, Emily voiced her committee's questions about her project as well as her uncertainty in answering them, calling on the group to help her find answers:

> EMILY: And, I guess, a question that I have for you guys, 'cause it's a question that I still have for myself. It's sort of, um, about my methodology, right? And so, this is a question that my committee is just like, "When you figure this out, you're, then you'll be good. But it will take you a while

to figure this out." So, I'm kind of calling this the "law and film" methodology, right? . . . People on my committee are really pushing me to say, to figure out, um, like, "Why are you putting law and film together?" And my real answer is, like, 'cause I want to.

Emily's comments to the group, giving voice to her professors' critical questions about her work, shaped the feedback she received. The group discussed her methodological choices at length. Multiple group members asked her pumping questions about how the legal cases she examined related to the films she was close-reading, while Radha, the group facilitator, took copious notes on Emily's answers. Through this process, Emily was forced to explain her choices and her thinking when it was not yet clear in her writing, and Radha did what she could to capture this thinking through note-taking. In the above examples, Emily refers to advisors as guides to the writing process, by voicing their questions and their assessment of the problems she needs to solve as a writer. Relaying their guidance served Emily by shaping the group conversation to fit her needs. In her interview, Emily valued the opportunity to talk through writing problems articulated by her advisors, so that she was able turn in a more thoughtful, polished draft.

Presentified advisor authority thus shaped the way group members collaborated across disciplinary boundaries and helps us understand their negotiations of authority. Aitchison (2014) reported that DWG members in her study made decisions about how to take up or reject feedback, based on judgments of the feedback giver's expertise in the discipline. Examining moments in which group members had to navigate disciplinary difference—when writers challenged feedback from the group—showed them referencing advisors as part of these challenging situations. Understanding the voice of the advisor as presentified in these situations shows writing group members not only referencing advisors as readers or sources of support but actually leveraging their authority to rhetorically sell their feedback or otherwise influence the course of group conversation. More productive instances linked advisor authority to fully articulated feedback or explanations of the rhetorical features of discipline-specific writing. Less productive instances challenged or deflected group feedback without offering such explanations that could help the group give better feedback.

In the following example, Ahmed relays his advisor's guidance and cites his advisor's work as a model, to gently reject feedback from Radha, the group facilitator. In responding to Radha, Ahmed handled the cross-disciplinary tension by citing his advisor as an expert, a strategy that allowed him to ask for more useful feedback:

> RADHA: You're selling yourself, I feel like, short. It doesn't—like, you don't seem super excited about this. [...] And I don't know if it's [that] you're trying to be more objective in terms of language?
>
> AHMED: Oh, yes. My advisor [said] don't try to say anything that is—why it is. This is not accepted generally in our field. [...] I was writing in a general language before, and encouraging new ideas [saying things like]: "this will change the field." [...] But this is not the way my advisor is, [or how] the rest of the community deals. So, you need to describe [the research] [...] and then let other people know how good you are. Don't say about yourself. So, that's why we are objective of anything we say.

Ahmed referenced his advisor to challenge feedback that conflicted with his understanding of writing conventions in his field. In doing so, Ahmed did not simply resist Radha's advice. He also explained the conventions of his field and his own process in learning them. By describing how his writing evolved, Ahmed positioned himself as a learner rather than pitting himself and his advisor against Radha. This strategy worked well for Ahmed because he had the backing of a credible source, but he did not outright reject group members' advice so much as help them understand how to give him better advice. Within this comment, Ahmed cited his advisor and positioned himself and his advisor together in "our field," while also reflecting on how he learned these disciplinary conventions. He showed how he was establishing himself as an expert in his field, and took an expert stance in the writing group.

Yet references to an advisor's guidance could also constrain productive feedback across disciplinary boundaries. In one particularly difficult group session, Holly struggled to communicate her goals and her advisor's expectations for her chapter. Her references to advisors were not linked to clear explanations about disciplinary conventions and showed her struggle to manage conflicting advice from her committee members. Throughout this conversation, discussing committee members' guidance was not especially effective, prompting Radha to encourage some resistance to the advisor voice and prompting other writers to provide Holly with a language for framing her work. The group thus functioned as a low-stakes space in which Holly had the opportunity to work out the problems she faced in structuring her chapter and to practice articulating her goals and choices as a writer. Holly introduced her chapter as one of three literature review chapters on key theoretical concepts, this one on the concept of "play." The chapter not only reviewed major philosophies of art and play but also included short sections narrating stories from her ethnographic study. The group was unsure of how to respond to Holly's chapter. Should a literature review include examples from her data? How might the primary data she included best help her articulate the problem or theory that her chapter was addressing? When Peter questioned whether narratives from her data collection even belonged in the chapter, Holly responded, "I don't know that it does. I've heard that I can use the data to help explain the concepts. [. . .] There's a lot more leeway in how—it's not necessarily science." She knew that her chapter, as "not necessarily science," would follow different disciplinary conventions than Peter's chapters but also did not seem committed to her own choices in structuring the chapter or to have a model to work from. She was uncertain in her own genre knowledge. Later in the conversation, she expressed ambivalence and uncertainty about her revision choices because she was not sure what her advisor wanted.

> HOLLY: And this is where—so to be—just to give you the background of me. My old advisor at [University X] is the narrative writer. My new advisor is more of a content analysis [person]. So, she likes the narrative and thinks I do a good job with it, but I think the old philosopher—er, the old advisor who I don't—I talk to a little bit, because she's remote. But I think she would be more inclined to see me just integrate the narrative down the way. But my new advisor is not—it's kind of like one of those things where she's, like, seventy-two, seventy-three, or something like that, and she's not—doesn't not trust me, but she's like, "If I haven't seen it and it hasn't happened," she's going to show me the way that makes sense to her. So, it's sort of—and I've never written a dissertation before, so I'm kind of like, "I don't know."

Holly recognized that her own understanding of conventions for dissertations in her field was incomplete, but she felt stuck negotiating conflicting advice from two different committee members and the feedback she received in group. As Emily, Peter, and the rest of the group debated how Holly ought to move forward with revising and perhaps restructuring her chapter, they tried to attend to disciplinary conventions and Holly's advisor's expectations, but because neither were especially clear to Holly, this was a difficult task.

Finally, Radha encouraged Holly to articulate her goals for the chapter and her purpose in including both theory and data throughout. In doing so, she acted as a kind of mediator, just as Marie did for Eleanor, encouraging Holly to develop her own voice in her writing and to negotiate with her advisor.

RADHA: So, not to say, like, forge new boundaries and get your spurs out and your cowboy hat, but, like—

HOLLY: But that, like, helps to hear.

RADHA: Is there a reason you're doing what you're doing? Because it feels like we're all on the same page in terms of, like, "Oh, here's where we'd like to see our examples." If there's a reason, I feel like you can kind of make that case to your advisor, and be like, "Hey, here's what I did." And show her, like, this lit review, because you've got it done. Be like, "Look, I did this lit review. Here's how I feel like this other version is more effective. Can I do this? Because it makes sense for me to do this in these ways."

HOLLY: And I don't think she would say no. I just think it's one of those things where "I haven't seen it done" and that wouldn't be the way she'd advise me to do it.

RADHA: But you're brilliant, so do what you want.

[*laughter*]

HOLLY: I just need it done. I'm scared and I need it done.

PETER: Do you know, like, so—so, you kind of have your definition of what play is. And then, like, I guess, what—I guess, what's the—do you know what the contribution is going to be? Is it going to be, like, "This is the way that practitioners should look at it?" or "I think this theory is strong, but it's weak in this area?"

Radha understood that her advice to Holly might be pushing boundaries, but she also asked, "is there a reason you're doing what you're doing?" and emphasized the group's general consensus thus far about Holly's chapter. As facilitator, Radha was more likely than other group members to encourage writers to articulate their own goals and choices as writers, even if that meant resisting or just reframing advisors' expectations. On one hand, this could open up a space for writers to articulate why their own writing choices are effective. On the other hand, Holly was "scared," anxious about meeting uncertain expectations with her text, prompting Peter to try to help Holly turn her literature review into an easily recognizable structure based on a gap in the field, a much safer route for quickly satisfying her advisor's expectations and graduating. Peter demonstrated his own expertise as he provided language for talking about Holly's research, suggesting ways she might articulate her contribution to the field. In this group meeting, however, Holly was still developing her sense of what her contribution was and how to communicate it in a dissertation chapter, particularly because she was trying to please committee members without a strong sense of what they wanted. Nevertheless, moments of resistance to presentified advisor authority, like this one, could invite writers to make conscious decisions about how to articulate their projects in their own voice and negotiate their relationships with advisors.

Developing and Practicing Genre Knowledge in Multidisciplinary Groups

So, where have we come to? Group members generally appreciated multidisciplinarity. And they were more nervous about reading across disciplinary difference and giving strong feedback than they were worried about the quality of the feedback they received. Facilitators attested, also, to the benefits of seeing writing across disciplines, for themselves and for the writers in their groups. For facilitators, the challenge was in getting buy-in and showing group members how to engage.

In practice, groups developed conversational strategies that allowed them to work together across difference. In these conversations, the writer and the rest of the group participants worked collaboratively on possible revisions—on lines of argument, on organization, on style—tinkering with words and phrases, and writing and rewriting together. I would argue that these sequences of feedback engaged writers in moments of co-authorship, even if that co-authorship was temporary. In *Across Property Lines: Textual Ownership in Writing Groups*, Candice Spigelman (2000) argued that writing groups require writers to give up ownership over their texts, at least briefly within the space of the writing groups. They require that group members exercise authority as readers to critique, to respond, and to make suggestions as though they themselves were the writer. We saw instances of this kind of collaboration when Peter offered suggestions (demonstrating Denny's "oral writing-revision space") and when groups deliberated over potential revisions, offering agreement and disagreement.

The collaborative process across disciplinary boundaries often hinged on the genre knowledge that group members, collectively, brought to and developed in the conversation. As research on genre and writing transfer has theorized, each act of composing is an act of recontextualization or integration of past genre knowledge for the unique rhetorical task at hand (Tardy et al. 2020; Nowacek 2011). By reading and offering feedback to help another writer revise, each group member was asked, then, to recontextualize their existing genre knowledge for the new situation, perhaps for an unfamiliar audience, about an unfamiliar subject, and according to unfamiliar formal conventions.

This was hard intellectual work, it was emotional work, and it offered a rich learning opportunity. As Tardy and colleagues write:

> Some new instances involve relatively simple adaptation (in similar situations and language settings), whereas others are more demanding (involving more significant changes to a rhetorical situation). . . . The more familiar the genre, the more automatic the recontextualization process, not necessarily requiring heavy engagement in genre awareness. When writers perform less familiar genres (or a genre in a new language and/or discourse community), genre awareness may become more important as they align and adapt existing knowledge to the new task. (301)

Because productive collaborations across disciplines require participants to engage in less familiar genres or discourse communities, they are also an opportunity to develop greater genre awareness, that is, a greater "understanding of rhetorical contexts and how writers may effectively respond to exigencies within such contexts" (Tardy et al. 2020, 296). By asking one another questions to elicit genre-specific knowledge (as well as subject knowledge) and listening for the "rhetorical resonances" (the shared formal and rhetorical features of specific academic genres), group members were both developing genre-specific knowledge and a broader genre awareness that would allow them to see their own writing with new eyes, as Emily explained in her interview.

The way that genre knowledge seemed to function in multidisciplinary writing group conversations underscores the social, collaborative, and distributed process by which genre knowledge develops. Similarly, in their study of transfer talk in writing center consultations, Nowacek and co-authors suggest that "transfer of learning is a strikingly social, even collaborative, cognition" (Nowacek et al. 2019). I did not set out to study transfer and didn't use Nowacek and colleagues' coding scheme, so I can't make a direct comparison to their study. However, I do think the way that genre knowledge was developed and negotiated in the writing groups aligns with the kinds of transfer talk that they noted in one-to-one writing center consultations.[6] Both the writing groups and individual consultations host conversations about in-progress writing, and both require participants to integrate or recontextualize past knowledge for the situation at hand, which includes both the writing itself (and its accompanying readership) and the ongoing group conversation. Nowacek et al. suggest:

---

6. Nowacek et al. define transfer talk as "the talk through which individuals make visible their prior learning (in this case, about writing) or try to access the prior learning of someone else" (n.p.).

> Perhaps facilitating transfer talk through asking questions and inviting stories can make writers more aware that they do indeed have some amount of previous knowledge and writing experience to draw on. Such conversations are a space where transfer talk can be cultivated to encourage writers not only to work productively on the assignment at hand, but also to become more confident in articulating and repurposing what they have already learned. (n.p.)

Accounts from interviews and surveys of writing group participants would suggest that the groups are one such conversational space. Both asking questions and giving answers about genre or about the specifics of the writing at hand engaged group participants in conversation that relied on genre knowledge, either explicitly or implicitly. The conversational sequences that drew out or surfaced each group member's prior genre knowledge opened up space in which the group, collectively, could deliberate about particular revision choices and, potentially, develop a stronger genre awareness.

Crucially, each individual group member was seen as bringing knowledge about their specific project, about their specific rhetorical situation, in their specific discipline. It was the writer's responsibility to explain the generic demands of their writing, the expectations and conventions that shaped writing in their field, as well as their own goals and inclinations as writers. Genre, in this case, wasn't treated as a static entity. That is, group members weren't asked to go find out what all dissertations in their field always look like and create a set of rules to follow, but instead they asked one another questions about audience, purpose, contribution, and process. Each writer was asked to participate in the position of expert and, through conversation, surface and exercise prior genre knowledge. At the same time, they also were negotiating ownership over the others' projects, based to some degree on judgments about others' expertise.

Participation in these negotiations of authority and expertise was distinctly emotional. It was complicated by group members' dispositions toward the task, their own confidence in themselves as readers and writers, their feelings about other group members, and their feelings about their relationships with "present others"—the advisors and committee members invoked in group conversation. For example, we saw how many study participants expressed apprehension at reading and offering feedback to those in other disciplines. We saw the feelings of competitiveness (lack of confidence?) that accompanied comparison in the UTG, particularly for the writers from the same and similar disciplines (and who were also young, white women who worked in the Writing Center). We heard the fear and uncertainty that Holly expressed as she anticipated needing to finish her degree that summer. And yet, there was also a great deal of laughter and playfulness that showed up in conversations across all three groups. There were authentic expressions of interest in and excitement about others' work. And there were rising feelings of confidence as both readers and writers. Clearly, working across disciplinary boundaries is both intellectual and emotional work, and it is identity work, as participants negotiate their emerging professional identities and their relationships with one another. In the next chapter, I dig further into the emotional lived experiences that characterized participation in the writing groups.

4
Storying the Difficulties

Emotional Labor in Writing Groups at a PWI

This chapter stories the difficulties of writing groups in the Writing Center, exploring group participants' emotional experiences in response to tension or conflict. To open this discussion, I'll share a story that Radha, the DWG facilitator, told me in her interview. This story reflects difficulties she experienced managing conflict in one of her writing groups.

Radha, the DWG facilitator, was an experienced consultant and writing group facilitator. She saw herself as a motivator, and often acted as a cheerleader, expressing interest in her group members' projects and excitement about their work together. She herself found inspiration as a graduate writer when she saw group members' progress. If I had to describe the emotions that she most often expressed to the group I observed, they would primarily be excitement, interest and curiosity, and joy in their projects. That's not to say that she wasn't fully aware of and responsive to problems or less comfortable emotions in academic writing. Radha's own dissertation work was focused on questions relating to race and education, and she was as likely as any of the group members to occasionally express anger at inequities in the university, frustration (often tinged with a bit of sarcasm) about problems with teachers or students, or anxiety about writing her own dissertation. These were expressions of emotion and responses to problems that could bring group members together, connecting through shared experience and offering opportunities for validation and for empathy.

The story Radha told me in her interview, however, relayed an experience of conflict with a group member. Her story reflects on managing emotion and on how to intervene if group members were acting in a way that didn't contribute to the productive and supportive community that she was helping her group to build. This wasn't something that I witnessed firsthand, as the story that Radha tells concerns a conflict in another of her writing groups, a conflict that came up between a white, male group member and the three other female group members, and how she and other group members dealt with that conflict.

> RADHA: I noticed that in one of these groups, I have, including me, four women and a dudebro. And dudebro is white, and dudebro has tended to be consistently loud and consistently cutting other people off. [. . .] And I was trying to figure out how to deal with it or how to, like, facilitate moving away from that. Other people in the group started voicing themselves and kind of being like, "no, this is how I think it's gonna be," and I think part of that is because [. . .] [I] say that this is a community and we're here for each other's benefit and not to put each other down but to be productive. And that is something that I do say a lot because it is something that I really strongly believe.

Radha points to the shared labor of establishing group norms and building productive relationships and also references racial and gender identity in reflecting on how she and others are able to do that emotional work. In this group, Radha saw both herself and the other women in her group taking responsibility, together, to establish the group norms of communication, to "not put each other down," and, presumably, to not interrupt others when they are offering their perspective. Although Radha's use of "dudebro" might strike some as flippant, I do think that it points to the way that this particular group member's behavior was representative of a larger pattern Radha had experienced with some white men in our predominantly white institution (PWI) who did not listen well to her, and who didn't perform the kind of emotional and relational work that was then performed by her and by other women in the group to help hold the community together.

Later in the interview, she explained that this writing group did build up a level of trust that allowed them to still be productive, despite some of the tensions at play. Her stories from this group, though, invite speculation about the different experiences that she and other group members may have had in managing various conflicts. For example, Radha recounted an experience in which the group had an informal but tension-filled conversation about affirmative action in education. In the conversation, she had shared an experience of talking with her first-year composition students about affirmative action in higher education. In sharing this story, Radha had expected to be met with a collegial kind of empathy but instead ended up in a debate about affirmative action and "reverse discrimination" with her group member. Radha explains that she struggled, in that conversation, to know how to engage politely and effectively, after they had engaged in an argument about the topic:

> RADHA: And he was like, "oh yeah, well, we think about histories and how they embed oppression, but y'know, at the end of the day, like, it's still unfair to me that this thing is happening for someone else." And that's the point at which I was [thinking,] "I'm used to talking about this with eighteen-year-old students." It's different when I'm talking to a forty-five-year-old adult who has children. [. . .] I was kind of getting a little at a loss of words, because the only thing that I wanted to say was "so, you're telling me that your privilege is the only privilege that matters. So, as long as you are getting what you want, you feel like you're being treated fairly, then it's all fine." And so, I was trying to figure out how to say that nicely, and somebody else ended up stepping in.

In this story, Radha's particular challenge points us to the ways that identifications of race, gender, and age are shaping the emotional work she was doing in this exchange. She is worried about politeness, how to say "nicely" the thing she really wants to say. She frames herself in a kind of one-down position to her male group member, who is also significantly older than she is and who is in a different life stage that, for Radha, seems to grant him a different kind of authority. At the same time, as facilitator, she was also in a role that meant that she was supposed to be creating an environment that served all of her group members productively. Entering into a contentious debate with a group member could have felt at odds with that goal. I don't want to say here that the group member should have just agreed with Radha and all would have been well, or to say that Radha should have just spoken her mind. I also don't have other group members' perspectives on the situation. Rather than debate what could or should have occurred, I'm interested in Radha's reflection on the kind of mental and emotional gymnastics that she was feeling compelled to perform—to decide if and how to enter fully into this conversation in a way that would preserve the community that she had tried hard to build with her group members. In the context of this group, where Radha did not feel that the one participant was attending as carefully as the rest to established group norms for communication (not interrupting each other, for example), her comments point to a discrepancy between the care that she felt she was showing in trying to be polite and the care she did not feel from the group member in attending to his effect on group interpersonal dynamics.

In exploring difficulty in writing groups, then, I attend to the different, individualized experiences of the difficulties or tensions that characterized the relational and intellectual work of writing group collaboration. In particular, I attend to the emotional labor that group members perform (or not) as they work through these difficulties. In this chapter, I draw on Arlie Hochschild's foundational definition of emotional labor, as well as recent scholarship that has taken up and theorized emotional labor in the writing center. In *The Managed Heart* (1983), Hochschild defines emotional labor as labor that "requires one to induce or suppress feeling in order to sustain the outward countenance that produces the proper state of mind in others" (7). Many of Hochschild's well-known examples come from Delta Air Lines flight attendants who were well versed in inducing friendliness, performed through pleasant smiles, and suppressing anger, frustration, and resentment in order to keep passengers calm, happy, and at ease. In the example that opens this chapter, we might think of Radha suppressing her own frustration in order to maintain a supportive environment. That's not to say that all emotional labor is problematic. Emotional work is critically important to how we live, work, and play together.[1] Hochschild's analysis, like others who have critically examined emotional labor in various spaces, makes this work visible *as work* and invites us to consider how that work is distributed in various communities, families, and workplaces.

More recently, writing center scholars have attended to emotional labor of writing center administrators (Caswell et al. 2016; Navickas 2020; Webster 2021) and of tutors (Giaimo 2023; Im, Shao, and Chen 2020; Mannon 2021; Nelson, Deges, and Weaver 2020). In *The Working Lives of New Writing Center*

---

1. Hochschild makes a distinction between *emotional labor*—"management of feeling to create a publicly observable facial and bodily display" that is "sold for a wage" and thus has an exchange value—and *emotion work* to "refer to these same acts done in a private context where they have use value" (7). I've used these terms somewhat interchangeably, though I've tried to use "emotional work" in reference to group members who aren't being paid to facilitate the groups. Both group members and facilitators, though, engaged in emotion work and shaped the emotional landscape of the writing groups.

Directors, Caswell, McKinney, and Jackson define emotional labor as work that involves "care, mentoring, or nurturing of others; building and sustaining relationships; work to resolve conflicts; managing our displays of emotion" (Caswell et al. 2016, 27). Clearly the work of taking part in and facilitating writing groups requires emotional labor, as we've already seen in a number of examples throughout this book. This chapter is particularly interested in how individual members of the group may have labored differently or experienced that emotional work differently, and in ways that were sometimes in tension with one another. The emotional experiences of writing groups were shaped by the same scripts that shape writing in the academy writ large.

In her essay "Resisting White, Patriarchal Emotional Labor Within the Writing Center," Nicole Caswell writes, "Writing centers are rich with affective economies that demand and shape directors' and consultants' emotional labor," inviting readers to consider how individuals' emotional labor takes place within our social systems (2022, 109). Drawing on work by Sara Ahmed (2014) and Laura Micciche (2007), Caswell reminds us that "while individuals have the same biological and chemical processes when an emotion has been triggered, the recognition and naming of that process is a social, cultural act. Individuals respond to their emotions based on how they have been socially and culturally conditioned to do so" (111). And so, Caswell and others ask us to think about how emotions are named, valued, and made meaningful according to the cultural conditioning in the context of the interaction itself and the institutional space. In writing center work, a number of authors have shown us already how race and gender fundamentally shape emotional labor and emotional experience in the writing center space.

In their critique of writing center spaces, Wonderful Faison and Anna K. (Willow) Treviño note the ways that writing center spaces often assume a white, middle-class aesthetic, rather than focusing on the lived experiences of people, particularly people of color, in the space. Critiquing the myth of the writing center as "cozy home," building on McKinney's (2013) work in *Peripheral Visions for Writing Centers*, they write, "a home is made a home through emotional labor and through acts of love, compassion, and empathy.... How can one make a home when the people who inhabit it have moderate, at best, and low, at worst, emotional connection to one another" (Faison and Treviño 2020, 104). Following their lead, I pay careful attention to the kinds of emotional connection and the emotional labor that upholds those connections in writing groups, particularly in how groups managed or worked through difficulties and were shaped by identitifications such as race, gender, class, and disability.

Attending to emotional labor is especially important in writing groups, which offer such rich possibilities for strong relationships and community building. Writing groups, particularly academic writing groups that grow in response or resistance to institutional spaces, are often storied as spaces of care, support, and camaraderie. They certainly have been one way that writers have carved out space for themselves in the landscape of the academy to "become part of an intellectual community, serve as disciplinary and emotional support, develop trust and respect in members, and recontextualize the writing process from an individual act to a socially embedded scholarly practice" (Kinney, Snyder-Yuly, and Martinez 2019) and to provide peer mentorship and "a sense of respect and accountability" (Sévère and Wilson 2020). They are one site in which to counter the isolation that so often characterizes graduate education, especially for students who have historically been excluded from spaces of US higher education or who are in the minority at a PWI like the one in this study (Lockett 2020). Yet, writing groups, like all writing center work, are also shaped by their institutional setting, and we can't assume that any and all writing groups will naturally develop the kinds of relationships that can be so valuable and supportive for students (Jackson 2004; Westbrook 2004).

This chapter, thus, stories the difficulties or tensions that characterized individual experiences of engaging in the writing groups I studied, and it also stories the tensions that characterize group collaboration in institutional spaces. Specifically, I'm interested in the difficulties of the writing group itself, rather than how students spoke about difficult emotions in relation to their writing projects. That is, students might have communicated to the rest of the group their sadness or stress about their writing projects, and the group may have offered empathy, validation, or support. Ultimately, this kind of process—the emotional labor that group members do for one another—is what forms such strong relationships, leading to feelings of intimacy and a sense of being cared for and supported. These things happened in the writing groups I observed, but they also happened amid interpersonal dynamics and difficulties of writing group practice itself. In this chapter, I focus on writing group difficulties: stories of inclusion and exclusion and of emotional labor experienced differently by different group members. When I coded emotions that participants expressed, I coded them initially as "writing emotion" and "group emotion," meaning feelings about the writing projects and feelings about the writing groups. This chapter focuses on feelings about difficulties in writing groups and particularly the way the groups were experienced differently by different individual participants in them.

Exploring emotion in the writing groups means not only naming and describing the feelings that individuals experienced in their bodies but also how those experiences related to one another and to the space of the group. The institutional space of the writing group in a writing center at a predominantly white institution created a particular context within which group participants worked together. Individuals experienced the groups differently, and some of those differences were shaped by negotiations of identity markers such as race, gender, age, disability, and linguistic background. In exploring the difficulties experienced by group members, I'm deliberately leaning into and highlighting the uncertainties, anxieties, conflicts participants had to negotiate as part of their emotional labor in the writing groups. This focus, I hope, will help address some of the risks of facilitating these groups in a writing center, and perhaps help offer perspectives to writing center directors and writing group facilitators that can help mitigate those risks in the design of the space and development of relationships.

The Emotional Landscape and Emotional Labor of the Writing Groups

Each of the writing groups I observed required emotional work from participants, as we've seen threaded throughout the previous chapters. We have already heard, for example, how facilitators described at least part of their work as providing stress relief, motivating writing, and inspiring confidence in the writers in their groups. They also noted the difficulty of "managing personalities" or holding group members accountable to one another. We've also heard group members express both growing feelings of confidence and gratitude for support, alongside anxiety about writing and about offering feedback across disciplines. Each group also was characterized by particular tensions or difficulties (large and small) stemming from the group practice and institutional context. In this section, I explore the emotional labor and experiences of those tensions in each group. First, I will attend somewhat briefly to the dissertation writing group and the second-year proposal group. For most of this chapter, however, I will focus on the undergraduate thesis group, which was the most fraught and offered the richest data for understanding emotional labor and how participants experienced and storied difficulty.

EMOTIONAL LABOR IN THE DISSERTATION WRITING GROUP: MOTIVATING WRITING, MANAGING ANXIETY, SETTING EXPECTATIONS

The dissertation writing group I observed, led by Radha, was generally a very supportive space. Although, in all three groups, both group members and facilitators offered expressions of praise, admiration, and interest that strengthened their relationships and reinforced writers' motivation for their projects, the dissertation writing group was particularly good at this, led both by Radha and by the group members who had taken part in previous groups (Emily, Peter, and Holly). The writers in this group were committed to the group process: they seemed to listen well to one another and to do their best to show up prepared to each meeting. In short, all participants in this group showed care for one another.

In the dissertation writing group, Radha was an enthusiastic facilitator. She was often upbeat, cheering on progress and expressing excitement about her group members' projects, and she invited this kind of enthusiasm from other group members. For example, at the end of one session, Emily was telling the group what to expect from her writing for the next week, and Radha expressed excitement about the project itself and the progress the group was making on their various writing projects:

> EMILY: So, hopefully it'll be, like, the first four pages of my chapter. My first chapter from the dissertation. So, it's, um, going to be about the Brown vs. Board of Education [*Radha claps*], the, like, oral arguments.
>
> RADHA: Sorry, I was excited. Um, reining it in.
>
> EMILY: Well, who knows if I'll get to that. But again, um, *Imitation of Life* and *The Defiant Ones*. So yeah.
>
> PETER: Cool.
>
> SARA: That'll be interesting.
>
> EMILY: Actually, it'll probably just be, like, the intro and me trying to say what I'm going to say.
>
> RADHA: Yeah, no, that's how this happens, I feel like. Yay! This is so exciting, you guys. Look at all this progress-making!

In this exchange at the end of a group meeting, mundane as it may be, Radha, Peter, and I do important relational work. We express actual interest in what Emily has to say about her topic. Radha cheers on the process of writing and frames the whole group process and dissertation writing process positively. Although reading others' work could be seen as a laborious and possibly anxiety-inducing chore, I want to underscore the importance of the positive attitude here both for participants and for Emily. The interest that we express in Emily's project reaffirms her commitment to her ideas and topic and reaffirms the group process as one that results in progress on the projects. And it reflects the mode in which Radha, in particular, tended to engage with writers in the groups.

In tension with the expressions of interest and excitement at reading others' ongoing work, were fears and anxieties about reading and offering feedback across disciplines. In the previous chapter, we saw how these anxieties were common. Here, I'd like to return to an example from the dissertation writing group (examined in chapter 3) to explore how the emotional experiences were linked to other markers of difference in the group conversations and how these emotions were discussed and responded to in the space of the group. In considering this exchange, I draw on both the conceptions of emotional labor considered above and on Stephanie Kerschbaum's 2014 *Toward a New Rhetoric of Difference*. In her study of student interactions in classroom peer-review sessions, Kerschbaum urges us to consider how difference is not fixed but instead is negotiated in context. She develops a way of examining how markers of difference are "dynamic, relational, and emergent" in the moment as individuals exercise rhetorical agency in identifying, interpreting, and acting upon "categorical identifications" such as race, disability, gender, etcetera. In the following exchange from an early group meeting, the first in which the group members came prepared to give feedback, having read Holly's writing, Ahmed explicitly takes a moment to address his own doubts about the makeup of the group and their ability to collaborate productively. In doing so, he alludes to differences of linguistic background as well as differences in disciplinary expertise.

> AHMED: I have a comment. I don't know—it's—it's, whether it's better at the end or the beginning, but it may help you, Sara, to have my impression about this. I was concerned about the formulation of the group, and the—the specialties of everyone. And I read this first sample, so I found it very—it's the first time to me to read English literature other than medical literature. It may be a problem for me, because I am an international student. I don't know. I enjoyed reading it, but I don't feel that I am able to give any critiques that may be useful to Holly or something that she could use. I enjoyed reading, I tried, but—and I got what she wrote, but I understand some words are new for me, because they are

like "epistemology" or something like this. [. . .] I think the greatest thing in our group is making a peer review, but the peer review has to be useful. For Holly, I don't think I would be useful at all for peer review. I don't know if you would be useful for me, I don't know if my writing will be hard for you to judge.

RADHA: Well, one of the things—I think—I noticed that you said that there were parts that you really enjoyed also, so I think that's—in terms of critique, that's actually the easiest way to start, right? Is to be like, "Look, this paragraph was really great because it was so clear, and I enjoyed reading it because this was the point that got across." But, for the purposes of the writing group, for the most part, I think—well, let's do today, and we'll see how you feel after it.

AHMED: OK.

Ahmed's remarks that open this topic episode demonstrate the generous and highly motivated stance he took toward the writing group (and my research project) alongside his concerns about the usefulness of the group. The fact that Ahmed explicitly raises this concern, framing it as a help to me as researcher-administrator, shows both his honesty, goodwill, and motivation to make this writing group useful. He takes care to state, "I think the greatest thing in our group is making peer review, but the peer review has to be useful." He clearly wants to do the work, even as he raises this concern.

Ahmed is also explicit about the way he "marks difference," as Kerschbaum might write, and raises the possibility of differences of nationality, linguistic background, and English literacies as possible salient differences in the reading experience. As explored in chapter 3, Ahmed considers whether his nationality or his lack of experience with reading humanities literature in English might be the thing that is causing a problem that he perceives in his ability to read critically and offer useful feedback. Though Ahmed frames his language background as a potential weakness, we can also see it as a strength. Ahmed draws upon and demonstrates awareness of how his genre knowledge might be tied to particular languages and literacies. Ultimately, though, the most salient difference that he lands on is disciplinary, as he also questions whether his writing will be too difficult for the other group members to assess.

In Radha's response, she does not engage with the explicit markers of linguistic difference that Ahmed has communicated. Rather, she focuses on the one positive emotion that he expressed: "I noticed that you said that there were parts that you really enjoyed also, so I think that's actually the easiest way to start," trying to use that positive feeling as a starting point for a way forward. At the same time, she mentions that she does think there are "ways to develop a way of reading that's not necessarily content-based" and then defers the conversation until the end of the meeting, presumably after Ahmed has had a chance to experience how it might actually work to give feedback across disciplinary difference. Her focus here is on motivating Ahmed to stay in the group, and she does that through drawing his attention to a positive feeling about the work (enjoyment) and through an argument focused on action—finding different ways to read.

Throughout the meeting, Ahmed did find ways in. He used the strategy of pumping questions (as discussed in previous chapters) to explicitly address disciplinary difference, asking Holly to explain the methodology guiding her project. He also asked her about children and play (key topics of her dissertation), grounding his question in his experiences parenting his own young child. Radha found Holly's answers to such questions quite useful. Radha took detailed notes as Holly answered, in case the notes might be useful in expanding sections of Holly's work. At the end of the meeting, Radha returned, as promised, to the concerns that Ahmed raised at the beginning of the meeting. If we read the following exchange for emotional work, we can see how Ahmed manages his own feelings and demonstrates care for others. We'll see how Radha attempts to motivate Ahmed and invites Holly into that motivational work as well:

> RADHA: Um, so, we are sort of running out of time, and I kind of wanted to back and address your [Ahmed's] concern about, like, criticism and what you can contribute? Um, this is actually not how my usual writing groups go, like, we usually just kind of go paragraph by paragraph. Like, we do the overall thing and then we just go paragraph by paragraph, um, and tighten things up. And I think your [Holly's] explanations were really useful, so I'm hoping that, like, having those typed up is going to be useful to you as you, kind of, go back and rearrange this. Um, but in terms of, like, critiques as more about, like, "hey, this idea wasn't, like, complete here," or "hey, this was a really great question that you asked here, maybe you could like build on it more." Um, so, it's not—I mean, I guess it's not, like, always meant to be, like, negative critique or, like, "this always needs to be fixed," but, like, "hey, I don't understand this fully. Could you add more?" or, like, "hey maybe you could say this in this way, to make it more clear," kind of thing. Does that help?

AHMED: Um, yeah, yes, of course it helps, but I don't know if I'm aware, I have background about this, um, general background to know what's missing here or what's short here, so that's just—

RADHA: I think, just as, like, a general reader, for you to be able to say, like, like, 'cause I don't actually know a lot about this theory and I hate Kant. Um, and I really hate Deleuze, like, I really, really, with a passion, hate Deleuze. Um, but just kind of, you know being like—

AHMED: Also, my concern is that I, I wanted to be as useful to them as they will be, so—

RADHA: Yeah. This is, also remember two people have already done writing groups, um, so this is also like, I'm coming back to this after, it takes, like, awhile to even get into the role of it, I promise you, this is, like, right, 'cause it, Holly, this is your third one? Second one? Okay. Yeah. Did you feel like it took—

HOLLY: It was hard taking [English student's] the first day.

RADHA: Yeah.

HOLLY: He had dropped like a twenty-five-page English bomb on the table, and I was like, oh god, that took me, like, five hours to read through that thing. And I was like, I was like, I didn't even get all the way through, just cause his, and his writing was beautiful. But it was dense, and I have never heard of any of it before and I just, I tried and basically just "do your best."

RADHA: Yeah, it's not—

HOLLY: Fake it till you make it.
[laughter]

RADHA: Then with seeing different people's writing, it helps you put it into perspective in terms of what kind of feedback is useful. So, I think, who's going next week, by the way? Great! So, next week, we'll see how, how your writing—
[. . .]

AHMED: Okay. Also there's just the last thing that I have a full paper that is, complete, completed, so um, yeah, after that, I don't want you to, to be. I don't want it to be a difficult task for you so, um, I will send the whole paper, but you may, you may only go through the introduction, and if you found the introduction was hard for you, don't go further in the other parts, okay?

So, if we read these exchanges for emotional labor, we can see a few ways that the participants are engaging in emotional, relational work. First, Ahmed is addressing his concern with the group explicitly, opening up the possibility for the group to work together on this problem. He is also managing his own feelings as he probes to figure out how his difference in linguistic background and his difference in disciplinary expertise is salient in this particular group context. Ahmed also does some work to try to frame the task for other group members. He demonstrates care for them as he shares his writing for feedback: "I don't want it to be a difficult task for you," he says, telling them to limit the investment of time and energy in the task of reading and developing feedback for his work. Second, Radha tries to motivate Ahmed by arguing for the value of the feedback Holly received in the group that day and providing some potential scripts for giving feedback. Finally, she enlists Holly in trying to convince Ahmed of the value of this investment of labor. Holly responds with her own emotional work: she empathizes with Ahmed by sharing her own experience reading a difficult text in a previous writing group and suggests that just "trying" and "doing your best" is enough. She tries to take the pressure off, saying, somewhat facetiously, "fake it 'til you make it." I do wonder, though, about the emotional labor of "faking it" until you make it in a writing group. It seems to me that given the difficulties that we saw in the undergraduate thesis group in chapter 3—which arose as students were "faking" their way through using difficult theoretical concepts, putting them in competition with one another—that the group needs to foster authentic engagement. And this is why I think Ahmed's concerns should be welcomed and addressed, perhaps in even more depth than they were in this conversation. Slowing down and spending more time drawing explicit attention to different ways of offering feedback through group practice might have been helpful. The work of acknowledging concerns or apprehensions as well as positive encouragement were both important to relationship-building and learning in this group.

 The tension between anxiety and relief, sunny encouragement and deliberate reckoning with difficulty or uncertainty, seems to me to be one that will always characterize institutionalized groups like this. Emotional labor in this group was about motivating group practice and motivating writing, and this labor was shared and distributed among Radha and her group participants. This labor also entailed negotiating shared values around group feedback and managing expectations. Ahmed's perspective, above, points us also to the possible difficulties, even in a supportive group, that particular group members may face as they navigate membership in this multidisciplinary space. For group facilitators and administrators, part of the emotional work of a writing group is helping to set boundaries on expectations. No one should be spending five hours reading for their weekly writing group. Recognizing this labor, framing the task for group members, offering them strategies for reading, and offering encouragement and validation for what they are able to do in one to two hours of preparation is both emotional and intellectual work and contributes to strong group relationships. To do that work well, though, necessitates understanding that each group member will have a different experience of that labor and the time it takes, and that sometimes group members' needs may be in tension or conflict.

EMOTIONAL LABOR IN THE SECOND-YEAR PROPOSAL GROUP: MOVING FROM TRANSACTIONAL TO TRANSFORMATIVE

In the SPG, both the group difficulties and the emotions that group participants were experiencing were less obvious to me, perhaps because they were less difficult. The students in this group were pleasant with one another, sharing their excitement about their project ideas and spring break plans. The proposals they were writing asked them to include personal statements and to speculate about the way that the grant would enable them to have a "transformative" experience. So, there was certainly sharing of personal lives and backgrounds in the service of figuring out how to articulate those experiences in a way that would win them the grant. At the same time, this group had fewer meetings (by design), and the stakes did not feel as high for the proposals that these writers undertook as those for the dissertation writers, for example. In this group, then, I didn't observe tensions of the sort that characterized the stories of the other two groups. It is possible, of course, that I missed some of those tensions, as I was only able to interview one member of the SPG.

However, I do want to highlight the emotional work that these group members undertook for and with one another. They provided support through sharing resources but also through validating one another's experiences in their "transformative experience" program. The SPG was a place to vent about frustrations with the program as well as to share advice on managing relationships with advisors. The work they undertook together also helped frame the task of writing for group members, treating one another's writing with care and attention.

During the last meeting, the SPG members talked through the strengths of the group and the reason they valued taking part in it. Although they did not talk specifically about Elizabeth as facilitator, they explained that the writing group helped them by teaching them specific writing knowledge and helping them to take the writing more seriously.

> JENNY: I feel like I've come away with a lot better understanding of what a proposal is, how you go about writing one in the future, and, you know, actually considering, um, something bigger than just the [program] proposal. 'Cause a lot of people who do it [the program] are like, "yeah, you attend these meetings, you write a document, and you get $2,000." That's what people think of it as. They don't think of it like a grant.
>
> LINDSEY: Like, they call it a proposal, but they don't think of it that way. They think of it as a normal paper that they just have to turn in.
>
> ANA: Yeah, they think of it as, like, "oh, I have a paper due. I can, like, bang that out in a day," but, like, you can't.
>
> JENNY: I mean, with [program], you kind of can, which is part of the issue. Like, this introduces the idea of a proposal, but I don't think people appreciate it as much as they could. And I think coming to this writing group kind of helped me see it as kind of a transition from not knowing at all about proposal writing to actually being prepared to go ahead and write another one.

For these writers, the group helped them to develop knowledge of proposal writing. They emphasized their own transformation as writers and as people who took this kind of writing seriously as part of their intellectual and professional development. In the SPG, we see emotional work in encouraging particular dispositions toward the writing they were doing. That disposition was one that saw the proposal writing as aligned with the students' goals, not just of winning the grant but also of learning to use writing in new professional and academic contexts. The tensions at play in this group were far less obvious to me, though that doesn't mean they weren't there. One tension that seemed to exist in these proposal groups broadly, though, was the tension between seeing the group as a learning opportunity (in the way the writers framed it above) and seeing it as an extra, something that they didn't really need in order to do well enough on the proposal to win the grant money. Though there was no attrition in this group, there was in other similar groups, and I think one reason for this is that writing groups, in general, weren't necessarily aligned with second-year student goals.

EMOTIONAL LABOR IN THE UNDERGRADUATE THESIS GROUP: NAVIGATING INCLUSION, EXCLUSION, AND BELONGING IN THE ACADEMY

The undergraduate thesis writing group held a number of stories in tension that each related to questions about student identity, about interpersonal group dynamics, and about the students' emerging sense of themselves as researchers. For these writers, difficulties emerged around issues of inclusion and exclusion in the writing group and the academy more broadly. In this section, I layer the stories that students told me about their experiences in the group, pointing also to exchanges in group practice to illuminate those perspectives.

The individuals who participated in the undergraduate thesis group were, generally, thoughtful, committed emerging researchers, all of whom were generous with their support of one another's ideas and writing. All of these students were working on projects that engaged issues of identity, equity, and diversity in some way. As time went on, they also repeatedly had discussions about their own identities and positionalities in their research projects and in the Writing Center. In the following descriptions of them and their projects, I describe them as they communicated their identities to me and to each other at the time. Andrew, a white, male student of Women's, Gender, and Sexuality Studies, was working on a project about representations and stories of queer Mormons and ex-Mormons. Eleanor, an English student who spoke quite openly about her own identity as a white, heterosexual woman, as well as her particular experiences as someone with ADD, was interested in how disability, race, and gender were represented in postmodern fiction. Maggie, a white woman completing her thesis in English, was trying to understand how Harper Lee's *To Kill a Mockingbird* was responding to civil rights movements, how audiences responded to the novel, and its continued use in educational settings. Adanna, a Black woman majoring in Economics, was investigating relationships between immigration and economic inequality in African countries. Marie, the group facilitator, was a white woman majoring in Philosophy and Women's Studies who was also a first-generation college student. She was consciously thinking about equity, belonging, and safety in the group. All participants in the group were in their early to mid twenties.

Each member of this group had a different perspective and gave different insights into their experiences of events as they unfolded in the group. For Eleanor and Maggie, in particular, the group gave them an opportunity to reflect on their own identities and positionalities as young, white women undergraduate researchers committed to racial justice and feminism. Both were third-year students, just beginning their thesis research. Marie, the undergraduate group facilitator, and I were also emerging researchers, both interested in feminist practice and in developing expertise and an identity in our chosen fields. Andrew and Adanna each were working to complete their theses and graduate that semester and did not find the writing group as helpful in that endeavor. The stories that these students told me are stories about anxiety and regret, about building friendships and mutual support, and about coming to understand their own identities, positionalities, and commitments in their academic work. Some of these stories exist in tension with one another. And so, in this section, I tell four stories, each foregrounding the emotional experiences of different group members. It was impossible to tell just one story of this group, and so I hope what this section and this chapter contribute is a rich understanding of the way that these writing groups held multiple stories and were experienced differently by different participants.

Story 1: Setting the Scene

To set the scene for the stories of these difficulties, I want to return, first, to the exchange that opened this book. In this exchange from a group meeting early in the term, each participant was attending to who they were as researchers. It was shaped by students' understandings of academic work and their sense of belonging in the academy.

> ADANNA: How do you guys come up for titles for your work?
>
> MARIE: The night before when I'm really tired.
>
> [*group laughter*]
>
> ADANNA: 'Cause this has actually been an ongoing project since the summer and it's probably had, like, seventy different names, so like, I don't know, I know it can be changed as late as possible, but it'd be nice to, like, have something that I actually—like, that's catchy and I like.
>
> MAGGIE: I kind of wait until I'm done with the paper. Sometimes it comes out of something I said in a paragraph that relates to my thesis or something like that. Like, I know I wrote about *Gatsby* or something about the ships being beat endlessly into the past, because it was related to, like, biography and stuff like that. But that didn't come down until the end, so it was a last line thing that kind of tied back to the title, so I don't know.
>
> ELEANOR: I can't really help you, I'm horrible at titles, to be honest. Mine are always too long.

ADANNA: Yeah, and I can't say economists are very creative. I'll be like, "Immigration and Economic Inequality." Bam. That's it.
  [laughter]

MARIE: I wouldn't do a creative title because I don't know much about Economics, but every paper I have read—

ADANNA: Not creative in the sense that "oh my gosh!" like, but not boring. A little something and you see it and you're like [snaps fingers], "okay that sounds interesting," at the very least. Not "okay, that's nice."

MARIE: Yeah, I mean, titles in economics just seem a little more descriptive than they are anything else. So yeah, I wouldn't try too hard, I would just, in as few words as possible, describe what your project is and describe and use that as your title.

MAGGIE: I mean, I think your title sounds kind of cool right now.

ELEANOR: Yeah, I think it shows what your project's about, and that's what's important. It doesn't have to be something fancy. I mean it's economics, right?

ADANNA: I want to be a *cool* economist, guys.
  [laughter]

MARIE: Do that when you have a PhD, though, not before.

ADANNA: I can do it now.

If we focus, in this exchange, on the relationship between Adanna and Marie, we see two different stances toward academic writing and toward how to intervene in scholarly conversations. Adanna is ready to be a "cool economist," and she recognizes the work that a snappy title might do for her in helping craft that identity. Marie, in her suggestion to "in as few words as possible, describe" the project and save cool, snappy-sounding titles for after becoming credentialed and legitimized in a field, reflects her own experiences using her writing to show belonging in the academy. As we saw in the previous chapter, Marie and Eleanor voiced and repeated the advice from past professors to negotiate authority in the writing group space. In other conversations with the writing group, Marie also shared some of her past struggles as a writer at Big State. She shared, for example, an experience in which a professor told her she had "no talent," though she then went on to complete an undergraduate thesis and graduate with honors in that field. Marie was a first-generation college student, and she was a strong reader and writer who was learning the discourses of her field and of the academy more broadly. It doesn't take a lot of imagination to start tracing connections between some of Marie's more painful past experiences with writing, to her advice to carefully attend to the conventions of writing in a field and writing in a way so as not to stand out until you have the credentials to enhance your ethos.

And yet, in relaying that advice and that stance, Marie ends up in a negotiation of authority with Adanna that has her putting limitations on Adanna's goals for her writing. Adanna is actively looking for ways to use her writing to develop and show her identity as a "cool economist." Her question about process, "how do you guys come up with titles for your work?," gets taken up in a conversation about conventions of her field (in which she is the most expert person in the room) and about the appropriateness of what the rest of the group perceives as breaking or stretching the boundaries of those conventions. This early exchange shows us two things that contribute to the difficulties that shaped this group. The first is anxiety or worry about fitting in and showing belonging through writing (in this case, enacted by Marie), and the second is the way that this group led to Adanna perhaps not getting what she wanted or needed from the group. Rather than being wholeheartedly supported, in this moment, Adanna is advised to wait. Marie is trying to be supportive here but ends up replicating (to a far lesser degree than what she experienced) a mode of disciplining student writing to make it fit an idea of a particular academic mold.

Story 2: Attrition, Facilitator Anxiety, and Whiteness at Big State: Losing Andrew and Adanna

The next story is about how the group participants experienced the shrinking of the group. About five weeks into the term, after attending just three meetings, both Andrew and Adanna left the group. In their emails to Marie, both cited time constraints and the difficulty of balancing a full class load, their theses, and attending a weekly group on Monday nights. When I followed up with Adanna, who emailed me some of her thoughts on the group, she further explained that even though she appreciated the mix of disciplines in the group and the way that the group helped jump-start her writing, what she really needed at that time was closer attention to her drafts and some feedback from people with more experience working with quantitative data. She also thought that it would have been helpful to be working with more people who were at the same stage of thesis writing as she was.

Adanna wrote:

> The primary challenge I had with the writing group was with the specificity of the feedback. At this stage in my writing, I felt like having a very close reading of early drafts was as critical as building my content. Also the fact that the writing expertise was geared toward humanities students was challenging as quantitative social science projects have different requirements than an English thesis.

For Adanna, what she was able to receive from the group's first several meetings was not matching what she had expected or desired. She wanted more specific feedback and, though she was receptive to the idea of multidisciplinarity, also felt the need for more "writing expertise" in the room that came from social science disciplines.

In response to a question about the strengths and weaknesses of the group, Adanna further specified:

> I think one of the strengths is that it was organized and spanned disciplines. Some of the weaknesses include the wide array of students in different parts of the project (brainstorming ideas vs. writing drafts). Also I was surprised this group only started convening second semester as theses typically span one academic year. Perhaps having a year-long group would be helpful.

Both Maggie and Eleanor were just barely getting started (they wouldn't be completing their theses until the following academic year), whereas Andrew and Adanna were both working to complete their theses that semester. Marie had also tailored some of the resources she shared (particularly about funding opportunities) to Marie and Eleanor, because they were still early enough in the process to benefit from it. As Adanna wrote to me, many of the resources didn't feel like they applied to her because she was in her final semester, and, most of all, she just wasn't able to commit to the weekly meetings. For Adanna, this group wasn't worth the time and labor, because she wasn't getting the feedback she needed.

Marie was quite anxious about losing Andrew and Adanna as participants in the group. Even though both had assured her that they just couldn't fit it into their schedules, she expressed to me lingering concerns that she had failed as a facilitator to do two things: first, to manage the different needs of the participants, and second, to facilitate the conversations about race and gender identity that were woven through the participants' thesis topics. Marie explained:

MARIE: Sometimes I felt like Adanna didn't necessarily feel comfortable sharing, and sometimes I worried about it being a fact that she was the only Black woman in the group and everybody was pretty much talking about issues around race and gender and things like that. So, I think that could have been potentially uncomfortable for her, because I think people might assume that just because of the makeup of the group, like, none of, like, none of us there is, like, openly racist or something, but it doesn't mean that that's still a safe space for her. So, I think that that bothered me, because I wanted it to be [a safe space]. But in a way, I could never make it a safe space for her.

Marie's reflection here is helpful in understanding the dynamics of this group and the position that she and Adanna were placed in as participants in it. Marie was regretful. Whether or not Adanna was uncomfortable, Marie clearly was. She was "bothered," because she did not know how to make the space "safe," how to facilitate conversations about race and gender as a white woman in a predominantly white group in a way that would support Adanna. In my own observations, Adanna did not strike me as being uncomfortable sharing. In the second group meeting, for example, she actively gave feedback to Andrew, solicited feedback on her own work, shared her experiences with different research resources, and chatted with everyone about vegan snacks. She was also confident about the work she was doing and who she wanted to be—"I want to be a *cool* economist, guys," as she said in the exchange above. But, most importantly, Adanna herself cited the difference in project stages and the kind of feedback that she needed as the primary reasons for leaving the group. She did not mention any kind of discomfort with the conversations.

So how might we read these two stories of the group attrition? Marie's experience is one of anxiety about her possible failures as a white group facilitator. Adanna's is of a confident emerging researcher who wanted different kinds of feedback than this group was offering her. Also, these stories are based on what participants told me, a white researcher. Marie had worked with me in the Writing Center for some time, and so we had an existing relationship, and one that continued as peers after we both had graduated from Big State and moved on to other pursuits. Adanna had only met me in the context of this group, and I was only able to follow up with her about her experiences via email, rather than an in-person interview. I bring this up to acknowledge how my framing of these stories is inevitably impacted by my own role, identity, and positionality as a white woman researcher in relationship to these students. We could read this disconnect by questioning either of the stories. Marie is overly anxious or reading too much into things. Or Adanna didn't want to share more vulnerably or expend the emotional labor needed to share concerns about the makeup of the group or any discomfort she may have experienced. But rather than trying to resolve these two stories, I want to try to hold them in tension with each other and come to something more useful.

The stories of attrition from Marie's perspective, Adanna's perspective, and my perspective are also contextualized by a larger story about the institution of Big State, a predominantly white university. Already, the writing group was formed in an institution where many of the academic spaces are also predominantly white. In this small writing group that was ad hoc and came together primarily based on the interests of the writing consultants who took part (rather than in collaboration with another campus unit, like the Undergraduate Research Office), it isn't surprising that we only had one participant of color. We didn't take any intentional steps to make the space one that was more inviting of racial diversity or supportive of the labor that discussing research topics related to race, gender, and disability entails. What could the Writing Center have done differently to mitigate the institutional pull toward predominantly white spaces and to support the students in the writing group space? Advertising and organizing the groups differently, perhaps? Doing more to, at the very least, create a group that didn't have only one participant of color? Doing more to diversify the research expertise represented by each participant in the room, which wouldn't necessarily change the racial or gender makeup of the group, but would avoid having one person as representative of an entire mode of research? So, the stories that I have of this group also tell a story of the institution and the kinds of emotional experiences that might happen in a writing group in a predominantly white university.

It is simply true that Andrew and Adanna left the group. Marie storied that as confusing, unsure if it was a personal failing or because of dynamics beyond her control. Adanna storied it as an agentive decision to prioritize her own project and what she really needed, which she wasn't getting from the group. Marie's story, though, prompts us to ask about the dynamics of inclusion and equity in spaces of higher education. If, as D.-L. Stewart wrote in an *Inside Higher Ed* opinion piece, seeking equity in higher ed means asking not only, "Who is in the room?" but also "Who is trying to get in the room but can't? Whose presence in the room is under constant threat of erasure?" we might consider how, in this group anyway, Adanna's leaving meant an erasure of Black bodies from the group. Marie did not story Andrew's leaving in the same way, though she was worried about it too. I wasn't able to interview Andrew, though he provided Marie similar reasons to Adanna's for his departure. Their leaving was perhaps reflective not of open discrimination but of a sense from both of the them that it wasn't worth the investment of emotional or intellectual labor that it would have taken to help Maggie and Eleanor through the early stages of their projects, or maybe even to manage or mitigate the dynamic of competition that seemed to arise between these young women, which is the next story that I'll layer in here.

Story 3: Competition, Collaboration, and Friendship: Three White Women Engaging in Undergraduate Research

We might expect that once Andrew and Adanna departed from the group, the three white women remaining—all of whom were also consultants in the Writing Center—would become even more tightly knit. And that was true, to a degree. In this group, Marie and Eleanor frequently brought snacks to share; they chitchatted throughout meetings about favorite television shows, movies, and books; they talked about work in the Writing Center; and they were the only group of the three I observed that took themselves out to a restaurant at the end of the term to celebrate their accomplishments together. In other words, there was a friendship in this group that extended beyond the collegial working relationship that was typical of the other groups. Alongside this story of growing friendship, though, was also a story of competition and comparison, of feelings of inadequacy and irritation that were also, based on their own assessments, about feelings of belonging in the academy, about "sounding smart" and understanding complex topics.

In a follow-up interview, well after the group ended, Marie spoke of her own role with some regret. In addition to her worries over why Andrew and Adanna left, she mentioned the dynamics between herself, Eleanor, and Maggie.

> MARIE: Actually, thinking back on it now, I think I'm actually pretty disappointed at how the group turned out. I'm trying to figure out if it was just the circumstances of the group . . . or if it was something that I could have done better.
>
> SARA: Uh-huh. Why are you disappointed?
>
> MARIE: Well, Andrew and Adanna, they left pretty early on. [. . .] So, that was kind of difficult for me. And then it just kind of became a Writing

Center circle because it was Eleanor, Maggie, and you, and I, and all had very particular ideas about writing centers and writing groups and how the group should go. And I think sometimes that made it difficult to sort of keep conversation on topic. But not let one person talk more than the other. Sometimes I feel like Eleanor would slip way more into consultant Eleanor. [. . .] It was something that I, like, noticed happening, but I didn't know how to redirect it in some kind of way.

She further explained:

MARIE: I kind of felt like there was sort of a problem with, like, using terminology just to sound smart, and I wasn't quite sure how to respond to that. [Eleanor] would use, like, the word *intersectionality* and *positionality* and things like that all the time, and they didn't quite make sense in her sentences to me, but I didn't want to say that I didn't understand. I don't think anybody else really wanted to either. And then I think it kind of turned into doing the same thing with, like, Maggie and the rest of us, like, even me. Like, using words that maybe she wouldn't know, so I could sound smarter.

SARA: Yeah. Like a one-upmanship kind of thing?

MARIE: Yeah, and that's something I was really disappointed in myself in too, because I feel like, if you've been a consultant in the Writing Center. And you love what you do and are passionate about it and you want to help others, that's something that you should kind of have a handle on. And I feel like in my one-on-one consultations and even the writing group that I did before, I didn't do anything like that. I didn't have a struggle with that. I feel like something in that group brought it out in me.

In this slice of her interview, Marie gives us a sense of the competition that seemed to arise for her in relationship to Eleanor. Marie felt she needed to prove herself and her knowledge of feminist theory in comparison to Eleanor, while also trying to make sure that Maggie was getting what she needed and wanted from the group and had enough opportunities to talk. When I look back at transcripts and my own notes on my experiences in the group, I can see the dynamic that was at play, as Marie described it. At times, it could be challenging to keep the group on task. In moments when the group had agreed to have independent work time for about forty-five minutes before coming back together to discuss, Eleanor seemed to find it particularly challenging to remain quiet or to give other group members the time and space that they asked for before engaging in conversation again. There were times when group conversation was dotted with the kinds of "terminology" that Marie mentions—*intersectionality, heterotopia, postmodern, second- and third-wave feminisms, neoliberal*, etcetera. We saw a bit of this dynamic in the exchange between Marie and Eleanor explored in chapter 3, showcasing how advisors were made present in group authority negotiation and how group members directed one another to readings.

So far, this story could be a story of a challenging group member, whose style of verbal processing was sometimes at odds with the rest of the group. Or, it could be a story of agonistic competition. Yet, I really want to trouble those stories for a couple of reasons. The first story (the challenging group member story) plays into narratives about "problem" clients who don't use the writing center the "right" way, rather than thinking about how writing center practices (dis)invite writers to engage in particular ways (Kiedaisch and Dinitz 2007; Rinaldi 2015). Marie herself doesn't like that story, and in her interview, we hear her look back on the dynamic with regret, beginning to own her part in it. Eleanor also offered her own counterpoint. In her interview after the group ended, Eleanor told me that she found long periods of time dedicated to quiet work quite difficult for her own attention and processing. Eleanor was quite open about her experiences with ADD, and her experiences in the Writing Center and in school more generally. We can read that particular difficulty as one of a situation where the needs of each group participant were at odds and needed to be negotiated. For the group to be most accessible for Eleanor, it needed to break up activities and not expect long, dedicated, quiet, individual work time.

The rest of the observational data also offers alternative stories about these group dynamics. Although the feelings of academic competition were part of a difficult dynamic in the group, when I look back at the observational data, my analytic memos, and Eleanor's interview, another story also emerges: a story about the critical role that Eleanor played in helping Maggie, in particular, move toward more complex understandings of race and the reception of *To Kill a Mockingbird*. Eleanor contributed toward a more collaborative, less competitive, mode of understanding and using concepts from critical theory over the course of the term. For Eleanor, the group also eventually became an important source of emotional, as well as intellectual, support.

Story 4: A Turning Point for Maggie? Considering Race, Researcher Positionality, and Group Attrition, Again

During their meeting in late March, Eleanor provided Maggie a really important piece of feedback. Throughout the term, Maggie had been struggling to find sources on *To Kill a Mockingbird* and also to find useful archival materials about its reception and cultural context from major newspapers. In the following excerpt from the group, Eleanor provides Maggie with a contemporary article that put Harper Lee's work in conversation with that of James Baldwin and Ta-Nehisi Coates. Further, Eleanor prompts Maggie not only to consider how the publication outlets she was examining might skew white in the perspectives they published but also to consider how her own whiteness might play out in the research process, both in terms of the arguments she constructs and in how she is read by others. In this instance, Maggie is really receptive to the ideas, and Eleanor positions herself as a collaborator who also needs support while doing this work. This story gives a glimpse of a different dynamic than the one that Marie storied, and that even Eleanor herself alluded to, about feeling a kind of insecurity with particular concepts from feminist theory or postmodern literary criticism. Instead, it shows Eleanor in support of Maggie and taking on a collaborative stance. This moment also shows some of the emotional work that might come with supporting young white women who are coming to a new understanding of race and racism in the United States.

> MAGGIE: It just gets a little discouraging 'cause, like, just the fact that there's not much out there, so—
>
> ELEANOR: I found something really interesting. I found this article that, um, is talking about some responses by people of color to *To Kill a Mockingbird* and *Go Set a Watchman* and Baldwin's statement, which they mention is that he believes that people can never really understand what it's like to be in those positions, like, not being a person of color. And so, he very much, he quotes this line, "you never really understand a person until you consider things from his point of view, until you climb into his skin and walk around in it," and he's saying that you can't just do that. You can never really fully understand. So, his is very much, like, an extreme perspective—
>
> MAGGIE: So, he's against Atticus, then.
>
> ELEANOR: He's against Atticus. And so, it's interesting to see—also they talk about, um, that book that just came out. I totally can't say his name. It

makes me feel bad, but it's, um, let me find it. I can send this to you if you want [*looking at computer*].

MAGGIE: Yeah, that'd be good.

ELEANOR: It's like, Coates?

MAGGIE: Ta-neesi Coates?

MARIE: Ta-Nehisi?

ELEANOR: Yeah, Ta-Nehisi Coates. It's, um, where he's saying he's never read it, and he doesn't want to. So, it's kind of interesting to see that, and it might also be interesting to see, like, it's basically saying that this is a text for white people to talk about racism. So, it's, like, looking at it from the perspective of a white person in this time, trying to understand, trying to make sense of this horrible event, you know? [*Maggie: mmhm.*] So that's kind of interesting too. It's like, y'know, it does serve that purpose, but is it really doing it well? It's kind of interesting to see that kind of response. I don't know, sorry.

In this moment, Eleanor interrupts Maggie's story that "there's not a lot out there" to share a source with her and to do some conceptual work, prompting Maggie to consider whose perspective on the novel she has been seeking (represented in the major newspapers she had been consulting) and to consider searching for responses to the book from "people of color," in particular James Baldwin and Ta-Nehisi Coates (who had recently published *Between the World and Me*). In giving her suggestion, Eleanor asks critical questions in straightforward language that everyone in the group could understand. She also mitigates her own authority with, "I don't know, sorry," at the end of her suggestion. The fact that this group now was only made up of relatively young white women makes me wonder, too, whether and how this conversation emerged in this way, in part, because it was now a relatively homogenous group. As the conversation continues, Maggie and Eleanor discuss their own positions as white women doing this kind of research. In doing so, though, they also speak in ways that demonstrate their still-growing awareness of how to think and talk about race, and how much emotional work it might take to provide support for them through this process:

MAGGIE: No, I hadn't even considered that, how it might be important to include—to, like, do something about that, like, people of color's response. That would—that's a whole different area that I—Like, I'm talking about how, like, critical reception affected things—

ELEANOR: What's your email?

MAGGIE: [*Tells Eleanor email address*]. Um, how critical—um, yeah, that might be something to consider. 'Cause, like, [my advisor] had suggested awhile ago, like, how did the movie adaptation play into things, but I feel like that could get enveloped into just, like, the biggest section on *To Kill a Mockingbird*, yeah, so I'm wondering if people of color might be important.

ELEANOR: I think it would be. I know it's a difficult subject.

MAGGIE: Yeah.

ELEANOR: Like, for me, um, I want to study critical race theory. I'm really fascinated by it. But you do have to come about it in a way that is aware of your own privilege, and there is always gonna be tension. There's always gonna be people who say you can't do that. I've had people tell me that.

MAGGIE: Yeah.

ELEANOR: And you just kinda gotta be like, "I care. This is important. I have to say this." And I know it's awkward. I think this is a great space that we can work through those issues. And also maybe we can have someone from African American Studies come in and talk to us too about, like, standpoint theory or something, to maybe get a better sense of that. 'Cause I think I would definitely benefit from those kind of discussions, personally.

This exchange shows a moment when Eleanor's focus on feminist and critical race theory was deployed in a way that really served the other members of her group, as well as some of the ways that both she and Maggie, in their enthusiasm, show some lack of awareness of the potential effects of their words. Eleanor offers the article, explains it, and reinforces Maggie's idea to consider race in the responses to *To Kill a Mockingbird*. Further, she attends to the emotional experience of doing this kind of work—"I know it's a difficult subject," she says, even as she invites Maggie to say with her, "I care," and to make a commitment to learning how to consider her own privilege and positionality when doing this work. They could have this conversation about terminology, about their identities and positionalities, without fear of alienating Adanna or Andrew. This group had a number of conversations like this one. Later in this same meeting, for example, they discussed the reclamation of the word *queer* in academic and public discourse, and whether and how they felt comfortable using language that had once been used to oppress or degrade. What

I think these exchanges show are opportunities the group took to push one another, even just a little bit, to talk about complex, often difficult subjects that were important to their theses and also to their sense of themselves as young white women doing academic work.

At the same time, some of their language might prompt critiques of the ways that white people in particular sometimes try to engage in anti-racist work. Eleanor's suggestion is to invite a faculty member or perhaps a graduate student from African American Studies to talk to the group about standpoint theory. She is looking for mentors. And, at the same time, she isn't necessarily aware, or at least not demonstrating awareness, of the labor that this would entail from that representative. This would be free additional labor that, while appreciated by Eleanor, Maggie, and Marie, would generally have gone unrewarded in systems for promotion, for example. For Maggie's part, though she shows receptiveness to Eleanor's ideas, her statement "I'm wondering if people of color might be important" also shows that she is really just beginning to consider race as a factor in the way she approaches research for a project. It takes Eleanor's prompting to get Maggie to consider race and her own positionality more fully, and then, when both she and Eleanor are having this conversation, racial identity is discussed in ways that highlight how their own whiteness and inexperience in these conversations is influencing the work.

As this conversation continued, Marie and I both responded to some discomfort around how Maggie and Eleanor are discussing "people of color" and responses to *To Kill a Mockingbird*. Marie tells Maggie to be clear about who she means by "people of color," and I warn her against assuming a monolithic response by "people of color."

> MARIE: I would just be careful of using the term "people of color" in your work.
>
> MAGGIE: Yeah?
>
> MARIE: 'Cause I think most of the time you're talking about Black people, and there's still a difference.
>
> ELEANOR: There's, there are contested discussions about what *Black* means too. So, I think you do, kind of, have to define and have footnotes and everything like that, so [*Maggie and Eleanor chuckle*] . . . Yeah that's just, that's life, though, right?
>
> SARA: I think, just remember, when you're citing Baldwin and you're citing Ta-Nehisi Coates, you're citing two men, right? They're not speaking for an entire group of people.

MARIE: Yeah.

> [silence for about ten seconds, Maggie writing notes, Sara typing notes, Marie opens computer]

In this group of white women, there was a level of discomfort with how race was discussed and how to engage one another in learning how to talk about it. And I wonder how much more emotional labor it would have taken Adanna or Andrew to engage in these conversations in ways that were supportive of a productive group dynamic. How much labor did Adanna and Andrew save themselves by leaving the group when they realized that it wasn't serving them as well?

In his 2016 article "Writing While Black: The Black Tax on African-American Graduate Writers," Cedric Burrows argues that the experiences of African American graduate student writers in predominantly white spaces of higher education are subject to the "black tax." He defines the "black tax" as "the societal charges placed on African-Americans in order to enter and participate in white spaces," at the heart of which is the idea that "if African-Americans work hard and rise above their station without complaining about racism, they will gain privileges that whites already have" (Burrows 2016, 15). If we add the "black tax" to the emotional and intellectual labor it might cost Adanna to contribute to this particular predominantly white space in the Writing Center, in which the focus of many group conversations was race and identity in literary texts, we understand how Adanna may have been saving herself some work in a space that wasn't offering her what she needed. And we understand how Marie might struggle in this space to both reckon with her own whiteness and create a safe environment for all of her participants.

Overall, these four stories provide a layered understanding of inclusion and exclusion in the thesis group. As time went on, I noticed a growing level of intimacy among group members, especially in the vulnerability that Eleanor and Marie were willing to brave as they shared a bit more of themselves and their goals in the academy. This group showed both the most intimate connections of the three groups I observed and the most palpable conflict between members. And it was the only group that experienced attrition, losing two members. The group, I think, supported ongoing, holistic growth for Eleanor, Maggie, and Marie, even as it did not provide those things for Andrew and Adanna. The remaining group members discussed family, dating, and some of the challenges they were experiencing in and out of school. While I won't examine these discussions in detail, I do want to highlight their existence. During one meeting, Eleanor referred to their activities several times as "therapy," following a discussion, prompted by Marie, of whether and how the group was helping each of us meet our goals. In her interview after the group ended, Eleanor reflected further:

> ELEANOR: I like the fact that because it was all people that I knew, I felt comfortable talking to them and I felt like not only did it help me in my process with writing a thesis. And I think it was hopefully helpful for them too. I also felt like there was, kind of like, a little therapy moment that happened. Of, like, you can support each other and we could talk about, you know, what was stressing us out too. And I think that really helped with that process too. Because it is stressful and school is stressful and life's stressful, so it's nice to kind of have a space not only where you can be productive with something but also just kind of get out of that mindset and just relax a little bit. [...] I just really liked the sense of community that I felt with that, and I really felt like we were supporting each other, which is really, it's hard to do sometimes. So, I think it was nice that we got to that point.

For Eleanor, the group eventually became a strong support system, and she emphasized that this was a point that the group "got to" as they developed a sense of community and of support. It became a space where she felt comfortable talking about both her writing and her life.

The group took time to enthusiastically celebrate one another's progress, whether that was Maggie's excited explanation of how a source she found was helping her discover a new argument, or Marie's successful defense of her honors thesis. They also shared more vulnerable moments of the writing process. Marie, late in the term, opened up about some of the miscommunications with her advisor that had shaped the early stages of her thesis. She told us about her pride in graduating with honors despite that professor telling her that she had "no talent." She told us about her determination to remember how privileged she was to get to attend college full-time and dream of graduate study, when many of her family and friends back home hadn't had such opportunities. And I think, over time, the more that Eleanor, Marie, and Maggie were able to share these parts of themselves, the more they were able to let go of the comparison that could put them at odds, or at least cause small annoyances. The stories of inclusion and exclusion, of competition and collaboration, ask us to consider how the institutional context, the demographic makeup of the group, and the particular topics under discussion demand different kinds of emotional and intellectual labor from different participants.

Emotional Labor, Tensions, and Difficulties in Academic Writing Groups

Storying the difficulties of the writing group participants in this study shows us how integral emotional labor is to writing group work. Part of that emotional labor is what we might expect: attending to feelings about writing, motivating participants to write, and attending to relationships with professors, as well as building relationships based on shared experiences. But this isn't all of the story. The experiences in writing groups are not singular. The writing groups could ask different emotional labor of the participants, as we saw in Radha's story, and the dynamics that existed in relationships between participants weren't always easy, as we saw in Marie, Eleanor, and Maggie's work together.

So, for me, this chapter also raises a number of questions: How can writing centers support writing groups in doing this kind of emotional labor? How do we encourage supportive relationships and invite group members to both perform the emotional labor of the group equitably and value each other as whole people? How do we mitigate inequitable distributions of emotional labor, as we saw in Radha's story? Some answers to these questions lie in both administrative practices and in facilitator practices.

Writing center administrators can, I think, take a lesson from the dynamic at play in the undergraduate thesis group especially to ask not only who is in the room but also how are they supported? We can take care, in advertising and forming writing groups, that we don't place a single person from a marginalized identity category (whatever that might mean in our institution) in a group on their own. We can train and support group facilitators to mediate conflicts in their groups and to attend to emotions both about the writing and about group practice itself. We can follow Cedric Burrows's advice for writing centers to "create spaces for people of similar backgrounds, especially shared racial identifications, to work together," because "such spaces can reflect the needs of the group and allow members to discuss their experiences without the gaze of whiteness haunting their space" (Burrows 2016, 18). We also might work to advocate for the students outside of the writing center or, at least, to do what we can to encourage a particular disposition toward students and student writing among faculty (again, recognizing our own emotional and intellectual labor and what it might cost each of us in our particular contexts).

In actual group facilitation, we can check in regularly with group members to see how the groups are or are not fulfilling participant needs, as Marie did a bit later in the term. We can ask facilitators to be on the lookout for how one group participant's needs or preferences might be at odds with another's, and try to find ways to help negotiate that tension. The participants' experiences in these groups underscore again, for me, how important it is to do our best to design these writing communities with an eye toward understanding the ways that they might resist or reinscribe the inequities that exist in institutional settings. That is, it's important to do the messy, complicated, sometimes uncomfortable work of expressing and moving through the difficult emotions that come up around writing and negotiating authority and expertise with others. Yet, it can be easy for a writing group to fall into habits that ask for certain members to perform more or different emotional labor, as we saw with Radha, or that pit group members in competition with one another, as in the undergraduate thesis group. The stories that I share in this chapter raise more questions than they answer. But attending to the difficulties, not just the successes, of writing groups does help us understand and better theorize and practice the intellectual and emotional labor of writing center work.

5
Expanding the Boundaries of Writing Center Work

This project began with a practical problem: how to effectively facilitate writing groups in a writing center. When I first conceived of this project, as a graduate writing consultant, I had facilitated a number of writing groups: some wildly successful, some that just barely made it to the end of the term, and some that simply failed to cohere and last longer than a few weeks. This project thus began with the question of what makes writing groups work in a particular context and for particular writers. As I conducted the study and wrote the book, it became bigger, touching on key questions in multiple areas: how students come to develop expertise in their field's communication practices and how they come to feel confident in their abilities; how genre knowledge and expertise shape writing center collaborations; how writers together experience and work through emotions; how writing consultants understand and perform their expertise; how groups of writers negotiate authority; and finally, how practices like writing groups invite writers into the center and what kinds of roles and positions are offered to students through various writing group practices.

 The writing groups featured in this study offer a research site in which to understand how collaborative learning can work in the writing center and to expand our understanding of the practices that can make up writing center work. This book is not an argument that all writing centers should conduct this sort of writing group, nor is it a how-to manual for writing groups. Rather, it recognizes that writing groups are one method by which to do the work of the writing center: supporting writers, effecting change in our institutions, teaching and learning with the writers that practice in our spaces. I hope that this book has invited readers to consider how group practices invite writers and writing consultants into different roles and relationships in the writing center than those offered by one-to-one tutoring.

In *Radical Writing Center Praxis*, Laura Greenfield (2019) urges readers to resist defining writing centers by the methods that we use. We don't exist to deliver individual tutoring to students in the university or to set up writing groups, though both practices might be part of our methods. Greenfield reminds us, "the task of a radical writing center is . . . to maintain a critical relationship with methods in which methods are always engaged in a process of transformative interrogation or ethical reinvention" (117). So, the question for this study becomes how writing groups as method contribute to a "dynamic learning and writing culture and community" in which we work toward transforming how writing happens on our campus (Geller et al. 2007, 14). How might writing groups be one method to, as Greenfield writes, "more critically dive into rather than turn away from the negotiation intrinsic to *collaboration*—approaching the liberatory process as a shared endeavor"? How does a critical examination of writing groups, as I've tried to offer in this book, help us understand how student and facilitator experiences in these groups and in their various communities are both "mutually constituted" and that they "differ because we are positioned differently within the systems of power in which we all operate" (Greenfield 2019, 123).

So, in conducting these case studies, I sought to understand three key questions: (1) How do writing groups support the goals of group stakeholders (students, consultant-facilitators, and the Writing Center)? (2) How do group participants negotiate authority, navigate difference, and experience and manage emotions in the writing groups? (3) How do the practices that I identified and named ask us to extend our understanding of collaborations in the Writing Center? In what follows, I try to answer these questions by synthesizing the findings presented in the previous chapters and to pursue the implications of those findings for writing center and writing studies scholarship.

Writing Groups Can Cohere as Liminal Communities of Practice that Shape and Are Shaped by Their Local Contexts.

The writing groups in this study were situated in relation both to the Writing Center and to the writers' home disciplinary communities. Attending to the practices of these groups—the facilitators' practices, the group members' feedback practices, and the challenges that arose—extends existing literature theorizing writing groups as sites of collaborative learning and disciplinary enculturation.

Foundational studies of writing groups, like Ann Gere's *Writing Groups: History, Theory, and Implications*, Caroline Heller's *Until We Are Strong Together: Women Writers in the Tenderloin*, Candace Spigelman's *Across Property Lines: Textual Ownership in Writing Groups*, and Beverly Moss, Nels Highberg, and Melissa Nicolas's collection *Writing Groups Inside and Outside the Classroom*, draw writing studies' attention to the richness of writing groups as sites for studying writing as collaborative, socially situated process. In particular, these texts establish the importance of writing group location—in the classroom, in community spaces—to understanding how writers collaborate, especially in regard to authority negotiation.

Building on this work, I explored the writing groups in this study as communities of practice, located in a larger landscape of practice, made up of Big State, the writer's home disciplinary communities, and the Writing Center, a community of practice itself. I came to see authority negotiation not as a limitation but as an important practice for the collaboration and for writers' growth in this space. The writers in each of the groups considered in this study came together to support one another in the shared endeavor of composing pieces of writing in unfamiliar genres and, for some of them, high-stakes purposes. In the UTG and DWG, student participants sought to establish membership in scholarly discourse communities. In the SPG, students sought grant money to fund projects, internships, or experiences that would be meaningful to them personally and professionally. In their groups, they developed sets of shared practices that both nurtured their individual writing projects and allowed them to work together: reading one another's work and offering feedback that would, hopefully, be useful to the writer.

Previous scholarship on academic writing groups as communities of practice has emphasized their liminality in relationship to writers' home disciplinary communities or local writing contexts (Brooks-Gillies et al. 2020; Kim and Wolke 2020; Phillips 2012). The groups in this study also demonstrated some of the same benefits of this liminality. As Kim and Wolke write, multidisciplinary writing groups give writers "a sense of community in a collaborative and supportive environment from peers outside of their disciplines, away from the traditional—and often competitive/stressful—confines of their own disciplinary programs" (Kim and Wolke 2020, 232). Further, they found that multidisciplinarity benefited graduate writing group participants (in their case, English L2 graduate students) by inviting them into the space as experts in their fields, improving their sense of agency. In this multidisciplinary space, group participants "were able to raise their awareness of expectations of their immediate audience [their group members] as well as their disciplinary discourse communities" (227). This held true in my study as well, yet the groups in my study also struck me as particularly situated within or in relation to the writing center, itself a community of practice shaped by its own disciplinary discourses. Facilitators, steeped in writing center theory and practice, brought a particular understanding of writing and how to respond effectively to other writers. Because these groups were sponsored by the Writing Center and facilitated by writing consultants, they were shaped in quite particular ways by the Writing Center's practices.

Facilitators Scaffolded Writing Groups by Modeling and Encouraging Writing Center Practices.

As argued in chapter 2, facilitators, though they may have downplayed their role, actually shaped the writing groups in particular and important ways. They scaffolded the writing groups, using a number of strategies to model feedback practices, prompt group member feedback, reframe group member feedback, encourage strong feedback through praise, and encourage relationship building through regular check-ins and chitchat with group members. The facilitator role, then, was key to group practice in modeling how to engage as an "expert-outsider" (Nowacek and Hughes 2015). Facilitators modeled and shared the kinds of writing expertise that writing consultants bring to their reading of texts in the Writing Center. They modeled the genre knowledge that is exercised through asking questions about the rhetorical choices a writer has made and about the expectations that audiences might bring to a piece of writing. And they elicited the same kinds of questions and engagement from their group members.

As expert-outsider readers, as group leaders, and as motivators for group practice, though, the facilitators didn't, as I understand it, hold an authority that made them and their ideas unassailable. Rather, they negotiated that authority through interaction with group members. Though facilitators were scaffolding a particular mode of engagement, group members also shaped group practice as they gave feedback, deliberated over that feedback, and made decisions about their texts. Through group discussion, the facilitators' and other group members' ideas were up for deliberation and debate. Further, writers themselves were generally looked to as the experts on their subjects and in the disciplinary norms of their fields.

The writing groups, then, invited students into the Writing Center in different roles than individual tutoring. They asked group members to be givers of writing feedback, not just receivers. Writing groups don't completely flatten the hierarchy between writer and tutor. Facilitators are still there. Group members and facilitators still negotiate authority. But the role of a group member does more inherently and obviously require the participant to both act as disciplinary expert and to build writing and reading knowledge in order to provide effective feedback. Further, the ongoing nature of the groups invited group members and facilitators to develop stronger relationships and to share a bit more of their lives outside of the immediate writing task at hand. This work was characterized by difficulties and tensions, requiring a significant investment of intellectual and emotional labor from participants.

Group Members Were Challenged to Read across Disciplinary Boundaries, Grew in Confidence in Their Disciplinary Expertise, and Used the Group to Gain Critical Distance on Other Spaces in the Academy.

To navigate disciplinary difference, one of the key challenges of participating in these groups, group members and facilitators leveraged genre knowledge (Tardy et al. 2020) in both implicit and explicit ways. Both group members and group facilitators engaged in feedback practices: asking pumping questions, reading aloud, suggesting revisions, agreeing and disagreeing with others, explaining projects. These practices required group participants to draw on and collectively develop genre-specific knowledge and, potentially, broader awareness of how genres work.

As I argued in chapter 3, the writing groups surfaced participants' genre knowledge and also offered an opportunity to co-construct new genre knowledge or to attune their reading and writing with a greater genre awareness. This study thus adds to some of the existing research on genre and writing transfer in the writing center. A number of scholars have argued for studying transfer in the writing center because it offers one way to see transfer in action: we can see and hear how writers share and make use of their prior knowledge in conversations about in-progress writing (Hagemann 1995; Nowacek et al. 2019; Rounsaville et al. 2022). In doing so, we have a view of the relational, collaborative nature of transfer of writing knowledge.

Chapter 3 showed how group practice required members to make use of genre knowledge as they read, wrote, gave feedback, and explained their projects to one another. In the context of the dissertation writing group and the undergraduate thesis group, disciplinary difference could be an especially valuable resource for gaining greater genre awareness and co-constructing genre knowledge. Because the group members were coming from different disciplines, they had to make explicit the expectations that guided their disciplinary writing. Similarly, Nowacek and colleagues (2019) and Winzenried and coauthors (2017) establish co-construction as one means by which individuals together recontextualize existing knowledge, "each drawing on their own experiences in order to collaboratively develop a strategy for or an understanding of a phenomenon" (Nowacek et al. 2019). Winzenried and colleagues emphasize the value of co-constructing based on different domains of knowledge and experience—in which multiple individuals together "complicate and nuance one another's ideas" (Winzenried et al. 2017). Interestingly, Winzenried and coauthors found that in their focus groups of first-year students, when speaking about genre, students were likely to overgeneralize, using common language to mask important genre differences. They needed an interviewer to intervene and prompt the thinking about differences that would allow them to "come to a more complex articulation of genre features" (Winzenried et al. 2017). By contrast, most of the participants in this study had a few more years of experience writing in academic genres, and further, they were actively working to collaborate on textual revisions, often across disciplinary boundaries. They were confronting differences and working to nuance them and find the useful resonances in order to collaborate effectively. The examples of co-constructing genre knowledge from the writing groups in this study underscore the idea that writing transfer—understood as recontextualizing or integrating past knowledge and practices—is, in practice, often collaborative and benefits from bringing together writers with a range of diverse writing experiences.

If this collaborative co-construction of genre knowledge benefited from disciplinary difference, I would like to suggest that it also could benefit from language difference and perhaps other forms of difference—experience with different domains of knowledge that individuals bring to their writing. In their 2022 article on relationality in writing transfer, Rounsaville, Lorimer-Leonard, and Nowacek remind readers that, if we consider the synchronous nature of writing transfer and want to rethink how we understand transfer, we need to consider the "hidden experiential factors that have shaped writers' knowledge about writing context and activity over a lifetime," as well as the ephemeral, fleeting, sometimes automatic nature of writing transfer (152). If we understand the revisions that group members deliberated as enacting a recontextualization of genre knowledge and building greater genre awareness, we also, then, must consider how this recontextualization work was undertaken amid the relational and emotional work of both the group itself and the process of disciplinary becoming more broadly. Genre knowledge in these groups developed from writers' past experiences, from their advisors (mediated through the group), from facilitators, and, likely, from the rich and varied literacies that group members brought with them from beyond the academy.

Relational Work in Writing Groups Was Characterized by Tension and Included Difficulties That Were Experienced Differently by Individual Group Members

The relational work of the groups themselves was important but could also be a source of difficulty. The negotiations of authority and expertise in these groups were experienced differently by different group members and in ways that were tied to group members' various identities in the context of this predominantly white institution of higher education. Writing groups always entail emotional labor. They always include the work of building relationships built on vulnerability that comes from sharing one's work and inviting critical feedback. And so, they always include the tensions of this emotional experience: tensions between anxiety and relief, self-doubt and confidence, fear and gratitude. But the particular context of these groups—academic writing groups located in a predominantly white institution in the Midwestern United States—also gave rise to particular difficulties that group members experienced. The stories of inclusion and exclusion, of emotional labor undertaken or opted out of in the writing groups, that were detailed in chapter 4, invite us to consider how we might more critically design and implement writing groups to better support all of our students and writing consultants. The ongoing nature of writing groups offers an opportunity for deeper relational work among participants, and that work needs investment in supports for facilitators and ongoing attention to accessibility and equity in the distribution of labor (emotional and intellectual) and the actual practices of writing group work.

Practical Implications for Writing Center–Sponsored Writing Groups

The most obvious practical application of this work is in providing support for writing group facilitators. When framing the task of group facilitation, I would start with the metaphor of scaffolding. Like scaffolding in writing center tutorials, scaffolding writing groups involves understanding what the group is learning and where the group is in relation to that learning. What is the zone of proximal development for a writing group? The facilitators thus need to understand what the key practices of writing groups are, the knowledge and relationships needed to engage in them, how to assess how ready their group members are to participate in those practices, and what kinds of support to put in place for the group members.

Writing groups engage members actively in reading and responding to others' writing, developing new modes of reading, developing a new language for talking about writing, co-constructing genre knowledge, and writing collaboratively. They engage members in negotiations of authority and expertise that can offer student writers, in particular, opportunities for development and practice in expert roles that they might not usually get to take on. And writing groups are also groups of people, subject to the same kinds of conflicts that can surface in any relationship. Further, as institutionally sponsored, they are subject to the same negotiations of power that come in institutional settings and that can reinscribe or resist the raced, gendered, and disabling discourses and practices that shape practice in these settings. The goal, for group facilitators, then, is to do what they can to engage participants in building the kind of community that invites diversity and that, to the best of their ability, makes the space safe for its members (whatever that means in the particular context); co-constructing genre knowledge; mediating or offering critical distance from writers' other direct feedback networks; and providing emotional support and countering isolation.

SCAFFOLDING RELATIONSHIP-BUILDING

Before anything else can really happen, group members must begin to develop relationships that will nurture productive collaborations. They have to be comfortable enough to share writing, to offer feedback, to disagree with one another, and to voice a concern. So, facilitators can invite the kinds of low-stakes sharing and exchange (about the weather, schedules, snacks, music, movies, TV shows) through which relationships begin to cohere. They can also model expressions of gratitude, validation of feelings, and expressions of empathy along with exchanges of feedback and stories of experiences in the academy more broadly. Facilitators can also invite each member of the group to give feedback or to respond to the conversation at hand. And they can interrupt, when and where it might be necessary to hold group members accountable to respecting one another. As chapter 4 showed, this work is more complicated than it sounds and can require a great deal of emotional labor to continually check in about how the writing group is working, and to work through difficulties.

SCAFFOLDING FEEDBACK: USING GENRE KNOWLEDGE TO READ AND WRITE TOGETHER

Facilitators also scaffold group member feedback, bringing group participants into the practices of reading and offering feedback in the writing center. Often, much of tutor training de-emphasizes tutor expertise, instead making sure that tutors put student ideas and expertise at the center of individual writing center sessions. We are, at times, trying to counter the idea that a tutor needs to fix a student's paper, so we emphasize sticking to a peer role and nondirective methods. This study, though, showed me the need to make more explicit the literacy practices and writing expertise that tutors regularly engage in the writing center. Doing so would better allow those tutors both to reflect on their own writing center practices and to frame the tasks and benefits of a multidisciplinary writing group more clearly for their group participants.

The findings of this study underscore a need to provide tutors a framework for theorizing both writing and tutoring, one that transfers from method to method. To support writing group facilitators in the context of Big State, then, I began to use key concepts from writing studies, especially emphasizing genre and scholarship on disciplinary writing and enculturation. Using these as frameworks, I would engage students in reflection on their own development as "expert-outsider" readers and tutors. The findings of this study suggest to me that support for writing group facilitators in the writing center should

- use concepts from writing studies (especially *genre*) to make explicit what tutors already know implicitly.
- ask tutors to reflect on what they do when they read in the writing center.
- ask tutors to reflect on how they developed expertise and a strong tutoring practice.
- give tutors a framework for understanding disciplinary writing, genre knowledge, and language they can share with students.
- offer strategies, such as modeling, prompting, and praising and reframing group feedback and check-ins with writing groups, that facilitators can use to scaffold group feedback.
- recognize emotional labor as an important practice of both group members and facilitators and one that has a tendency to be unevenly distributed in groups in institutional settings.

This approach, asking tutors to reflect on their practice with key concepts from writing studies in mind, is also well aligned with approaches to tutor training grounded in transfer research. For example, Lauren Marshall Bowen and Matthew Davis suggest adapting the Teaching for Transfer curriculum, designed by Kathleen Blake Yancey, Liane Robertson, and Kara Taczak (2014), for training writing center tutors. Bowen and Davis emphasize three core components of the curriculum: (1) reflection as tutors "simultaneously develop their own writing knowledge and practice *and* develop and employ tutoring strategies to guide others' learning transfer"; (2) key terms, or a vocabulary that helps them "develop flexible conceptual frameworks" for writing and tutoring; and (3) a theory of writing and theory of tutoring assignment that allows tutors to develop a "flexible roadmap" to guide their understanding of how writing works in various domains of their lives (school, work, home, religious institutions, etc.), and how they and other students use prior knowledge and experiences of writing in new situations (n.p.). To be clear, I did not use a Teaching for Transfer course to prepare and support the tutor-facilitators in this study, but I do think the findings of this study indicate the potential usefulness of that approach, both to train tutors as they begin work in the writing center and to continue developing support for them that transfers from one mode of writing center work to another.

The writing groups offered facilitators a space in which to recognize how concepts and practices from tutoring transferred from one set of practices (one-to-one tutoring) to another (group facilitation). Graduate tutors from rhetoric and composition also reflected in interviews, as we saw from Elizabeth, upon how their teaching practices in composition classrooms were influencing their work. The Writing Center could help facilitators continue that reflective work, giving them time and space to revise their theories of writing and tutoring to consciously integrate their writing group experiences. Further, they could have benefited (and I could have benefited!) from more structured opportunities to develop understandings and awareness of genre, in particular. Because explicit discussions of genre and the integration of genre knowledge were so important to group work across disciplinary boundaries, understanding genre as social action and genre knowledge as enacted through writing and group practice would, I think, be one of the core concepts for a theory of writing, tutoring, and writing group work. Having the language readily available to describe that for group members could be invaluable.

The tutor-facilitators I interviewed often downplayed the expertise that they enacted in the writing groups. That expertise included being able to read and offer feedback across disciplinary boundaries; respond appropriately to another writer's emotions; invite, model, and reframe effective feedback; and continue to collaborate with their group members to build knowledge of the specific genres under consideration and a broader understanding of how writing works in academic spaces. To more effectively help students in their groups learn to read and offer feedback to others in ways that were sustainable (not taking five hours to read one other person's piece of writing, for example), group facilitators needed to recognize how they themselves did this work and how they had developed their own expertise.

Finally, I hope that support for writing group facilitators would prompt them also to consider how power is at work in academic spaces and in the writing groups in their institution. They need time and space to reflect on how emotional labor is distributed in their groups and the difficulties that can arise in these spaces. I've come to think about emotional work that these groups can do as integral to any of the other work that they allow for group members. The literature on students' lived experiences of education emphasizes the importance of spaces that counter epistemic injustice, that is, spaces that run counter to much of the institution because they invite and affirm students' ways of knowing, especially when those ways of knowing come from lived experience. This has major implications for the ways that I think about the space that the writing groups create.

In my study, I saw both affirmations of students' ways of knowing and attempts to shift students' ways of thinking and knowing. For example, Radha, in particular, affirmed Holly's interest in taking a more creative approach to dissertation writing, one that valued and highlighted storytelling over a strict progression from literature review to a presentation of her data. In contrast, Marie's advice to be a bit more conservative in title choice, for example, might be an example of an impulse to fit into existing discourses rather than reshaping them. I still think that genre knowledge—especially a critical genre knowledge that accounts for and values multilingualism and multiple literacies—is important. But I also think it important to create a space in which writers feel able to make the best decisions for themselves. Which brings me to something I didn't see in the groups.

What I didn't see was resistance to what we might call productivity norms. Everyone assumed that it was best to get as much writing done as possible, always. It seems like a no-brainer. We're a writing center. We were in writing groups. Most people came with the goal of getting writing accomplished. But, if we truly are supporting students in understanding their goals, I also think there is room for supporting students in rest as well as labor. That is, productivity in writing doesn't have to mean writing all the time, working all the time. We might read the student chitchat about vacations, the UTG group's somewhat frequent digressions, as resistance to the idea that they needed to be working, on task, all the time—it was OK to talk about and to take vacations! Especially for graduate groups, I would like to see writing groups that make explicit space for rest and that affirm students in listening to their own bodies, their own need for rest and care. Students who feel supported in all of their emotions and needs—the good feelings, the bad feelings, the joy and energy of experiencing flow in writing, the exhaustion of a "hitting a wall," the relief of doing something restorative, the need for a nap—will be able to make the best decisions for themselves. They will be able to do the work they want to do. They will be able to make an informed decision to take a break or to do their work in a different way.

To that end, I would also like to see more explicit attention in these groups to the body. The UTG did attend in implicit ways to their bodies. They shared snacks. They got up and used the whiteboard. They talked about embodied experiences. But none of the groups made explicit the embodied labor and experience of writing and reading. Of course, group members and facilitators are going to have varying comfort levels with talking about and engaging their bodies, performing with their bodies in front of others in writing groups. So, I don't want to make prescriptions, but future work might look for various ways that group facilitators might engage the body.

Limitations of the Study, Questions for Future Research, and a Note on Methodology

This book is built upon case study, and as such, it falls prey to the same limitations as all case study research. It's mostly focused on three groups sponsored by a single academic writing center. The participants in the study are particular to this site, a large research institution in the Midwest. I myself am a white woman writing center professional who has always attended or taught at large, public, research-intensive universities. And so, my findings, particularly about the ways that these groups functioned for group members within this institutional space, aren't necessarily directly applicable to other academic contexts, let alone other spaces beyond academic institutions. How, for example, might writing groups look different or do different work at Historically Black Colleges and Universities (HBCUs) or Hispanic-Serving Institutions (HSIs)? Scholars such as Karen Keaton Jackson, Hope Jackson, Dawn N. Hicks Tafari, Kendra Mitchell, and others have called upon writing center and composition studies more broadly to better account for and highlight work in contexts like HBCUs, HSIs, or other minority-serving institutions (Jackson et al. 2019; Jackson and Hand 2024; Jackson and Howard 2019; Mitchell 2019). This scholarship critiques the way current scholarship heavily features predominantly white research institutions, like the one featured in this study, and offers the rich insights and practices that come out of writing programs in HBCUs. Beyond calling on the field to diversify the programs highlighted in its journals, though, they remind us that HBCUs have long been contributing to the development of rhetorical knowledge and writing pedagogies. As Beverly Moss writes, "HBCU contributions are part of the foundation upon which composition studies is built" (Moss 2021, 145). Throughout this study, I've attempted to highlight how the relational, affective work that Karen Keaton Jackson, Amara Hand, and Kendra Mitchell describe in HBCU writing centers shows up (or doesn't) in this PWI, following the lead of contributors to collections like *Counterstories from the Writing Center*. However, this study is still limited by its location in a single writing center at a PWI.

This study is also focused fairly narrowly on academic writing. How do group members perform or emerge as experts in other kinds of discursive contexts—writing, reading, and listening to fiction, poetry, podcasts, or other compositions composed for communities beyond the university? Although it was outside the scope of the project to explore these questions, I do hope that the foci I've brought to the study—understanding authority negotiation as a key practice; attending to difficulty, conflict, and tension as part of collaboration and community; and considering how facilitator and participant roles and expertise play out locally—are useful across contexts.

Finally, I've attempted to do "data-driven" work in a way that doesn't erase people in favor of data. What I've tried to do in this book is use qualitative methods to open practice up to deep, rich observation; foreground participant perspectives; establish reciprocal relationships with my research participants; and account for my own role as a participant in the groups, as observer of group practice, and as analyst. Of course my own positionality as an emerging researcher and my actual participation in the groups as participant-observer has shaped this study. I am sure that I have only just scratched the surface of understanding how identity, power, and positionality are at work in participants' lived experiences of writing groups. When I first began this project, I did not have race, gender, disability, or any other identity marker at the forefront of my research questions. I waited to see if and how these things would emerge in observations and in interviews. Of course they did, and I did my best to follow up, but because I did so in a more reactive rather than proactive way, I do think my treatment of them began a bit haphazardly, as is reflected in the dissertation version of this project. Over time, I have deepened that analysis, asked follow-up questions, and generally done a lot more reading and thinking, guided by ongoing scholarship in the field and by mentors and friends. Still, I think that my data collection was likely limited by both my own positionality and my focus at the time. Future research could open up the ways that race, gender, disability, sexuality, and other identifications are at play in writing groups.

Given the challenge that group members articulated in reading across disciplinary boundaries, another of the questions for future research that this study raised for me is about the role of genre knowledge in *reading* in the writing center. That is, how do consultants develop and make use of genre knowledge when they read clients' writing? How can we frame and scaffold reading as a core practice in writing groups or other modes of writing support in the center? Although this study couldn't fully take up that question, it does emphasize the importance of understanding reading in the writing center and in writers' disciplinary emergence. Further, the study emphasizes the way that disciplinary expertise emerges in collaboration with people beyond our discipline, and the importance of such relationships in navigating the emotional experience of disciplinary learning.

On the Indescribable in Group Work

Much of this book has been an attempt to demystify group work for other writing center practitioners and scholars. I've tried to describe in some detail how facilitators scaffold group practice. I've highlighted the expertise of writing center work—the ways of reading and ways of engaging with writers—that facilitators enact and model in the writing groups. I've explored how the writing groups challenge both the facilitators and the group members to develop new practices. I've described the negotiations of authority that constitute writing group collaborations, particularly those across disciplinary divides. And I've tried to describe and hold in tension the sometimes contradictory stories of lived emotional experience from individual participants in the writing groups. And it is there, I think, that the attempt to demystify begins to show its limits.

As I was finishing the initial draft of chapter 4, I happened to listen to an episode of the podcast *Poetry Unbound*, hosted by Pádraig Ó Tuama. The episode centered on a poem by Benjamin Gucciardi, titled "The Rungs." The poem's speaker, presumably a social worker, teacher, or school counselor, narrates a meeting for a group of teenage boys, in which the boys provide loving support for one another. What strikes me most about this poem is how it highlights the bodies of the boys in relation to each other, rather than the conversational moves or facilitator practices. The facilitator's practices—reminding the boys how to listen, and to pass around green foam dice (to indicate who has the floor)—are just setup, background to the more central images of the poem. With their bodies, hearts listening, backs straightening, a hand reaching over to a back, the boys are able to offer a support, a ladder, for one another, and a moment in which one of them may "sit in the sun" (Gucciardi). In short, what I think this poem does is to remind me that there is still something mystical—knowable, yet indescribable through academic prose—that can happen when groups of people come together in mutual love and support.

In his reflections in the podcast episode, Ó Tuama also attends to the bodies of the boys, the backs that straighten in response to the softness of B.'s quivering lip as he holds the green foam dice, perhaps his own stories, heavy as boulders in his hands. The poem goes:

When they reach B., who walked here, unaccompanied,
from Honduras three months ago, he holds them like boulders.

We straighten when his lip begins to quiver.
It's not my place to tell you what he shared that day.

But I can tell you how M. put his hand on B.'s back
and said, *maje desahogate*,

which translates roughly to un-drown yourself,
though no English phrase so willingly accepts

that everyone has drowned, and that we can reverse that gasping,
expel the fluids from our lungs.

There is strength and softness in that image of the boys forming the ladder and offering support for B. to "expel" the story that had him drowning. Ó Tuama reflects that for him, this image is about "being looked at in friendship and acceptance," being "held in positive regard," and "looking for a posture of support in the room." When I take this image back to the groups in my study, I think that it rings true for some of the experiences there. We might expect that because the group members in my study are highly privileged compared to the boys in this poem (all successful undergraduate and graduate students), they are often looked at in friendship and acceptance. Yet, we know that, so often, spaces of higher education can make these brilliant people feel less than positively regarded. In this poem, the words the boys offer are spare. It is their bodies, working in solidarity, that offer the moment in which B. can unburden himself and "sit in the sun." The boys create that space for him as much as, or more than, the facilitator.

Yet Ó Tuama also reflects on the speaker's practice in this poem, relating to it through his own experiences as a group facilitator. He says,

> This is a poem that's set in a room that's very familiar to me, group facilitation, where you go into the room as a group leader, and you have something set in place. You have an opening question, you have a hope that the room knows the way that the conversation's going to go. [. . .] And you just think, "I hope we get through this, and I hope we can have enough structure here that if someone says something that's really important, that everyone in the room can offer the kind of support that's needed." And that really is building on an economy and a hope of love and trust that's happening in the room. [. . .] It's as difficult and as simple as consistency. And opportunity.

And enough ritual and dependability to know that when somebody needs the trust, the people are in the room to show it and to offer that kind of love.

What I take away from this poem and from Ó Tuama's reflections on it are both the importance of the facilitation practices—the creation of ritual dependability, as he says—and the incompleteness of those practices for what can happen in group relationships. Each group meeting has a potential, when its members come together, to create meaning through the exchange of love and trust, and that is part of the telling of stories and the offering of feedback. Something happens when groups come together that is still something of a mystery to me, and sometimes it feels like a kind of magic.

And so, at the end of this book, while I argue for the importance of the demystifying in the early chapters—the descriptive work that I hope would help offer a theory and a sense of concrete practices that new group facilitators might work from—I also want to keep the mystery of what happens when people form relationships based on mutual trust and support. I hope that, in holding the stories of conflict and competition alongside those of gratitude and growth, I keep the richness of these group collaborations, and the possibilities for love and care that make them so worthwhile.

This kind of love and care seems to me to be more important than ever. I wrote much of this book through the COVID-19 pandemic, through multiple pregnancies, through the births of two babies, through parenting toddlers, through developing relationships with new colleagues at work, and through moving to a new home and meeting new neighbors. There were times when it felt especially isolating to be writing at home in my office, disconnected from the original context of this work and from the version of myself that I was when I began it. And there were times when I established or re-established community with colleagues, friends, and other writers, with whom I could have the kinds of exchange that would allow this project to come to fruition. That experience, and the findings of this research, have underscored for me how important it is to write in community, even when that work is messy, complicated, and sometimes uncomfortable. For writing centers, I hope this book contributes to the design of collaborative learning experiences in expansive and innovative ways, inviting writers into the space in new roles and inviting them to join in reshaping our centers and our institutions.

APPENDIX A
Interview Questions

The following questions served as a guide for semi-structured interviews.

1. What were your motivations and goals when you joined a writing group?
2. Did these remain consistent throughout your involvement with the group?
3. How would you characterize the benefits of Writing Center–sponsored writing groups?
4. What were some of the challenges that you faced in Writing Center–sponsored writing groups?
5. Have you been a part of writing groups or exchanged writing with others outside of the Writing Center? How did the Writing Center–sponsored groups compare to your other experiences?
6. How would you characterize the role of the facilitator in your group? Were they helpful to group interactions or to your writing development? How or why?
7. Many of our Writing Center–sponsored writing groups are multidisciplinary. What was your experience like working with writers from multiple disciplines?

8. How has participation in a writing group influenced your writing practices?
9. Has participation in writing groups changed or influenced your understanding of what it means to write or how you write best?
10. Do you feel that your involvement in Writing Center–sponsored writing groups has improved your writing / writing process? In what ways?
11. How do you use the feedback you receive in writing group? Do you use notes or written/verbal feedback from your group members as you make your revisions?
12. What kinds of feedback were the most useful for you?
13. Did you feel that the writing group met your needs as a writer?
14. Was there anything unexpected or something that surprised you in your experience with the writing groups?
15. Would you recommend Writing Center writing groups to others?
16. Had you used other Writing Center one-on-one services before you joined the writing group?
17. Before you joined a writing group, how did you think about what the Writing Center is/does on campus?
18. Since you've been involved in the writing group, would you be more likely to come in to the Writing Center for other kinds of consultations?
19. Has your participation in the writing group changed your perception of the Writing Center?
20. What kinds of changes would you make to our Writing Center–sponsored writing groups?

APPENDIX B
Survey Questions

Q1 *This is a consent form for research participation. It contains important information about this study and what to expect if you decide to participate. Your participation is voluntary.*

You are being asked to participate in a survey of writing group participants at BSU's writing center. This survey is one part of a larger study which aims to increase knoweldge about: (1) the affordances and constraints of writing groups in supporting the learning and motivation of students, staff, and faculty at BSU and (2) the different dimensions of peer-review in a writing group versus those that occur in one-on-one consultations in writing centers across the country.

This survey should take no more than 10–15 minutes and will ask you about your motivations and experiences in your writing center-sponsored writing group. Any identifying information will be kept confidential.

By clicking "Continue" (>>) you agree that you have read this form and are aware that you are being asked to participate in a research study, and you voluntarily agree to participate in this survey.

Q2 *In which writing group are you participating?*

Q3 *What is your major or department?*

Q4   *What is your rank at BSU?*

- o   Freshman
- o   Sophomore
- o   Junior
- o   Senior
- o   Graduate Student
- o   Post-Doctorate researcher
- o   Faculty
- o   Staff

Q5   *Is English your native language?*

- o   Yes
- o   No

Q6   *Are you an international student?*

- o   Yes
- o   No

Q7   *What were your motivations for joining a writing group?*

Q8   *How has your participation in a writing group helped you improve your writing and/or meet your goals?*

Q9   *Many of the Writing Center's groups include participants from multiple disciplines. Please describe your experience working with writers from different disciplines in your writing group.*

Q10 *In what ways might your writing group have better served your needs as a writer? How might you improve your writing group?*

Please rate the extent to which you agree or disagree with the following statements:

Q11 *My group facilitator was friendly and welcoming.*

- o   Strongly Disagree
- o   Disagree
- o   Neither Agree nor Disagree
- o   Agree
- o   Strongly Agree

Q12 *My facilitator explained things clearly.*

- o Strongly Disagree
- o Disagree
- o Neither Agree nor Disagree
- o Agree
- o Strongly Agree

Q13 *My facilitator was interested in hearing my writing concerns.*

- o Strongly Disagree
- o Disagree
- o Neither Agree nor Disagree
- o Agree
- o Strongly Agree

Q14 *I would work with the same facilitator again.*

- o Strongly Disagree
- o Disagree
- o Neither Agree nor Disagree
- o Agree
- o Strongly Agree

Q15 *I felt comfortable asking questions during my writing group meetings.*

- o Strongly Disagree
- o Disagree
- o Neither Agree nor Disagree
- o Agree
- o Strongly Agree

Q16 *I felt comfortable stating my opinions during group meetings.*

- o Strongly Disagree
- o Disagree
- o Neither Agree nor Disagree
- o Agree
- o Strongly Agree

Q17 *My group members were interested in hearing my writing concerns.*

- ○ Strongly Disagree
- ○ Disagree
- ○ Neither Agree nor Disagree
- ○ Agree
- ○ Strongly Agree

Q18 *I felt that my group members' comments were useful.*

- ○ Strongly Disagree
- ○ Disagree
- ○ Neither Agree nor Disagree
- ○ Agree
- ○ Strongly Agree

Q19 *The time allocation of each meeting was appropriate.*

- ○ Strongly Disagree
- ○ Disagree
- ○ Neither Agree nor Disagree
- ○ Agree
- ○ Strongly Agree

Q20 *Please make any additional comments about the previous questions or about your experience in your writing group.*

APPENDIX C
Survey Data

There were a total of thirty-seven responses to the end-of-term survey. The response rate was 38 percent.

TABLE C.1. Survey respondents' demographics

		Number of Respondents	Percentage of Respondents
Group	Dissertation	11	30%
	Postdoc	9	24%
	Graduate Open-Genre	4	11%
	Second-Year Proposal	3	8%
	Undergraduate Thesis	3	8%
	Personal Statement	1	3%
	Master's Thesis	1	3%
	Graduate Sit-Down-and-Write	1	3%
	Unclear	2	6%
Discipline	STEM Fields	15	41%
	Humanities	13	35%
	Social Sciences	9	24%
Academic Rank	Staff	1	3%
	Postdoc	9	24%
	Graduate Student	20	54%
	Senior	3	8%
	Junior	1	3%
	Sophomore	3	8%
	Freshman	0	0
Nationality	International Student	8	22%
	Domestic Student	29	78%
English Language Background	Non-native English Speaker	12	32%
	Native English Speaker	25	68%

TABLE C.2. Survey response data: Questions 11–19

	Strongly Disagree		Disagree		Neither Agree nor Disagree		Agree		Strongly Agree	
	n	%	n	%	n	%	n	%	n	%
The time allocation of each meeting was appropriate.	0	0%	2	5%	2	5%	12	32%	21	57%
I felt that my group members' comments were useful.	0	0%	1	3%	3	8%	9	24%	24	65%
My group members were interested in hearing my writing concerns.	0	0%	0	0%	1	3%	8	22%	28	76%
I felt comfortable stating my opinions during group meetings.	0	0%	0	0%	0	0%	11	30%	26	70%
I felt comfortable asking questions during group meetings.	0	0%	0	0%	0	0%	8	22%	29	78%
I would work with the same facilitator again.	1	3%	1	3%	1	3%	3	8%	31	83%
My facilitator was interested in hearing my writing concerns.	0	0%	0	0%	1	3%	4	11%	32	86%
My facilitator explained things clearly.	0	0%	1	3%	0	0%	8	22%	28	76%
My group facilitator was friendly and welcoming.	0	0%	0	0%	0	0%	4	11%	33	89%

APPENDIX D
Codebooks

TABLE D.1. Codebook for facilitator role and practices

Category	Code	Description	Example
Participant Perspectives on Facilitator Role			
Facilitator Perspectives on their Role	Authority vs. Non-authority	Facilitators discuss their authority in groups	"I try not to be too authoritarian" "I don't want to be a teacher"
	Emotional Support	Facilitators aim to make the group a supportive emotional environment	"to be a stress relief" Helping students to "feel more confident"
	Logistical Support	Facilitators talk about their work as timekeepers, emailing reminders, etc.	"Just be a timekeeper in a lot of ways"

continued on next page

TABLE D.1—*continued*

Category	Code	Description	Example
Participant Perspectives on Facilitator Role (*continued*)			
Facilitator Perspectives on their Role	Managing Personalities	Holding people accountable for showing up and preparing for group, knowing how/whether to intervene when a group member dominates conversation or seems hesitant to participate	"There are going to be individuals who are really committed and really involved, and really into it and just fantastic, and then there are others who just flake" "And I think he [group member] was just a little bit quieter personality wise"
Group Members on Facilitator Role	Providing Writing Expertise	Facilitators as providing expertise in writing	"people that are maybe thinking differently about writing than I do" "you guys know what you're doing" [regarding giving feedback and writing proposals]
	Modeling Reading	Facilitators modeling different reading strategies	"Hearing from [facilitators] 'well, but wait a minute, why is that there?'"
	Providing Feedback	Providing more feedback than was expected; providing useful feedback	"a person who provides a lot of feedback"
Facilitator Practices			
Facilitator Practices: Logistical Support	Timekeeping	Tracking the amount of time spent per person, per activity, or per topic	"we're almost out of time" "for the sake of time, let's come back to that when ..."
	Agenda-Setting	Discussing plan for the day or future meetings, initiated by facilitator	"we have Emily's chapter today" Marie: asking group members what they brought or if they want time to write
	Get back "on task"	Bringing conversation back to the writing; moving on from chitchat	"to get back to the writing" Marie: setting timer for quiet work
	Invite guest expert(s)	Invited guest experts to speak to the group	Marie invited two experts—a graduate student from literary studies and a GA from the libraries to talk to writers

continued on next page

TABLE D.1—*continued*

Category	Code	Description	Example
Facilitator Practices (*continued*)			
Facilitator Practices: Cognitive Scaffolding	Prompting Group Feedback	Asking questions that invite group members to give writer feedback, can be formulaic or non-formulaic, to individuals or to the group as a whole	"Thoughts?" "Would you [group] prefer to know that further up as a reader?"
	Reframing Group Member Feedback	Re-phrasing feedback or summarizing/paraphrasing group conversation	"But the way you [Ahmed] describe it out loud [vs. in draft] it's just not likely. Like, it's nearly impossible, and I think that's what Emily said"
	Prompting Writer to Ask for Feedback	Asking writer what they are most interested in working on / what kind of feedback they want	"Do you also want attention to sentence-level polishing, or do you want just concepts?" "I guess start with, you know, what kind of feedback are you looking for on the statement"
	Notetaking	Facilitator takes notes on the whiteboard (publicly) or explicitly tries to note suggestions and ideas for/from writer (creating a kind of session transcript)	"I typed that into a comment that you can go back to"
Facilitator Practices: Emotional and Relational Scaffolding	Praising Group Member Feedback	Praising feedback given by other group members	"I think that's good advice." "That's beautiful."
	Inviting Group Metacommentary	Asking for feedback on group practices; inviting reflection on how the group is/isn't meeting goals	Marie: invited group members to free write and share about how group was/wasn't helping meet their initial goals
	Checking In	Facilitator checks in about group members' projects and feelings	"Let's hear how you guys are actually doing and how writing is going" "How's it going for the internships and research projects?"

TABLE D.2. Codebook for group feedback practices

Category	Code	Description	Example
Cognitive Strategies	Pumping	Asking questions that pump the writer for information, asking them to think out loud or clarify information	"So, maybe just explain that a little bit to me. Is it, are you basically saying nothing's really changing? These films really aren't a break from previous films?"
	Reading aloud	Facilitators or group participants read sections of text aloud	"I will start reading out loud. We'll go through the abstract. [reads abstract aloud]"
	Responding as a reader	Narrate reading experience	"I know you can do the lit review, but how is this applying in your data, and I kept waiting for it"
	Suggesting revision	Making suggestions to writer for revision of text	"My thoughts would be, I mean looking at the prompt, to expand and really add as much detail there as possible"
	Agreeing	Agreeing with another's feedback	"So I, like I agree with you on adding something of interest I guess at the beginning"
	Disagreeing	Disagreeing with another's feedback	In response to another group member's suggestion to expand on Emily's literature review: Peter: "But I feel like we're just like so pumped to like, get to your analysis."
	Notetaking	Taking notes based on group conversation, sometimes discussed and sometimes not, but recorded in field notes	"I typed that into a comment that you can go back [to]"

continued on next page

TABLE D.2—*continued*

Category	Code	Description	Example
Cognitive Strategies	Articulating a writing problem	Writer explains the problem they are trying to solve in their writing or the problem they want suggestions for	"I didn't really know how to say, like it would—it would help me expand academically, because I was like, I know it's supposed to, but like, I don't know how, cause like it's an internship." "Right. So I could revisit this, or I could pull this out and put it in my data section, or I could take small chunks. It's just sort of how to help it make sense as you're reading it. [...] But that's sort of another question. Does it need to go here?"
	Explaining the writing project	Writer explains something about their project, background information, methodology, or what they intended for a particular section of text; often in response to pumping question; demonstrates specialized expertise of writer	"But I'm saying that it's the crisis alone is not sufficient, there's also in these, um, these legacies bits and pieces, alternatives" Emily (pumping question): And so, you talk about bacteria and fungi versus viruses, and so, I was just wondering what—it seemed like that was the first time we were reading that and I was—maybe it's because I don't understand, but what was your purpose with differentiating between those two? Ahmed (explaining): So, bacteria and fungi, the gold standard for them, for the detection, is the phenotypic instincts...

continued on next page

TABLE D.2—*continued*

Category	Code	Description	Example
Cognitive Strategies	Discussing genre or disciplinary expectations	Explicitly talking about genre conventions and disciplinary expectations	Andrew: I think also, uh, just considering what your abstract will look like at the end of the project is going to be very different from what you're submitting to the Denman cause that's something that I'm keeping in mind and my advisor has told me. Radha: So this might be a broader question for everybody.... Like, what exactly is the purpose of the introduction for the purposes of dissertations? Other than to be a giant lit review to be like, well look at all these things I read.
Relational Strategies	Resource-sharing	Sharing resources for writing process (technologies, secondary sources, information about events or funding opportunities)	"If you guys are looking for good citation managers, I've used Zotero..."
	Sharing writing experiences	Empathizing with other group members by sharing writing experiences	Emily: That's a good point. And then also the justification for the films. So beyond that, also other than sort of I think that they're good films, I need to find that kind of good justification for it. Radha: This is—this bothers me actually, this justification idea because I'm also struggling with that right now.

continued on next page

TABLE D.2—*continued*

Category	Code	Description	Example
Relational Strategies	Chitchat	Group participants engage in small talk and informal conversations unrelated to the writing	Radha: Um, I guess let's hear how you guys are actually doing, and how writing is going, and that. Um, everybody's writing going super fabulously and everybody's life is full of bon-bons and cream puffs? Peter: [chuckles] Yes. [inaudible cross-talk] Have you ever seen the nutrition information on cream puffs? [Laughter] Radha: No. Sara: A little scary, yeah? Radha: Yeah. Peter: It's like oh, I just took three years off of my life.
	Gratitude	Participants express gratitude for the writing group or for specific feedback	Radha: But hopefully this was helpful and I'm glad we had this group. I feel like this was such a good solid group and we all just stuck together. I really appreciated that. Um— Ahmed: I'm really appreciating that you're supporting me.
	Expressing emotion about writing group	Expressing feelings about the group itself (gratitude, anxiety, concern, excitement, etc.)	Maggie: I liked how last week went, just how we were—like had time to talk about what we were doing. Cause like, I kind of have to like talk-therapy my way through things. So last week was especially productive for me. Ahmed: I'm feeling kind of shy toward you guys . . .
	Expressing emotion about the writing	Expressing feelings about the writing (anxiety, worry, excitement)	Holly: I just need it done. I'm scared, and I need it done.

TABLE D.3. Codebook for advisor talk

Code	Description	Example
Advisor as Guide	Advisors referred to as guides for the writing process	"they're all telling me I need to write the analysis now"
Advisor as Reader	Advisors referred to as primary readers or audience of a text	"I feel like that's probably what my advisor does when she's reading my stuff..."
Advisor as Discipline	Advisors referred to as providers of disciplinary knowledge	"I have two advisors. So I have one, [Advisor 1], who is the postmodernist and he's been giving me a lot of information about what postmodernism is in literature and how I can connect feminism with it through [Advisor 2]."
Advisor as Point of Resistance	Advisors referred to as individuals distinct from writer; group mediates between writer and presentified advisor voice, resisting or reframing advisor's guidance, encouraging writer to articulate own voice	"It's OK to want what your advisors want but I think that maybe sitting down and really thinking about what you want from this project might be helpful"

References

Ahmed, Sara. 2014. *The Cultural Politics of Emotion*. 2nd ed. Edinburgh University Press.
Aitchison, Claire. 2009. "Writing Groups for Doctoral Education." *Studies in Higher Education* 34 (8): 905–16. https://doi.org/10.1080/03075070902785580.
Aitchison, Claire. 2010. "Learning Together to Publish: Writing Group Pedagogies for Doctoral Publishing." In *Publishing Pedagogies for the Doctorate and Beyond*, edited by Claire Aitchison, Barbara Kamler, and Alison Lee, 83–100. Routledge.
Aitchison, Claire. 2014. "Learning from Multiple Voices: Feedback and Authority in Doctoral Writing Groups." In *Writing Groups for Doctoral Education and Beyond*, edited by Claire Aitchison and Cally Guerin, 51–64. Routledge.
Artemeva, Natasha. 2008. "Toward a Unified Social Theory of Genre Learning." *Journal of Business and Technical Communication* 22 (2): 160–85. https://doi.org/10.1177/1050651907311925.
Artemeva, Natasha. 2009. "Stories of Becoming: A Study of Novice Engineers Learning Genres of Their Profession." *Genre in a Changing World*, edited Charles Bazerman, Adair Bonini, and Débora Figueiredo,158–78. WAC Clearinghouse; Parlor Press. https://doi.org/10.37514/PER-B.2009.2324.
Beckstead, Linda, Kate Brooke, Robert Brooke et al. 2004. "The Thursday Night Writing Group: Crossing Institutional Lines." In *Writing Groups Inside and Outside the Classroom*, edited by Beverly J. Moss, Nels P. Highberg, and Melissa Nicolas. Routledge.
Benoit-Barné, C., and F. Cooren. 2009. "The Accomplishment of Authority Through Presentification." *Management Communication Quarterly* 23 (1): 5–31.

Berkenkotter, Carol. 1984. "Student Writers and Their Sense of Authority over Texts." *College Composition and Communication* 35 (3): 312–19. https://doi.org/10.2307/357459.

Block, Rebecca. 2016. "Disruptive Design: An Empirical Study of Reading Aloud in the Writing Center." *Writing Center Journal* 35 (2): 33–59.

Boquet, E. H., and N. Lerner. 2008. "After 'The Idea of a Writing Center.'" *College English* 71 (2): 170–89.

Bowen, Lauren Marshall, and Matthew Davis. "Teaching for Transfer and the Design of a Writing Center Education Program." In *Transfer of Learning in the Writing Center: A WLN Edited Collection*, edited by Bonnie Devet and Dana Lynn Driscoll. WLN.

Broad, B. 2012. "Strategies and Passions in Empirical Qualitative Research." In *Writing Studies Research in Practice: Methods and Methodologies*, edited by L. Nickoson and M. P. Sheridan, 197–209. Southern Illinois University Press.

Brooks, Jeff. 1991. "Minimalist Tutoring: Making the Student Do All the Work." *Writing Lab Newsletter* 15 (6): 1–4.

Brooks-Gillies, Marilee, Elena G. Garcia, and Katie Manthey. 2020. "Making Do by Making Space: Multidisciplinary Graduate Writing Groups as Spaces Alongside Programmatic and Institutional Places." In *Graduate Writing Across Disciplines: Identifying, Teaching, Supporting*, edited by M. Brooks-Gillies, E. G. Garcia, S. H. Kim, and T. Smith, 191–209. WAC Clearinghouse; University Press of Colorado.

Bruffee, K. A. 1984. "Collaborative Learning and the 'Conversation of Mankind.'" *College English* 46 (7): 635–52.

Burrows, Cedric D. 2016. "Writing While Black: The Black Tax on African-American Graduate Writers." *Praxis: A Writing Center Journal* 14 (1): 15–20.

Carillo, Ellen. 2015. *Securing a Place for Reading Studies in Composition: The Importance of Teaching for Transfer*. Utah State University Press.

Carillo, Ellen. 2016. "Creating Mindful Readers in First-Year Composition Courses: A Strategy to Facilitate Transfer." *Pedagogy: Critical Approaches to Teaching Literature, Language, Composition, and Culture* 16 (1): 9–22.

Carino, Peter. 2003. "Power and Authority in Peer Tutoring." In *The Center Will Hold*, edited by Michael A. Pemberton and Joyce Kinkead, 96–113. University Press of Colorado. https://doi.org/10.2307/j.ctt46nxnq.9.

Caswell, Nicole I. 2022. "Resisting White Patriarchal Emotional Labor Within the Writing Center." In *Counterstories from the Writing Center*, edited by W. Faison and F. Condon, 109–19. Utah State University Press.

Caswell, Nicole I., Jackie Grutsch McKinney, and Rebecca Jackson. 2016. *The Working Lives of New Writing Center Directors*. Utah State University Press.

Charmaz, K. 2008. "Grounded Theory as an Emergent Method." In *Handbook of Emergent Methods*, edited by S. N. Hesse-Biber and P. Leavy, 155–70. The Guilford Press.

Chihota, C., and Lucia Thesen. 2014. "Rehearsing 'the Postgraduate Condition' in Writers' Circles." *Risk in Academic Writing: Postgraduate Students, Their Teachers and the Making of Knowledge*, edited by Luscia Thesen and Linda Cooper, 131–47. Multilingual Matters.

Colombo, Laura, and Elizabeth L. Rodas. 2021. "Interdisciplinarity as an Opportunity in Argentinian and Ecuadorian Writing Groups." *Higher Education Research and Development* 40 (2): 207–19.

Corbett, Steven J. 2008. "Tutoring Style, Tutoring Ethics: The Continuing Relevance of the Directive/Nondirective Debate." *Praxis: A Writing Center Journal* 5 (2). http://www.praxisuwc.com/corbett-52.

Corbett, Steven J. 2011. "Using Case Study Multi-Methods to Investigate Close(r) Collaboration: Course-Based Tutoring and the Directive/Nondirective Instructional Continuum." *Writing Center Journal* 31 (1): 55–81.

Corbett, Steven J. 2013. "Negotiating Pedagogical Authority: The Rhetoric of Writing Center Tutoring Styles and Methods." *Rhetoric Review* 32 (1): 81–98. https://doi.org/10.1080/07350198.2013.739497.

Cui, Wenqi, Jing Zhang, and Dana Lynn Driscoll. 2022. "Graduate Writing Groups: Evidence-Based Practices for Advanced Graduate Writing Support." *Writing Center Journal* 40 (2): 85–102.

Cuthbert, Denise, Ceridwen Spark, and Eliza Burke. 2009. "Disciplining Writing: The Case for Multi-Disciplinary Writing Groups to Support Writing for Publication by Higher Degree by Research Candidates in the Humanities, Arts and Social Sciences." *Higher Education Research and Development* 28 (2): 137–49.

Day, Kami, and Michele Eodice. 2004. "Coauthoring as Place: A Different Ethos." In *Writing Groups Inside and Outside the Classroom*, edited by Beverly J. Moss, Nels P. Highberg, and Melissa Nicolas. Routledge.

Denny, Harry, Robert Mundy, Liliana M. Naydan, Richard Sévère, and Anna Sicari, eds. 2019. *Out in the Center: Public Controversies and Private Struggles*. Utah State University Press.

Denny, Harry, John Nordlof, and Lori Salem. 2018. "'Tell Me Exactly What It Was That I Was Doing That Was so Bad': Understanding the Needs and Expectations of Working-Class Students in Writing Centers." *Writing Center Journal* 37 (1): 67–100.

Denny, Melody. 2018. "The Oral Writing-Revision Space: Identifying a New and Common Discourse Feature of Writing Center Consultations." *Writing Center Journal* 37 (1): 35–66.

Denzin, N. K., and Y. S. Lincoln. 2011. *The Sage Handbook of Qualitative Research*. Sage.

Dias, Patrick, Aviva Freedman, Peter Medway, and Anthony Paré. 1999. "Situating Writing." In *Worlds Apart: Acting and Writing in Academic and Workplace Contexts*, edited P. Dias, A. Freedman, P. Medway, and A. Paré, 17–46. Routledge.

Dinitz, Sue, and Susanmarie Harrington. 2014. "The Role of Disciplinary Expertise in Shaping Writing Tutorials." *Writing Center Journal* 33 (2): 73–98.

Driscoll, Dana Lynn, and Sherry Wynn Perdue. 2012. "Theory, Lore, and More: An Analysis of RAD Research in 'The Writing Center Journal,' 1980–2009." *Writing Center Journal* 32 (2): 11–39.

Driscoll, D. L., and J. Wells. 2012. "Beyond Knowledge and Skills: Writing Transfer and the Role of Student Dispositions." *Composition Forum* 26. http://compositionforum.com/issue/26/beyond-knowledge-skills.php.

Faison, Wonderful, and Frankie Condon, eds. 2022. *Counterstories from the Writing Center*. Utah State University Press.

Faison, Wonderful, and A. K. Treviño. 2020. "Race, Retention, Language, and Literacy: The Hidden Curriculum of the Writing Center." *Learning from the Lived Experiences of Graduate Student Writers*, edited Shannon Madden, Michele Eodice, Kirsten T. Edwards, and Alexandria Lockett, 92–107. Utah State University Press.

Farkas, Kerrie, and Christina Haas. 2012. "A Grounded Theory Approach for Studying Writing and Literacy." *Practicing Research in Writing Studies: Reflexive and Ethically Responsible Research*, edited K. M. Powell and P. Takayoshi, 81–95. Hampton Press.

Garcia, Elena Marie-Adkins, Seung hee Eum, and Lorna Watt. 2013. "Experiencing the Benefits of Difference within Multidisciplinary Graduate Writing Groups." In *Working with Faculty Writers*, edited by Anne Ellen Geller and Michele Eodice. Utah State University Press.

Geller, A. E., M. Eodice, F. Condon, M. Carroll, and E. H. Boquet. 2007. *The Everyday Writing Center: A Community of Practice*. Utah State University Press.

Geller, Anne Ellen, Frankie Condon, and Meg Carroll. 2011. "Bold: The Everyday Writing Center and the Production of New Knowledge in Antiracist Theory and Practice." *Writing Centers and the New Racism: A Call for Sustainable Dialogue and Change*, edited Laura Greenfield and Karen Rowan, 101–123. Utah State University Press.

Geller, Anne Ellen, and Michele Eodice. 2013. *Working with Faculty Writers*. Utah State University Press.

George, Diana. 1984. "Working with Peer Groups in the Composition Classroom." *College Composition and Communication* 35 (3): 320–26. https://doi.org/10.2307/357460.

Gere, Anne Ruggles. 1987. *Writing Groups: History, Theory, and Implications*. SIU Press.

Gere, Anne Ruggles. 1994. "Kitchen Tables and Rented Rooms: The Extracurriculum of Composition." *College Composition and Communication* 45 (1): 75–92. https://doi.org/10.2307/358588.

Gere, Anne Ruggles, and Robert D. Abbott. 1985. "Talking about Writing: The Language of Writing Groups." *Research in the Teaching of English* 19 (4): 362–85.

Giaimo, Genie Nicole. 2023. *Unwell Writing Centers: Searching for Wellness in Neoliberal Educational Institutions and Beyond*. Utah State University Press.

Gillespie, P. 2002. "Beyond the House of Lore: WCenter as Research Site." *Writing Center Research: Extending the Conversation*, edited Paula Gillespie, Alice Gillam, Lady Falls Brown, and Byron Stay, 39–52. Lawrence Erlbaum.

Godbee, Beth. 2020. "The Trauma of Graduate Education: Graduate Writers Countering Epistemic Injustice and Reclaiming Epistemic Rights." In *Learning from the Lived Experiences of Graduate Student Writers*, edited by Shannon Madden, Michele Eodice, Kirsten T. Edwards, Alexandria Lockett, 35–51. Utah State University Press.

Gradin, Sherrie, Jennifer Pauley-Gose, and Candace Stewart. 2006. "Disciplinary Differences, Rhetorical Resonances: Graduate Writing Groups Beyond the Humanities." *Praxis: A Writing Center Journal* 3(2). https://doi.org/10.15781/T2P55DZ88.

Greenfield, Laura. 2019. *Radical Writing Center Praxis: A Paradigm for Ethical Political Engagement*. Utah State University Press.

Greenwell, Amanda, Renée Lavoie, Gissel Campos, Sarah Gerrish, and Mary Joerg. 2020. "Reading and the Writing Center: Tutor Education and Praxis." *Praxis: A Writing Center Journal* 17(2): 7–19.

Grimm, Nancy. 1999. *Good Intentions: Writing Center Work for Postmodern Times*. CrossCurrents, New Perspectives in Rhetoric and Composition. Boynton/Cook-Heinemann.

Grimm, Nancy. 2011. "Retheorizing Writing Center Work to Transform a System of Advantage Based on Race." *Writing Centers and the New Racism: A Call for Sustainable Dialogue and Change*, edited by Laura Greenfield and Karen Rowan, 75–100. Utah State University Press.

Guerin, Cally, Vicki Xafis, Diana V. Doda, Marianne H. Gillam, Allison J. Larg, Helene Luckner, Nasreen Jahan, Aris Widayati, and Chuangzhou Xu. 2013. "Diversity in Collaborative Research Communities: A Multicultural, Multidisciplinary Thesis Writing Group in Public Health." *Studies in Continuing Education* 35 (1): 65–81. https://doi.org/10.1080/0158037X.2012.684375.

Haas, Sarah. 2014. "Pick-n-Mix: A Typology of Writers' Groups in Use." In *Writing Groups for Doctoral Education and Beyond*. Routledge.

Hagemann, J. 1995. "Writing Centers as Sites for Writing Transfer Research." In *Writing Center Perspectives*, edited by B. L. Stay, C. Murphy, and E. Hobson, 120–31. NWCA Press.

Hall, R. Mark. 2011. "Theory in/to Practice: Using Dialogic Reflection to Develop a Writing Center Community of Practice." *Writing Center Journal* 31(1): 82–105.

Hall, R. Mark. 2017. *Around the Texts of Writing Center Work: An Inquiry-based Approach to Tutor Education*. Utah State University Press.

Hartelius, E. J. 2010. *The Rhetoric of Expertise*. Lexington Books.

Heller, Caroline E. 1997. *Until We Are Strong Together: Women Writers in the Tenderloin*. Teachers College Press.

Hixson, C., W. Lee, D. Hunter, M. Paretti, H. Matusocivh, and R. McCord. 2016. "Understanding the Structural and Attitudinal Elements That Sustain a Graduate Student Writing Group in an Engineering Department." *WLN: A Journal of Writing Center Scholarship* 40 (5–6): 18.

Hochschild, Arlie Russell. 1983. *The Managed Heart: Commercialization of Human Feeling*. University of California Press.

Ianetta, Melissa, and Lauren Fitzgerald. 2016. *The Oxford Guide for Writing Tutors: Practice and Research*. Oxford University Press.

Im, Hohjin, Jianmin Shao, and Chuansheng Chen. 2020. "The Emotional Sponge." *Writing Center Journal* 38(1): 203–30.

Jackson, Karen Keaton, and Amara Hand. 2024. "Effectively Affective: Examining the Ethos of One HBCU Writing Center." *Writing Center Journal* 41 (3): 38–54.

Jackson, Karen Keaton, and Mick Howard. 2019. "From the Editors: MSIs Matter; Recognizing Writing Center Work at Minority Serving Institutions." *Praxis: A Writing Center Journal* 16 (2).

Jackson, Karen Keaton, Hope Jackson, and Dawn N. Hicks Tafari. 2019. "We Belong in the Discussion: Including HBCUs in Conversations about Race and Writing." *College Composition and Communication* 71 (2): 184–214.

Jackson, Rebecca L. 2004. "'I Don't Talk to Blacks,' or Contextual Constraints on Peer Writing Groups in the Prison College Classroom." In *Writing Groups Inside and Outside the Classroom*, edited by Beverly J. Moss, Nels P. Highberg, and Melissa Nicolas. Routledge.

Jackson, Rebecca, and Grutsch Jackie McKinney. 2012. "Beyond Tutoring: Mapping the Invisible Landscape of Writing Center Work." *Praxis: A Writing Center Journal* 9 (1): 1–11. https://doi.org/10.15781/T2RR1Q34T.

Julien, Karen, and Jacqueline L. Beres. 2019. "Cheaper than Therapy: The Unexpected Benefits and Challenges of an Academic Writing Partnership." In *Critical Collaborative Communities*, edited by Nicola Simmons and Ann Singh, 3–16. Brill. https://doi.org/10.1163/9789004410985_001

Kaufhold, Kathrin, and Daniel Egil Yencken. 2021. "Writing Groups as Dialogic Spaces: Negotiating Multiple Normative Perspectives." *Journal of Academic Writing* 11 (1): 1–15.

Kerschbaum, Stephanie L. 2014. *Toward a New Rhetoric of Difference*. CCCC Studies in Writing and Rhetoric. Conference on College Composition and Communication; National Council of Teachers of English.

Kiedaisch, J., and S. Dinitz. 1993. "Look Back and Say 'So What': The Limitations of the Generalist Tutor." *Writing Center Journal* 14 (1): 63–74.

Kiedaisch, Jean, and Sue Dinitz. 2007. "Changing Notions of Difference in the Writing Center: The Possibilities of Universal Design." *Writing Center Journal* 27 (2): 5.

Kim, Soo Hyon, and Shari Wolke. 2020. "Graduate Writing Groups: Helping L2 Writers Navigate the Murky Waters of Academic Writing." In *Graduate Writing Across Disciplines: Identifying, Teaching, Supporting*, edited by M. Brooks-Gillies, E. G. Garcia, S. H. Kim, and T. Smith, 211–42. WAC Clearinghouse; University Press of Colorado. https://doi.org/10.37514/ATD-B.2020.0407.2.09.

King, Carolyne M. 2018. "Tutors as Readers: Reprising the Role of Reading in the Writing Center." *Praxis: A Writing Center Journal* 16 (1): 63–74.

Kinney, Tiffany, Julie Snyder-Yuly, and Sumiko Martinez. 2019. "Cultivating Graduate Writing Groups as Communities of Practice: A Call to Action for the Writing Center." *Praxis: A Writing Center Journal* 16 (3): 16–24. https://doi.org/10.26153/tsw/3175.

Kjesrud, Roberta D. 2015. "Lessons from Data: Avoiding Lore Bias in Research Paradigms." *Writing Center Journal* 34 (2): 33–58.

Kramer, T. 2016. "Writing Circles: Combining Peer Review, Commitment, and Gentle Guidance." *WLN: A Journal of Writing Center Scholarship* 40 (7–8): 20–28.

Kranek, A. A., and M. Paz Carvajal Regidor. 2021. "It's Crowded in Here: 'Present Others' in Advanced Graduate Writers' Sessions." *Praxis: A Writing Center Journal* 18 (2): 62–73.

Lassig, Carly J., Lisette H. Dillon, and Carmel M. Diezmann. 2013. "Student or Scholar? Transforming Identities Through a Research Writing Group." *Studies in Continuing Education* 35 (3): 299–314. https://doi.org/10.1080/0158037X.2012.746226.

Lave, J., and E. Wenger. 1991. *Situated Learning: Legitimate Peripheral Participation*. Cambridge University Press.

Lawrence, Susan, and Terry Myers Zawacki. 2018. *Re/Writing the Center: Approaches to Supporting Graduate Students in the Writing Center*. Utah State University Press.

Li, Linda. 2014. "Scaffolding the Thesis Writing Process: An Ongoing Writing Group for International Research Students." In *Writing Groups for Doctoral Education and Beyond*, edited by Claire Aitchison and Cally Guerin, 145–61. Routledge.

Lockett, Alexandria. 2020. "Graduate Writing in Communities: Critical Notes on Access and Success." *Learning from the Lived Experiences of Graduate Student Writers*, edited Shannon Madden, Michele Eodice, Kirsten T. Edwards, and Alexandria Lockett, 125–30. Utah State University Press.

Lunsford, A. 1991. "Collaboration, Control, and the Idea of a Writing Center." *Writing Center Journal* 12 (1): 3–10.

Mackiewicz, Jo, and Isabelle Kramer Thompson. 2015. *Talk About Writing: The Tutoring Strategies of Experienced Writing Center Tutors*. Routledge.

Maher, D., L. Seaton, C. McMullen, T. Fitzgerald, E. Otsuji, and A. Lee. 2008. "'Becoming and Being Writers': The Experiences of Doctoral Students in Writing Groups." *Studies in Continuing Education* 30 (3): 263–75.

Mannon, B. O. 2016. "What Do Graduate Students Want from the Writing Center? Tutoring Practices to Support Dissertation and Thesis Writers." *Praxis: A Writing Center Journal* 13 (2).

McKinney, Jackie Grutsch. 2013. *Peripheral Visions for Writing Centers*. Utah State University Press.

McMurray, Claire. 2017. "A Systematic Approach to Graduate Writing Groups: Facilitator, First Meeting, and Feedback Structure." *Praxis: A Writing Center Journal* 14 (2): 44–49.

McMurray, Claire. 2019. "Writing Groups: An Analysis of Participants' Expectations and Activities." *Praxis: A Writing Center Journal* 17 (1): 52–67.

Merriam, Sharan B., and Elizabeth J. Tisdell. 2016. *Qualitative Research: A Guide to Design and Implementation*. 4th ed. Jossey-Bass Higher and Adult Education Series. Jossey-Bass.

Micciche, Laura R. 2007. *Doing Emotion: Rhetoric, Writing, Teaching*. Portsmouth, NH: Boynton/Cook Publishers.

Miles, Matthew B., and A. M. Huberman. 1994. *Qualitative Data Analysis: An Expanded Sourcebook*. 2nd ed. Sage Publications. http://catdir.loc.gov/catdir/enhancements/fy0655/93041204-t.html.

Mitchell, Kendra. 2019. "Liminally Speaking: Pathos-Driven Approaches in an HBCU Writing Center as a Way Forward." *Praxis: A Writing Center Journal* 16 (2): 75–81.

Mortensen, P., and G. E. Kirsch. 1993. "On Authority in the Study of Writing." *College Composition and Communication* 44 (4): 556–72.

Moss, Beverly J. 2021. "Where Would We Be? Legacies, Roll Calls, and the Teaching of Writing in HBCUs." *Composition Studies* 49 (1): 144–48.

Moss, Beverly J., Nels P. Highberg, and Melissa Nicolas, eds. 2004. *Writing Groups Inside and Outside the Classroom*. International Writing Centers Association (IWCA) Press Series. Routledge.

Murphy, C., and S. Sherwood. 2011. *The St. Martin's Sourcebook for Writing Tutors*. Bedford / St. Martin's.

National Research Council. 2000. *How People Learn: Brain, Mind, Experience, and School: Expanded Edition*. National Academies Press. https://doi.org/10.17226/9853.

Navickas, Kate. 2020. "The Emotional Labor of Becoming: Lessons from an Exiting Writing Center Director." In *The Things We Carry: Strategies for Recognizing and*

Negotiating Emotional Labor in Writing Program Administration, edited by C. A. Wooten, J. Babb, K. M. Costello, and K. Navickas, 56–74. Utah State University Press.

Negretti, Raffaella. 2021. "Searching for Metacognitive Generalities: Areas of Convergence in Learning to Write for Publication Across Doctoral Students in Science and Engineering." *Written Communication* 38 (2): 167–207.

Nelson, Matthew T., Sam Deges, and Kathleen F. Weaver. 2020. "Making Visible the Emotional Labor of Writing Center Work." In *The Things We Carry: Strategies for Recognizing and Negotiating Emotional Labor in Writing Program Administration*, edited by C. A. Wooten, J. Babb, K. M. Costello, and K. Navickas, 161–76. Utah State University Press.

Nicklay, Jennifer. 2012. "Got Guilt? Consultant Guilt in the Writing Center Community." *Writing Center Journal* 32 (1): 14–27.

Nordlof, John. 2020. "Vygotskean Learning Theory." In *Theories and Methods of Writing Center Studies: A Practical Guide*, edited by Jo Mackiewicz and Rebecca Day Babcock, 11–19. Routledge.

Nowacek, Rebecca S. 2011. *Agents of Integration: Understanding Transfer as a Rhetorical Act*. Southern Illinois University Press.

Nowacek, Rebecca, Bridget Bodee, Julia E. Douglas et al. 2019. "'Transfer Talk' in Talk About Writing in Progress: Two Propositions About Transfer of Learning." In *Composition Forum* 42. https://compositionforum.com/issue/42/transfer-talk.php.

Nowacek, Rebecca S., and Bradley Hughes. 2015. "Threshold Concepts in the Writing Center: Scaffolding the Development of Tutor Expertise." In *Naming What We Know: Threshold Concepts of Writing Studies*, edited by Linda Adler-Kassner and Elizabeth Wardle, 171–85. Utah State University Press.

Paré, Anthony. 2011. "Speaking of Writing: Supervisory Feedback and the Dissertation." *Doctoral Education: Research-Based Strategies for Doctoral Students, Supervisors and Administrators*, edited by Lynn McAlpine and Cheryl Amundsen, 59–74. Springer Dordrecht.

Paré, Anthony. 2014. "Writing Together for Many Reasons: Theoretical and Historical Perspectives." In *Writing Groups for Doctoral Education and Beyond*, edited by Claire Aitchison and Cally Guerin, 18–29. Routledge.

Pemberton, Michael A. 2018. "Rethinking the WAC / Writing Center / Graduate Student Connection." *Re/Writing the Center: Approaches to Supporting Graduate Students in the Writing Center*, edited by Susan Lawrence and Terry Myers Zawacki, 29–48. Utah State University Press.

Phillips, Tallin. 2012. "Graduate Writing Groups: Shaping Writing and Writers from Student to Scholar." *Praxis: A Writing Center Journal* 10 (1): 1–7.

Powell, Katrina M., and Pamela Takayoshi. 2003. "Accepting Roles Created for Us: The Ethics of Reciprocity." *College Composition and Communication* 54 (3): 394–422.

Prior, Paul. 1994. "Response, Revision, Disciplinarity: A Microhistory of a Dissertation Prospectus in Sociology." *Written Communication* 11 (4): 483–533.

Prior, Paul. 1998. *Writing/Disciplinarity: A Sociohistoric Account of Literate Activity in the Academy*. Taylor and Francis.

Reiff, M. J., and A. Bawarshi. 2011. "Tracing Discursive Resources: How Students Use Prior Genre Knowledge to Negotiate New Writing Contexts in First-Year Composition." *Written Communication* 28 (3): 312–37.

Rinaldi, Kerri. 2015. "Disability in the Writing Center: A New Approach (That's Not So New)." *Praxis: A Writing Center Journal* 13 (1): 9–14.

Roozen, Kevin, and Joe Erickson. 2017. *Expanding Literate Landscapes: Persons, Practices, and Sociohistoric Perspectives of Disciplinary Development.* Computers and Composition Digital Press; Utah State University Press. https://ccdigitalpress.org/book/expanding/.

Rounsaville, Angela, Rebecca Lorimer Leonard, and Rebecca S. Nowacek. 2022. "Relationality in the Transfer of Writing Knowledge." *College Composition and Communication* 74 (1): 136–63.

Ryan, L., and L. Zimmerelli. 2010. *The Bedford Guide for Writing Tutors.* Bedford / St. Martins.

Saldaña, J. 2016. *The Coding Manual for Qualitative Researchers.* Sage Publications.

Sévère, Richard, and Maurice Wilson. 2020. "Voices from the Hill: HBCUs and the Graduate Student Experience." *Learning from the Lived Experiences of Graduate Student Writers*, edited Shannon Madden, Michele Eodice, Kirsten T. Edwards, and Alexandria Lockett, 73–91. Utah State University Press.

Shanahan, C., T. Shanahan, and C. Misischia. 2011. "Analysis of Expert Readers in Three Disciplines: History, Mathematics, and Chemistry." *Journal of Literacy Research* 43 (4): 393–429. https://doi.org/10.1177/1086296X11424071.

Simpson, Steve. 2018. "On the Distinct Needs of Multilingual STEM Graduate Students in Writing Centers." *Re/Writing the Center: Approaches to Supporting Graduate Students in the Writing Center*, edited by Susan Lawrence and Terry Myers Zawacki, 66–85. Utah State University Press.

Smith, Trixie G., Janice C. Molloy, Eva Kassens-Nor, Wen Li, and Manuel Colunga-Garcia. 2013. "Developing a Heuristic for Multidisciplinary Faculty Writing Groups: A Case Study." In *Working with Faculty Writers*, edited by Anne Ellen Geller and Michele Eodice, 175–88. Utah State University Press.

Spigelman, C., and L. Grobman. 2005. *On Location: Theory and Practice in Classroom-Based Writing Tutoring.* Utah State University Press.

Spigelman, Candace. 2000. *Across Property Lines: Textual Ownership in Writing Groups.* Studies in Writing and Rhetoric. Southern Illinois University Press.

Stewart, D.-L. 2017. "Language of Appeasement." *Inside Higher Ed*, March 29. https://www.insidehighered.com/views/2017/03/30/colleges-need-language-shift-not-one-you-think-essay.

Tardy, Christine M., Bruna Sommer-Farias, and Jeroen Gevers. 2020. "Teaching and Researching Genre Knowledge: Toward an Enhanced Theoretical Framework." *Written Communication* 37 (3): 287–321.

Thesen, Lucia. 2014. "'If They're Not Laughing, Watch Out!': Emotion and Risk in Postgraduate Writers' Circles." In *Writing Groups for Doctoral Education and Beyond*, edited by Claire Aitchison and Cally Guerin, 162–76. Routledge.

Thomas, Sharon, Leonora Smith, and Terri Trupiano Barry. 2004. "Shaping Writing Groups in the Sciences." In *Writing Groups Inside and Outside the Classroom*, edited by Beverly J. Moss, Nels P. Highberg, and Melissa Nicolas, 79–94. Lawrence Erlbaum Associates.

Waring, H. Z. 2005. "Peer Tutoring in a Graduate Writing Centre: Identity, Expertise and Advice Resisting." *Applied Linguistics* 26 (2): 141–68.

Webster, Travis. 2021. *Queerly Centered: LGBTQA Writing Center Directors Navigate the Workplace*. Utah State University Press.

Wenger, Etienne. 1998. *Communities of Practice: Learning, Meaning, and Identity*. Learning in Doing. Cambridge University Press. http://catdir.loc.gov/catdir/toc/cam026/98202423.html.

Wenger, Etienne, Richard McDermott, and William M. Snyder. 2002. "Seven Principles for Cultivating Communities of Practice." *Cultivating Communities of Practice: A Guide to Managing Knowledge*, 49–64. Harvard Business School Publishing.

Wenger-Trayner, E., M. Fenton-O'Creevy, S. Hutchinson, C. Kubiak, and B. Wenger-Trayner. 2015. *Learning in Landscapes of Practice: Boundaries, Identity, and Knowledgeability in Practice-Based Learning*. Routledge.

Wenger-Trayner, E., and B. Wenger-Trayner. 2015. "Introduction to Communities of Practice." Wenger-Trayner professional website. http://wenger-trayner.com/introduction-to-communities-of-practice/.

Westbrook, Evelyn. 2004. "Community, Collaboration, and Conflict: The Community Writing Group as Contact Zone." In *Writing Groups Inside and Outside the Classroom*, edited by Beverly J. Moss, Nels P. Highberg, and Melissa Nicolas. Routledge.

White, Stephanie, and Elisabeth Miller. 2015. "Senior-Thesis Writing Groups: Putting Students in the Driver's Seat." *WLN: A Journal of Writing Center Scholarship* 39 (5–6): 1–5.

Wilder, Sara. 2021. "Another Voice in the Room: Negotiating Authority in Multidisciplinary Writing Groups." *Written Communication* 38 (2): 247–77.

Wilmot, Kirstin. 2018. "Designing Writing Groups to Support Postgraduate Students' Academic Writing: A Case Study from a South African University." *Innovations in Education and Teaching International* 55 (3): 257–65.

Wilmot, Kirstin, and Sioux McKenna. 2018. "Writing Groups as Transformative Spaces." *Higher Education Research and Development* 37 (4): 868–82.

Winzenried, Misty Anne, Lillian Campbell, Roger Chao, and Alison Cardinal. 2017. "Co-Constructing Writing Knowledge: Students' Collaborative Talk Across Contexts." *Composition Forum* 37.

Yancey, Kathleen, Liane Robertson, and Kara Taczak. 2014. *Writing Across Contexts: Transfer, Composition, and Sites of Writing*. University Press of Colorado.

Index

Page numbers followed by *t* indicate tables. Page numbers followed by *n* indicate notes.

academic space, 134
academic writing groups. *See* dissertation writing group (DWG); multidisciplinary writing groups; second-year proposal group (SPG); undergraduate thesis group (UTG); writing groups
accessibility, 7, 154
accountability: academic writing groups, 35, 36, 48, 118–19
Across Property Lines: Textual Ownership in Writing Groups, 11, 108, 149
active/passive role, facilitators, 37–38, 46–47, 50
activities, group facilitator training, 33
advisor authority. *See* negotiation of authority
African American students, 134, 142
age identity, 115, 118–19
agenda setting, 42–43, 53, 62, 65, 176*t*
agreement/disagreement feedback, 55–56, 83, 178*t*
Ahmed, Sara, 117
Aitchison, Claire, 8, 9, 38–39, 104
anti-racist writing, white perspective, 141
anxiety, 47, 119, 131–35
Around the Texts of Writing Center Work, 14
attendance, participant-observer, 8, 23, 27*n*2

attrition, 10, 51, 127, 131–35, 138, 142
authoritarian negotiation. *See* negotiation of authority
authority vs. non-authority facilitator role, 5–6, 32, 42–43, 175*t*

Baldwin, James, 138, 139, 141
belonging, sense of, 128, 129, 131, 135
benefits of writing groups, 9–12
best practices: authority negotiation, 160; group facilitators, 23; tutoring, 7, 8; writing center administrators, 8
black tax in white spaces, 142
Block, Rebecca, 56–57
Bowen, Lauren Marshall, 156
Brooks-Gillies, Marilee, 17–18, 68
Burke, Eliza, 68
Burrows, Cedric, 142, 144

Carillo, Ellen, 77
Carino, Peter, 19–20
case study research, 159
Caswell, Nicole, 117
challenges for writing groups, 10–12, 18–19, 37, 52–53, 75–76, 137
check-ins, 52–53, 126, 144–45, 150, 156, 177*t*

Chihota, Clement Mapfumo, 39
chitchat feedback, 52–53, 150, 181t
citing, advisor authority, 97–100
class identity, 118
class rank, 168
classroom-based writing groups, 11–12
co-construction, genre knowledge, 83n4, 84–85, 108, 152
Coates, Ta-Nehisi, 138, 139, 141
codebook, facilitator role and practices, 175t–82t
coding. *See* data collection and analysis
cognitive scaffolding: agreement/disagreement, 83, 178t; collaborative authorship, 55; discipline/genre expectations, 83n4, 84–85, 180t; emotional labor, 40, 41, 82; group facilitators, 177t; notetaking, 65, 178t; praise, 57; pumping, 40, 83, 85, 88–90, 178t; reader response, 56, 83, 85, 90–91, 178t; reframing, 57, 62; revision suggestions, 40, 83, 85, 90–91, 178t; rhetorical reading, 52; writing projects, 179t
collaborative learning process: challenges, 160; co-construction, 152; cognitive scaffolding, 55; communities-of-practice, 8, 51; disciplinary expertise, 49, 65–66, 73n1, 160–61; emotional support, 33, 41, 82, 138–39; facilitator role, 36, 38; feedback, 54–55; genre knowledge, 84–85, 108–9, 147–48, 152–53; multilingual writing groups, 66–67, 80–81, 108, 149–50; negotiation of authority, 5–9, 11, 43, 148–49; participant-observer researchers, 8, 29; relationship-building, 154–55; student-teacher relationship, 40; suggestions, 55, 62, 83, 85, 90–91, 139; textual ownership, 108; transfer of learning, 109–10, 151–52; undergraduate thesis group (UTG), 137; writing conferences, 9–10; writing transfer, 71–72, 108, 151–53
Colombo, Laura, 68
Colunga-Garcia, Manuel, 10
commitment, second-year proposal group (SPG), 120
communities of practice (CoP): disciplinary, 16–17; engagement, 18–19; expertise, 16, 19, 49, 73n1; framework, 8, 13–15; hierarchy, 17–18, 41, 45; learning, 13; memberships, 16, 33; newcomers, 42, 47, 79; reification, 14; transactional process, 15; trust-building, 161, 163
community service projects, 26
community writing groups, 11
competition among group members, 100, 110, 135t, 136, 143, 163

composition studies, 20, 79, 84–85, 108–9
conflict mediation, 11, 18–19, 103–8, 113–14, 117, 142, 144, 160, 163
consent forms from research participants, 167
constraints, advisor authority, 101, 104–6
contextualized documents, 8, 27, 28t, 30
controversial discussions, 142
conventions, undergraduate thesis group (UTG), 131
conversation analysis, 31n3, 38, 40, 52, 65–66, 83n4, 87–88, 108
core practices, 160
creative approach writing process, 158
creative work projects, 26
critical race theory, 140
critique follow-up, 62
cross-disciplinary groups. *See* multidisciplinary writing groups
Cui, Wenqi, 38
cultural conditioning, 117
Cuthbert, Denise, 68

data collection and analysis: coding, 30–31, 31n3, 40–41, 83n4, 87–88, 119; contextualized documents, 27, 28t; field notes, 28t, 65; limitations, 160; participant-observer, 8, 27, 28t, 29–30; patterns, 31; qualitative approach, 8, 26–27; semi-structured interviews, 8, 27, 29, 165–66; surveys, 8, 27, 28t, 51, 74n2; video recordings, 27, 28t
Davis, Matthew, 156
demographics, group members, 23–24, 143, 172t
Denny, Melody, 87, 108
department/major of research participants, 167
dependability, group members, 163
differences, negotiation of authority, 20–21, 39, 121, 122
difficulties, writing groups, 113, 118–19, 144–45, 160
directive/nondirective tutoring methods, 36, 43–45, 46, 51, 155
disability identity, 118, 119, 134, 160
disagreement/agreement feedback, 55–56, 83, 178t
disciplinary communities: advisor authority, 100–2; collaborative learning process, 84–85, 152–53; communities of practice, 16–17, 51, 70; disciplinary differences, 51, 65–66, 83; feedback, 16, 39, 84–85, 180t, 182t; genre knowledge, 70–72, 83, 84–85, 90, 106, 151–53; peripheral engagement, 16–17; writing conventions, 39, 102–8

disciplinary expertise. *See* expertise
dissertation writing group (DWG): advisor authority, 39, 97–98, 103–8; cross-disciplinary constraints, 39, 68–69, 76, 83, 104–6; expertise, 49, 69–70; genre knowledge, 81, 83*n*4, 84–85, 106, 122, 152. *See also* multidisciplinary writing groups; second-year proposal group (SPG); undergraduate thesis group (UTG); writing groups
diversity in writing groups, 9–11, 18–19, 128, 134, 144
doctoral students, 9, 16–17
domestic student research participants, 74*n*2, 172*t*
Driscoll, Dana Lynn, 38

effective feedback, 157
email logistical support, 52
embodied experiences, 158–59
emerging scholarly identities, 5, 128, 129, 130
emotional labor: attrition, 51, 135; collaborative suggestions, 83, 90–91, 138–40; exchange value, 116*n*1; genre awareness, 81, 109; group facilitators, 32, 39, 41*n*1, 63, 161–63, 175*t*, 177*t*; group norms, 48, 114, 115, 143, 144; identity markers, 116, 116*n*1, 119, 134, 142; inclusion/exclusion, 153–54; inequities, 143; negotiation of authority, 51–53, 115–16; predominantly white institutions (PWIs), 33; relational work, 41*n*1, 153–54; relationship-building, 117; student writing, 9; use value, 116*n*1; writing centers, 17, 116–17; writing groups, 8, 9, 67, 153–54, 157, 175*t*
emotions feedback, 181*t*
empirical research, 6–7, 26–27, 30–31, 38
end-of-term survey data, 51, 74*n*2, 171*t*–73*t*
engagement feedback, 16–17, 62, 108, 121, 125, 142, 154
English as a Second Language (ESL) writing groups, 22, 38
English thesis writing, 84–85
enthusiasm, group facilitators, 120
epistemic injustice, 9–10
equity, 7, 128, 154
Erickson, Joe, 33
Eum, Seung Hee, 9
The Everyday Writing Center: A Community of Practice, 14–15, 18
exclusion/inclusion, 33, 153–54
expansion of writing center programs, 21–22
expert-outsider facilitator, 50, 63, 150–51, 155–56
expertise: collaborative learning process, 73*n*1, 160–61; communities of practice, 16, 19, 51;

disciplinary writing, 73*n*1, 147; negotiation of authority, 70; scaffolding group practice, 63; tutor-facilitators, 36, 49, 52, 63, 155, 157. *See also* genre knowledge

facilitators. *See* group facilitators
faculty writing group, 6*n*1, 10, 167
Faison, Wonderful, 117–18
feedback practices: advisor authority, 97–98, 104, 106–8, 182*t*; anxiety, 131–35; cognitive practices, 32, 178*t*–80*t*; collaborative learning process, 36, 38, 39, 41, 54–55; critique follow-up, 62; cross-disciplinary constraints, 101, 104–6; engagement, 38, 40, 52–53, 58–62, 121, 158–59; group feedback, 22, 32, 60–61, 151, 168–70, 175*t*, 177*t*; notetaking, 65, 177*t*; oral writing-revision space (OR), 87–88, 108, 182*t*; praise, 52, 57–60, 62, 156; prompting, 54–57, 156; pumping questions, 40, 83, 85, 88–90, 104, 123, 151; reading practice, 57, 77–79, 151–52, 176*t*; recontextualization, 72, 77, 80, 108–9; reframing, 57–58, 62, 156; relational practices, 32, 41*n*1, 180*t*–81*t*; revision suggestions, 62, 83, 85, 90–91, 138–39, 150–51; scaffolding, 32, 39, 41*n*1, 52, 61, 62, 63, 155–57, 177*t*; shared practices, 14, 58–59, 161; signposting, 49, 59–60; usefulness, 50, 76*n*3, 79, 80, 121–25
feminist co-mentoring, 9–10
feminist theory, 20, 138, 140
field notes, 28*t*, 65
first-year writing students, 22
Fitzgerald, Lauren, 39, 43
focused praise, 59–60
freshman research participants, 74*n*2, 172*t*
friendships, 135

Garcia, Elena G., 9, 17–18, 68
Geller, Anne Ellen, 14–15, 18, 42
gender identity, 18–19, 114–15, 118–19, 132–34, 160
genre awareness: disciplinary differences, 152; emotional labor, 76–77, 81, 109; expectation, 84–85, 180*t*; group feedback, 55–56, 84–85, 152; intellectual labor, 39, 76–78, 81; multidisciplinary writing groups, 72, 81, 109–10; undergraduate thesis group (UTG), 84–85, 152
genre knowledge: advisory authority, 106; co-construction, 152; collaborative learning process, 41, 84–85, 108–9, 147–48, 152–53; expertise, 69–70; genre-specific knowledge, 72; group facilitators, 63; multilingualism,

73, 80–81, 158; oral writing-revision space (OR), 87–88, 108; reading activities, 155–58, 160–61; recontextualization, 72, 77, 80; rhetorical resonances, 50, 78–79, 83, 85, 109; scaffolding, 155–58; writing transfer, 71–72, 108, 151–53. *See also* expertise
Gere, Anne Ruggles, 11, 149
Gevers, Jeroen, 72
Gillespie, Paula, 56
goals of group facilitators, 33, 35, 39, 43–44, 177t
Godbee, Beth, 9
graduate student research participants, 74n2, 172t
graduate writing groups, 6n1, 9–10, 22, 23, 38–39
gratitude, 119, 181t
Gradin, Sherrie, 85
Greenfield, Laura, 20, 21, 148
grounded theory analysis, 30
group facilitators: active/passive role, 36–38, 46–47; best practices, 23; codebook, 175t–82t; directive/nondirective methods, 6, 36, 43–45, 46, 51, 155; emotional labor, 39, 52–53, 63, 114–15, 116n1, 154, 161–63, 177t; expectation boundaries, 126; expert-outsider, 50, 63, 150–51, 155–56, 176t; expertise, 32, 73n1, 176t; intellectual labor, 39, 52, 76, 78, 154; logistical support, 32, 38–41, 46, 52, 53, 60–63, 176t; managing personalities, 119, 136–37, 176t; mediator role, 102–5, 106–8, 144; metacommentary, 177t; motivator role, 113; negotiation of authority, 5–8, 35–37, 42–45, 51, 63, 175t; on task, 71–72, 176t; participant-observer role, 57–58; peer tutoring, 42, 46; peripheral role, 6, 16–17, 37, 38, 63, 70, 79, 117; positivity, 120–21; research interviews, 8, 30; timekeeping, 35, 36, 43, 50, 176t; trust-building, 162–63; white perspective, 133. *See also* feedback practices
group members: accountability, 35, 36, 48, 119; agreement/disagreement, 55–56, 83; challenges, 37, 137; collaborative learning process, 41, 108; competition, 143; controversial discussions, 142; conversational practices, 40, 65–66, 83n4, 108; emotional labor, 67, 116, 116n1, 119, 142, 144; engagement, 58–62, 80–82, 108, 142, 154; equity/inequity, 33, 39, 76, 143, 145; facilitators, 32, 169–70, 177t; feedback practices, 6, 6n1, 22, 31, 52–53, 57–61, 108, 150–51; genre awareness, 55–56, 81; genre knowledge, 71, 81, 158; giving feedback, 67–68, 75–76; inclu-

sion/exclusion, 39, 76, 143, 144; intellectual labor, 39, 67, 138–40; needs, 126, 132, 137; norms, 48, 114, 116; perspective on facilitators, 36; positionality, 138–40; prompting, 54–57; receiving feedback, 67–68, 75–76; relationship-building, 117–19, 154–55; research processes, 138–40; scaffolding, 57, 77, 155–58, 161; students of color, 134, 142; suggestions, 83, 85, 90–91, 139; support systems, 143–44; textual ownership, 108; transfer of learning, 156
group sessions, 52–53
Grutsch McKinney, Jackie, 6, 6n1, 117
Gucciardi, Benjamin, 161–62
guest experts, 176t
guides, advisor feedback, 182t

Haas, Sarah, 36
Hall, R. Mark, 14, 15
Hartelius, Johanna, 73n1
Heller, Caroline, 149
hierarchy. *See* negotiation of authority
Highberg, Nels, 149
Hispanic-Serving Institutions (HSIs), 159
Historically Black Colleges and Universities (HBCUs), 159
Hochschild, Arlie Russell, 116, 116n1
home disciplines, 16–17, 39, 74, 77
How People Learn: Brain, Mind, Experience, and School, 70
Hughes, Bradley, 50, 63
humanities discipline research participants, 74n2, 172t
hybrid teaching, 7

Ianetta, Melissa, 39, 43
identity markers, 13, 14, 18–21, 40, 121–22, 128–29, 134, 142, 160
impact of writing group location, 12
improving writing groups, 168
in vivo codes, 30–31
inclusion/exclusion, 117–19, 128, 134, 142–44, 153–54
inductive research approach, 26
inequities among group members, 113, 145
influence of group facilitators, 23, 150
informal conversation. *See* chitchat feedback
informed practices, 20
institutional context, 11, 118
intellectual labor: attrition, 51, 135; facilitators, 39, 52, 154; genre awareness, 76, 81, 109; group members, 138–40, 143; inclusion/exclusion, 143; multidisciplinary groups, 8,

32, 67, 76–78, 111; student writing, 9; suggestions, 83, 85, 90–91, 139; writing groups, 9, 126, 137–40
international scholarship on writing groups, 38–39
international students, writing groups, 22, 39, 74n2, 79–80, 121–22, 172t
International Writing Centers Association 2021, 7
internships, 26, 27t
intersectionality, 16–17
interview questions, 8, 27, 28t, 30, 165–66
iterative research approach, 26

Jackson, Rebecca L., 6, 6n1, 11, 117
Jackson, Hope, 159
Jackson, Karen Keaton, 159
junior research participants, 74n2, 172t

Kassens-Noor, Eva, 10
Kerschbaum, Stephanie L., 20, 121–22
keywords. *See* vocabulary framework
Kim, Soo Hyon, 150
Kinney, Tiffany, 17
Kirsch, Gesa E., 20
knowledge in practice, 70–72, 75

land-grant universities, 21–22, 167–70
landscape of practice, 75
leadership roles, group facilitators, 36, 50
Learning in Landscapes of Practice: Boundaries, Identity, and Knowledgeability in Practice-Based Learning, 75
learning through collaboration. *See* collaborative learning process
learning transfer. *See* transfer of learning
learning communities of practice, 13–14, 51
legitimating feedback, 97–100
Li, Linda, 10, 39
Likert scale, 76n3
liminality, multidisciplinary writing groups, 68, 149–50
limitations: case study research, 159; data collection and analysis, 160; writing groups, 167; classroom-based writing groups, 11–12; linguistic background identity, 119, 121–22, 125; literacy learning, 8, 33, 70, 84; lived experiences, 6, 10–11, 26, 117, 126, 128–31, 143, 153, 156–57; writing center research, 6–7
logistical support: agenda setting, 42–43, 53, 62, 65; email, 52; facilitators, 32, 38, 41, 46, 52, 175t, 176t; feedback, 39, 52, 59–61; structure, 22, 39, 150–51; task at hand, 53, 71–72; timekeeping, 43, 50, 52
Lorimer-Leonard, Rebecca, 71–72, 153

Mackiewicz, Jo, 31n3, 39–41, 56
The Managed Heart, 116
Manthey, Katie, 17–18, 68
marginalized identities, 144
Martinez, Sumiko, 17, 69, 118
master's thesis research participants, 172t
McDermott, Richard, 13
McMurray, Claire, 10
mediator role of facilitator, 102–5, 106–8
meeting locations for writing groups, 149
mentoring, 9–10
metacognition, 72
metacommentary, 52, 177t
Micciche, Laura, 117
Mid-Atlantic Writing Centers Association 2021, 7
Miller, Elizabeth, 37
Misischia, Cynthia, 77
Mitchell, Kendra, 159
modeling, 156
Molloy, Janice C., 10
Mortensen, Peter, 20
Moss, Beverly J., 149, 159
motivational scaffolding. *See* relational scaffolding
motivator role of facilitator, 113
multidisciplinary writing groups: benefits, 68, 73–75; co-authorship, 108; collaborative learning process, 5–8, 41, 66–67, 108, 149–50; conversational practices, 40, 65–66, 83n4, 108, 131; cross-disciplinary constraints, 39, 51, 73–76, 102–8; emotional labor, 8, 32, 67, 82, 110–11; expectations, 18–19; feedback, 4–5, 39, 63–64, 67–68, 75–76, 108, 110; genre knowledge, 71–72, 106, 108–11, 152–53; home disciplines, 68–69; intellectual labor, 8, 32, 39, 67, 76–78, 111; international students, 22, 27t, 39, 79–80, 121–22; liminality, 68, 149–50; receiving feedback, 67–68, 75–76; recontextualization, 72, 77, 80, 108–9; rhetorical resonances, 50, 78–79, 83, 85; subdisciplines, 68; support, 149–50; transfer of learning, 69, 71–72, 108, 109n6, 109–10, 151–53. *See also* dissertation writing group (DWG); second-year proposal group (SPG); undergraduate thesis group (UTG); writing groups
multilingualism, 73, 80–81, 152–53, 158
Murphy, Christina, 43
mutual engagement, 18–19

Naming What We Know: Threshold Concepts of Writing Studies, 50
native English speaker research participants, 168, 172*t*
needs of group members, 126, 144–45
negotiation of authority: advisor feedback, 182*t*; best practices, 160; collaborative learning process, 41, 46, 148, 149; communities of practice, 15–17, 51; directive/nondirective tutoring, 36, 43, 46, 51; disciplinary writing, 97–98, 101, 103–5; dissertation advisors, 106–8; feedback, 98–100; group facilitators, 14, 20, 35–38, 42–45, 63, 115–16, 150–51; home disciplines, 16–17; identity markers, 20–21; mutual engagement, 18–19; participant-observer, 8, 30; relational work, 41, 153; writing groups, 5–9, 11–14, 16–18, 99–103
Negretti, Raffaella, 71
Nicklay, Jennifer, 44
Nicolas, Melissa, 149
non-autonomous writing groups, 11
non-native English speaker research participants, 168, 172*t*
nondirective/directive methods, 6, 36, 43–46, 51, 155
Northern California Writing Centers Association 2021, 7
notetaking feedback, 65, 177*t*, 178*t*
Nowacek, Rebecca, 50, 63, 71–72, 109, 109n6, 152–53

Ó Tuama, Pádraig, 161–63
on task, 71–72, 176*t*
one-to-one tutoring, 8, 46, 156–57
online teaching, 7
oral writing-revision space (OR), 87–88, 108
outdoor leadership experiences, 26
The Oxford Guide for Writing Tutors, 43

Pacific Northwest Writing Centers Association 2021, 7
Paré, Anthony, 9
participant-observer: collaborative relationships, 8, 29; data collection and analysis, 8, 27, 28*t*; facilitators, 57–58; meeting attendance, 23, 27n2; negotiations of authority, 29–30; positionality, 133–34; reciprocity, 160
passive/active role, facilitators, 37–38, 46–47, 50
patterns in data collection and analysis, 31
Pauley-Gose, 85
peer review, 9, 38–39, 118, 155, 167, 170
peer tutoring, 19–20, 35–36, 42, 46

Pemberton, Michael A., 37
people of color, writing groups, 6, 26, 142
peripheral facilitator role, 6, 16–17, 37–38, 63, 70, 79, 117
Peripheral Visions for Writing Centers, 6, 117
personal statements, 172*t*
personalities in writing groups, 176*t*
Phillips, Talinn, 16–17
Poetry Unbound, 161
point of resistance, 182*t*
point-predict reading aloud method, 56
positionality in writing research, 128–29, 133–34, 138–42, 160
positivity, 120–21
postdoctoral scholars, 22, 172*t*
postmodern literary criticism, 138
praise feedback, 57–60, 150, 156
predominantly white institutions (PWIs): academic space, 114, 134, 153; African American graduate students, 142; exclusion/inclusion, 33; identity markers, 114, 115, 118, 119
primary readers, 182*t*
prison writing groups, 11
process codes, 30–31
productivity norms, 37, 48, 158
professional development, 10, 33, 39, 63–64
project explaining, 83
prompting, 54–57, 156
proposal projects. *See* second-year proposal group (SPG)
pumping questions, 40, 83, 85, 88–90, 104, 123, 151, 178*t*

qualitative research approach, 8, 26–27, 160
questionnaires, 167–70, 173*t*
quiet time, 137

race and racism, 11, 18–19, 132–34, 138–40, 142, 160
racial identity, 114, 115, 118, 119
Radical Writing Center Praxis: A Paradigm for Ethical Political Engagement, 20, 21, 148
reader response feedback, 83, 85, 90–91, 178*t*
reading aloud, 41n1, 53, 56, 63, 151–52, 155–58, 160–61
reading practice models, 77–79, 176*t*
reciprocity, participant-observers, 160
recontextualization of genres, 72, 77, 80, 108–9
reflective activities, 156
reframing feedback, 41, 52, 57–58, 62, 150, 156
relational scaffolding: emotional labor, 41, 82, 117, 124–25, 153–55, 180*t*, 181*t*; facilitators, 32, 52, 120–21, 177*t*; group members, 117–19,

144–45; interest, 120–21; negotiations of authority, 153; praise, 62; reframing, 57
research methods: case studies, 159; coding, 30–31, 40–41, 83n4, 119; contextualizing documents, 30; data collection and analysis, 8, 26–27, 28t; interviews, 8, 30, 165–66; observation, 14; qualitative, 160
research participants: class rank, 168; consent forms, 167; demographics, 172t; emerging findings, 31; facilitators, 30, 32, 168, 175t; land-grant universities, 167–70; response rates, 51, 171; writing groups, 8, 25, 29–30
research processes, 138–40
research projects, 89–90, 128–29
researchers, positionality, 8, 29–30, 138–40, 160
resource-sharing, 100–2, 180t
response rate, surveys, 51, 74n2, 171t–73t
retention rates. *See* student retention
reverse outlining, 49
revisions suggestions, 83, 85, 87–91, 150–51, 178t. *See also* collaborative learning process
The Rhetoric of Expertise, 73n1
rhetorical reading cognitive support, 41n1, 52
rhetorical resonances, 50, 78–79, 83, 83n4, 85, 109
Robertson, Liane, 70, 79, 156
Rodas, Elizabeth L., 68
role of group facilitators. *See* group facilitators
Roozen, Kevin, 33
Rounsaville, Angela, 71–72, 153
"The Rungs," 161–62
Ryan, Leigh, 56

safe space, 133
The Saint Martin's Sourcebook for Writing Tutors, 43
scaffolding: cognitive, 32, 40, 41n1, 55, 56, 177t; emotional, 32, 41n1, 82, 177t; facilitators, 36, 39, 61–63; genre knowledge, 39, 83n4, 155–58; group members, 52, 54, 57, 155–58, 161; motivation, 167–68; oral writing-revision space (OR), 87–88, 108; relational, 32, 41n1, 177t; relationship-building, 154–55; writing groups, 150–51; zone of proximal development, 40
scholarship, writing center studies, 5–6, 26–27, 30–31, 33, 38, 148
scholarly identity, 67
second-year proposal group (SPG): commitment, 120; group process, 53, 120–21; project proposal, 25–26, 90, 126–27, 151; relational work, 41n1, 124–25; transformation, stories of, 89–90, 126. *See also* dissertation writing group (DWG); multidisciplinary writing groups; undergraduate thesis group (UTG); writing groups
semi-autonomous writing groups, 11
semi-structured interviews, 8, 27, 28t, 30, 165–66
senior research participants, 172t
Shanahan, Cynthia, 77
Shanahan, Timothy, 77
shared experiences, writing groups, 10–11, 13–14, 113, 152–54
shared feedback language, 58–60
shared trust. *See* trust-building
Sherwood, 43
signposting, 49, 59–60
Simpson, Steve, 38
small talk. *See* chitchat feedback
Smith, Trixie, 69
Snyder, William M., 13
Snyder-Yuly, Julie, 17, 69
social conditioning, 117
social sciences discipline research participants, 172t
Sommer-Farias, Bruna, 72
sophomore research participants, 172t
Southeastern Writing Centers Association 2021, 7
Spigelman, Candace, 11, 108, 149
staff research participants, 172t
STEM field discipline research participants, 38, 172t
Stewart, Candace, 85
Stewart, D.-L., 134
structural support. *See* logistical support
student retention, 8, 24, 25
student writing, 9–10, 16–20, 25, 39, 128, 147, 157
study abroad programs, 26, 27t
suggestions. *See* collaborative learning process
support for writing groups, 143–44, 149–50, 154, 175t
survey data, 8, 27, 28t, 30, 51, 73, 74n2, 167–70, 171t–73t

Taczak, Kara, 6, 70, 156
Tafari, Dawn N. Hicks, 159
Talk About Writing: The Tutoring Strategies of Experienced Writing Center Tutors, 39–40
Tardy, Christine M., 72, 80, 109
targeted praise, 62

task at hand, 53, 71–72
teacher authority, 19, 157
tension, group member, 39, 144–45
text engagement, 56
textual ownership, 108
theoretical framework. *See* communities of practice (CoP)
theoretical text resources, 84
theory of tutoring/writing, 156
Thesen, Lucia, 17, 39
thesis writing groups. *See* undergraduate thesis group (UTG)
thingness, 14
Thompson, Isabelle Kramer, 31n3, 39, 40–41, 56
timekeeping, 35–36, 43, 52, 175t, 176t
topic discussions, 143
Toward a New Rhetoric of Difference, 20, 121
traditional research projects, 25–26
training group facilitators, 33, 39
training. *See* professional development
transactional process, 15
transcriptions of writing group meetings, 27–28
transfer of learning, 79, 109, 109n6, 110, 156
transformation, stories of, 89–90, 126
Treviño, Anna K. (Willow), 117–18
trust-building, 18, 161–63
tutor-facilitators; best practices, 7, 8; communities of practice, 13–14, 51; directive/nondirective methods, 43, 46, 51, 155; emotional labor, 63, 116–17; genre knowledge, 36, 50, 52, 63, 155, 157; group facilitators, 22; hierarchy, 19–20, 45; one-to-one tutoring, 8, 46, 156–57; peer tutoring, 35–36, 39, 46, 155; reading material, 63, 77, 156; research observation, 14; scaffolding, 39–40, 43; training, 45–46; transfer of learning, 156; valued practices, 14; writing center theory, 19, 23; writing groups, 19–21. *See also* group facilitators

unclear research participants, 172t
undergraduate thesis group (UTG): academic space, 134; belonging, 128–31, 135; collaborative learning process, 55, 85, 90–91, 135–38; disciplinary differences, 16, 83n4, 83–85, 102–3; emerging researchers, 128–30; group dynamics, 53, 128, 132, 137; inclusion/exclusion, 117–19, 128, 134, 142–44; intellectual labor, 76–78, 126, 137–40; lived experiences, 126, 128–29, 130–31; research processes, 128–29, 138; safe space, 133; shared experiences, 142–43; survey responses, 51, 74n2, 172t;

verbal processing, 137; white perspective, 138, 142. *See also* dissertation writing group (DWG); multidisciplinary writing group; second-year proposal group (SPG); writing groups
Until We Are Strong Together: Women Writers in the Tenderloin, 149
usefulness of feedback, 50, 76n3, 79, 80, 121–25

valued practices, 14
verbal processing, 137
video recordings, 27, 28t
vocabulary framework, 156
Vygotskian learning theory, 39, 40

Waring, Hansun Zhang, 96
Watt, Lorna, 9
Wenger-Trayner, Beverly, 13–14, 75
Wenger, Etienne, 13–14, 18
Westbrook, Evelyn, 11
white perspective/white privilege, 117, 133, 138–42
White, Stephanie, 37
Wilmot, Kirsten, 68
Winzenried, Misty Anne, 152
Wolke, Shari, 150
Women's Gender, and Sexuality Studies (WGSS) thesis writing, 48, 84–85
The Working Lives of New Writing Center Directors, 116–17
workshopping, facilitators, 3–4
writing across the curriculum programs, 21–22
writing activities, 83n4, 84–85, 155–58
writing center administrators, 7, 8, 116–17
writing center research: academic writing groups, 149; emotional labor, 116; empirical research, 5–7, 26–27, 30–31, 38; expansion, 21–22; facilitator role of, 37; graduate students, 22; group attrition, 10, 51; increase, 8–9; lack of, 10; lived experiences, 6–7, 26, 117; prison classrooms, 11; theoretical frameworks, 14–15; tutoring practices, 19–20, 23, 63; writing center-sponsored writing groups, 17–18; writing group scholarship, 148
writing centers: collaborative practice, 5–6, 8, 15; emotional support, 17; exclusion/inclusion, 33; faculty writing groups, 6n1; feedback, 150–51; graduate tutors, 23; group practice, 6n1; hybrid/in-person teaching, 7; international students, 22, 39, 79–80; lived experiences, 6, 26; negotiation of author-

ity, 20, 51; reification, 13–14; scholarship, 33; support for writing groups, 144; writing groups, 6n1. *See also* communities of practice (CoP); writing groups
writing conferences, 9–10
writing development, 8, 33, 156, 168
writing experiences, 180t
writing expertise, 32, 49, 73n1, 176t
Writing Groups in the Writing Center, 13
Writing Groups Inside and Outside the Classroom, 149
Writing Groups: History, Theory, and Implications, 11, 149
writing groups: challenges, 77, 137; conflicts, 11, 106–8, 113–14, 163; diversity, 9–11, 22–24, 144; embodied experiences, 158–59; emotional labor, 41, 76–77, 82, 123–27, 129, 134–39, 143–45, 153–57, 175t; feedback, 31–32, 57–62, 84, 97, 100–1, 120–22, 131–32, 138–39, 178–81; group facilitators, 5–10, 19–21, 24, 25t, 26, 27t, 36, 39, 62, 175t–82t; group norms, 37, 48, 116, 158; hierarchy, 19–20, 45; identity markers, 18–19, 114–15, 121–22, 128–29, 134, 160; logistical support, 32, 41, 46, 175t; membership, 22, 149; negotiation of authority, 5–9, 11–14, 16–18, 31, 51, 97–102, 110–11, 130–31, 135–37; participant-observer, 23, 27n2, 28t, 29–30; peer review, 9, 39, 118, 167, 170; perspectives, 32, 175t; predominantly white institutions (PWIs), 114, 134, 153; pumping questions, 40, 83, 85, 88–90, 104, 123; reading practices, 53, 77–80, 160–61; relationship-building, 18, 117–19, 153; research participants, 8, 24, 25t, 27, 28t, 29–30, 73–74, 74n2, 75, 167t–72t; scaffolding, 150–51; structure, 39, 52–53; workshopping, 3–4; writing-center sponsored, 5–6, 6n1, 15–18, 144, 147–51, 154, 170. *See also* dissertation writing group (DWG); second-year proposal group (SPG); undergraduate thesis group (UTG)
Writing Groups for Doctoral Education and Beyond, 39
writing process, 4–5, 8, 22, 82, 143, 158, 163, 182t
writing studies, 83n4, 84–85, 156
writing transfer, 71–72, 108, 151–53
writing tutors. *See* group facilitators; tutor-facilitators

Yancey, Kathleen Blake, 70, 156

Zhang, Jing, 38
Zimmerelli, Lisa, 56
zone of proximal development, 40

About the Author

SARA WILDER is an assistant professor of English at University of Maryland, College Park, where she teaches rhetoric and writing and directs the Writing Center. Her research also appears in journals such as *Written Communication*, *WLN: A Journal of Writing Center Scholarship*, and *Literacy in Composition Studies*.

www.ingramcontent.com/pod-product-compliance
Lightning Source LLC
Chambersburg PA
CBHW060602080526
44585CB00013B/654